PACIFIC SHORE FISHING

PACIFIC SHORE FISHING

Written and Illustrated by
MICHAEL R. SAKAMOTO

Foreword by Stan Wright

A Kolowalu Book
UNIVERSITY OF HAWAII PRESS
Honolulu

COPYRIGHT © 1985 BY MICHAEL R. SAKAMOTO
ALL RIGHTS RESERVED
PRINTED IN THE UNITED STATES OF AMERICA

10   09   08   07   06   05   11   10   9   8   7   6

Library of Congress Cataloging in Publication Data
Sakamoto, Michael R.
  Pacific shore fishing.

  (A Kolowalu book)
  Bibliography: p.
  Includes indexes.
  1. Saltwater fishing—Hawaii. 2. Surf fishing—
Hawaii. I. Title.
SH679.H3S35   1985   799.1'6659   84-16372
ISBN 0-8248-0892-4

University of Hawai'i Press books are printed on acid-free paper and meet the guidelines for permanence and durability of the Council on Library Resources.

PRINTED BY THE MAPLE-VAIL BOOK MANUFACTURING GROUP

www.uhpress.hawaii.edu

Dedicated to
Kat,
Paul,
and
Stefanie

CONTENTS

Foreword by Stan Wright	xi
Preface	xiii
Acknowledgments	xv

1 The Art of Handpole Fishing — 1
- *Bamboo Poles* — 1
- *Fiberglass Extension Poles* — 5
- *Using the Right Monofilament and Hooks* — 6
- *Knots for the Handpole Fisherman* — 9
- *Floaters* — 9
- *Other Techniques for the Handpole Fisherman* — 13
- *Catching Bait* — 15

2 Reels for the Shore Fisherman — 17
- *The Evolution of the Reel* — 17
- *How to Choose a Reel* — 19
- *Spinning Reels* — 21
- *Bait-Casting Reels* — 24
- *Surf Casting Reels* — 26
- *Maintaining Your Reels* — 31
- *Your Emergency Repair Kit* — 36

3 Fishing Rods — 39
- *A Rod for Every Job* — 41
- *Ultralight Rod* — 45
- *Mighty Midget Rod* — 49
- *Bait-Casting Rod* — 51
- *Medium-Action Spinning Rod* — 53

Heavy-Weight Spinning Rod	55
Ulua *Pole*	57
Fiberglass Ulua *Rod*	61
Graphite and Boron Rods	64
Half-and-Half Rod	66
Rod Cases	67
Rod Sacks	71
4 Monofilament and Monofilament Knots	72
Knots and the Leader	76
The Knots	77
The Leaders	92
5 The Art of Bait Fishing	116
Dead Bait Whipping	116
Live Bait Fishing from Shore	132
6 Lures for the Shore Fisherman	143
Plugs	144
Adjustable Plugs: The Mirro-Lure	146
Tin Squids	148
Lai Skin Jig	149
Spoons	152
Leadhead Jig	154
Plastic Body Jigs	156
Homemade Lures	158
7 The Art of Whipping the Shoreline	160
Casting with Accuracy	162
Spinning Presentation and Techniques	163
Skipping the Plug	167
Surface Plugging for Big Ulua	168
Jigging and Deep Jigging from Shore	174
Working the Spoon	176
Daily Fishing Patterns	179
8 Slide-Bait Fishing	181
The Stop Ring	182
Working the Baits	183
Fishing for Ulua	184
Gaffs	191

9 **Fishing Accessories and Other Paraphernalia**	198
Swivels	200
Hooks	201
Lead and Sinkers	202
Leader Material	204
Pliers and Other Fishing Tools	207
Shore Fishing Lights	210
Tackle Boxes—Big or Small?	216
Ice Chests and Insulated Fish Bags	218
Tail Carriers and Meat Hooks	219
10 **Shoreline Gamefish**	221
Glossary	247
References	249
Gamefish Index	251
General Index	253
About the Author	256

FOREWORD

A good fishing trip is sharing the experience with a friend. Good company can turn a cold, wet, whitewash day into a warm, happy, dream-come-true outing. It is my pleasure to introduce to you Mike Sakamoto, someone who has given me much knowledge and companionship in fishing.

Shore fishermen of the Hawaiian Islands have some mystical fascination for *pāpio* and their older brothers, the *ulua*. Oldtimers guard their secrets of success, revealing these "black magic" fishing methods to only a fortunate select few. Mike has written a book for the angler who has or would like to fish the Hawaiian shoreline. He reveals secrets and techniques he learned from personal observations and investigations, as well as invented out of pure necessity.

No matter what your style of fishing, Mike has something to help you succeed in the interesting and exciting sport of shore fishing. At times the technical descriptions and detailed diagrams of Mike's gear may seem bewildering, even intimidating to the beginner, but believe you me, if the only thing around to fish with were a hook, line, and bamboo pole, Mike would be right in there having just as much fun as the rest of us. I feel this book fills a long neglected need. It not only will help the novice get started but it will inform, entertain, and win a nod of approval from the pro.

STAN WRIGHT

PREFACE

Fishing from shore is where it all begins. At one time or another we all will have the opportunity to pick up a bamboo pole and drop a bait into the water. The moment you have, you've become a fisherman. Once the bait is in the water, the angler's soul slowly emerges, the rolling surface of the water hypnotizes you and you begin to dream of incredible strikes, powerful determined runs that scream your reel and make your heart pound. You dream of fantastic trips and adventures that will take you to exotic lands in search of the ultimate strike and trophy.

Later, some of us drift off to different hobbies, but some of us continue to be fishermen. We return trip after trip, adventure after adventure and continue to strive to unravel the secrets of the sea and the moment of the strike. We dig deeper and deeper and develop theories, ideas, and techniques in an effort to find the patience and oneness with the sea that fishing requires. The special mystique of the ocean, the uncertainty that lies in the openness of the shoreline and the vastness of the horizon, the sounds of thundering waves and the musty smell of the ocean air keep all of us going back and back and back.

Every fisherman has a theory or an idea for his sport. I have always believed that fishermen are some of the most ingenious people in the world: anglers have designed their own rods, reels, leaders, gaffing equipment, special plugs. One angler even invented a floater that sets your hook for you, lights up when a fish bites, and even winds itself up when a trigger is tripped. It is for these people that I have written this book: the anglers who are inventors and innovators, and are unafraid of the taunting and chiding that come with being different; and the individuals that see angling as being pure, unadulterated fun.

The true treasure we all find in angling is fellowship. This bond is intangible but very real. The fisherman who speaks your language and shares his knowledge and the excitement of the strike with you becomes more than a friend: he is someone with whom you will share memories for years to come.

And in the years to come, fishing techniques, tackle and fish fighting savvy will evolve tenfold. The fish one will be able to hook and land will become larger and larger, and therefore the challenge will be to land these monsters on lighter and lighter tackle. The size of the tackle will continue to diminish and the challenge will therefore be renewed again and again.

With these developments must come the caring for the shoreline. There must be cultivated the idea that "a fish is too valuable to hook and land only once"; that the sea's bounty is not unlimited; that if we anglers are not going to eat our catch, then it must be released to fight again. The true trophy in angling is the memory of the strike, the battle, the final landing of the fish. Beyond this there is no reason to keep a fish that has given you an experience no man can take away from you.

Fishing, after all, is really nothing but a lot of tales of the one that got away.

ACKNOWLEDGMENTS

I want to thank those people who have helped me through the hard times by reminding me that I should "finish writing the fishing book." Without their faith and constant prodding, I would never have written the last word of *Pacific Shore Fishing;* it would still be confined to the rusty back burners of my mind and never have reached the shelves. These people include my wife Kathleen (Kat), my mother Peggy, my father Paul, and my children Stefanie and Paul. They all supported me through the hard, quiet hours at the typewriter.

I wish to thank Stan Wright, who reminded me for several years that such a book needed to be written. He never let me down and always instilled determination in me.

Special thanks also go to Lefty Kreh, Mark Sosin, Dick Gaumer, Capt. Rick Gaffney, Gary Ranne, Jim Rizzuto, Glenn Ikemoto, Bobby Nii, Ernie Theodore, Bruce Kaya, Betty Bushnell, Bob Pritchard, Mike, Earl, and Ethel Tokunaga, Chuck Johnson, Dominic Uyetake, and Kathy Matsueda.

1
The Art of Handpole Fishing

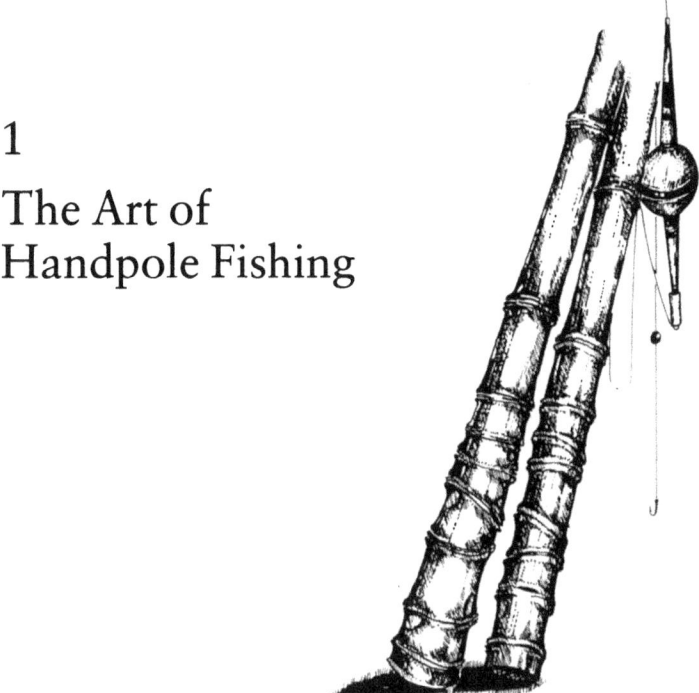

Bamboo Poles

Bamboo pole fishing is one of angling's simplest art forms. Its earliest tackle possibly consisted of a broken branch, a homemade braided cord, a handcarved wooden or bone fishhook, and freshly dug earthworms. Although the tackle of today is essentially the same, fishing styles and techniques have become much more innovative and productive. But all in all the angler determines the state of the art. He develops his own inner force, his delicate touch or "supreme feel," which extends far down the length of his rod and finally down the line. So, handpole fishing is a delicate art and really a bridge both to fishing that requires more sophisticated tackle and to further skills and ideas.

If you are a beginner, selecting the inobtrusive bamboo pole is the foremost step to developing angling skills. By using this simple pole you can learn many things: the way to tie monofilament knots, rig and tie leaders, maintain tackle, read productive waters, and learn the habits of the fish you hope to catch.

Once these valuable basic skills are mastered and refined, you can rely on them when you use the cane pole to catch valuable bait for hang baits or for heavy spinning tackle and slide-bait surf casting tackle.

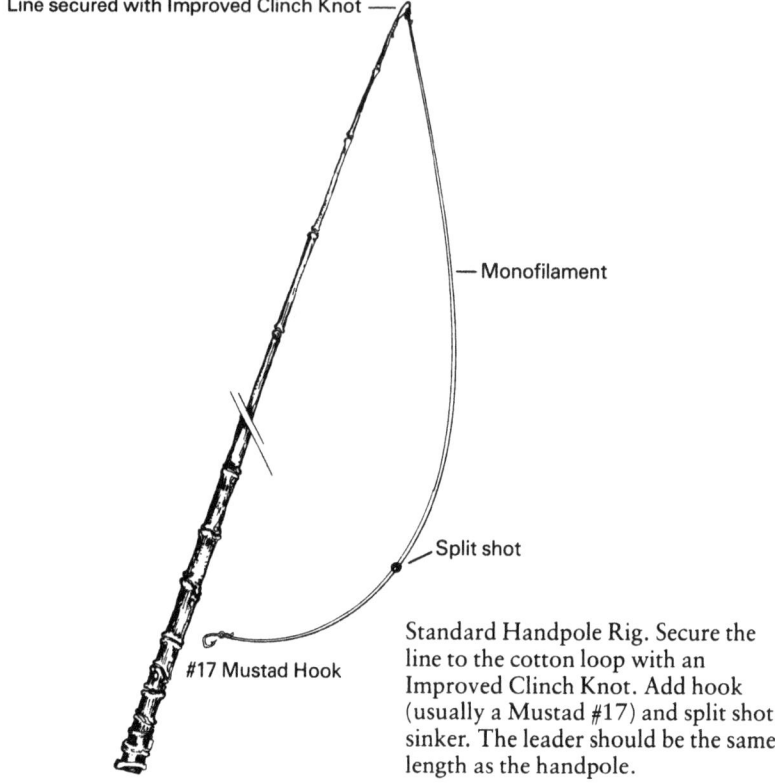

Standard Handpole Rig. Secure the line to the cotton loop with an Improved Clinch Knot. Add hook (usually a Mustad #17) and split shot sinker. The leader should be the same length as the handpole.

Selecting the Bamboo Pole

The bamboo fishing pole is possibly the most rudimentary piece of equipment for fishing, short of a handline. It's inexpensive, durable, has a fine taper, and will last for many trips. It will give you and your children adventures you can look back on with pride. Just about anyone can use a handpole and catch fish, but the handpole can do so much more. It can start you on a road to endless achievements and challenges, and acquaint you with the ocean around you. But you should get to know even this simple tool before you select and purchase one.

When selecting a bamboo pole, look for the pole that has the most "knuckles" (also called dams) per stalk. The knuckle is a natural joint on the stalk and its strongest part. If the pole you select has very few knuckles, then the pole is on the weak side and may collapse under severe stress. This is not to say that you're out to purchase a bamboo pole that can literally haul up an Allison tuna. What it is, is that you're out to find a handpole that will last trip after trip and that will be able to land a stubborn *pāpio* (juvenile trevally) when the time comes.

The next thing to look for are wormholes and crusty or soft sections of the pole, clues that the rod may have dry rot. If the pole has dry rot, it will collapse and a fine powder will come out at the break. This rod is definitely no good. A fairly dependable way to test a bamboo pole is to hold the tip against a ceiling or doorsill. Flexing the pole this way will show you the taper of the rod and will also expose a rotten or collapsed section, or a split stalk. It's always a good idea to flex the pole at the fishing store before you pull out your wallet. This way you are assured that your pole won't suddenly shatter into a million pieces when you finally hook your first fish.

Another thing to check when selecting a bamboo pole is color. The stalk should have a golden-yellow tint to it. It shouldn't look whitish or severely water-stained. The skin of the stalk should have a nice gloss to it, even seem slightly slippery. If the stalk looks and feels dry and bumpy, it's old and very brittle and would make for better firewood than a fishing pole. To keep the bamboo from becoming dry and brittle, varnish it once or twice a year. Give it a good coat of spar varnish or plain rod varnish, available in most fishing supply stores.

Good bamboo will actually take at least a year to cure; if possible, it should be cured even longer. Tonkin cane (*Arundinaria amabilis,* 'the lovely bamboo'), used for building split-cane rods, may have been cured since before the Second World War. Some culms (a bunch of select bamboo stalks) will have small splits in them. For stalks that measure three inches in diameter and that are going to be split and glued into finely crafted fly rods, splits actually aid in the curing process. But on a handpole, splits indicate a stress point that may cause future problems.

So select good bamboo poles and they will last you many a fishing season. I know of one guy who caught so many *'oama* (juvenile goatfish) with his one bamboo pole, he finally decided to hang it up and buy another one. But a bamboo pole cost much less in the old days than it does now. After seriously comparing today's price with the price he paid so many years ago, he decided to take the old bamboo pole out of the trash can and go back to using it. Since then he has caught more fish, and the bamboo pole is still going strong. One day he'll save enough money to buy a new one, but until then he'll just go on using the pole that he bought for 5 cents.

The distance you usually maintain between you and the fish naturally determines the length of the bamboo pole you'll want to purchase. When you go to the local fishing supply store, you'll find a vast array of bamboo poles, from the short five-footers to the monster stalks that are anywhere from ten to twenty-five feet long. The long ones are usually used as surf casting poles and are extremely heavy. Unless you're thinking of fishing from high cliffs and for big game, the super-long poles aren't for you.

Most of the bamboo poles you find on the open market come with some kind of cotton cord loop at the end of the tip to which you tie your line. If yours does not, you'll either have to tie your fishing line directly to the tip of the rod or add your own loop. If you'd like to add your own loop, simply get a cotton cord, form a loop, and tie it off with some thin sewing thread. Rod-wrapping nylon thread works perfectly because it stretches and is very strong. Dental floss is also good for wrapping on rod tip loops. Coat the wrapping with fingernail polish (shocking pink is a good choice) or rod-wrapping varnish. This will keep the thread from unraveling and forming a horrible tangled mess, not to mention keep you from losing your fish, which might pull it off.

For bamboo tips another good thing to do is get some white paint and paint the top three feet of the tip. This will make it easier to see the tip during some dark night when the fish are only tapping the bait. It can also help you find the tip when you're stomping all around a pier or in lava fields. The white paint will keep you from breaking a

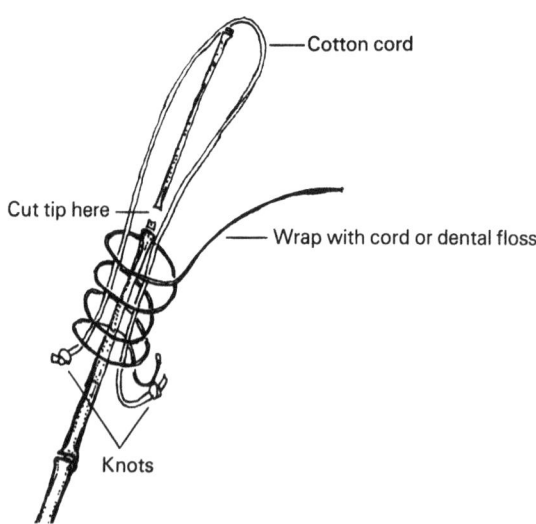

Preparing the tip

lot of shafts, butts, and tips—and from becoming frustrated. White paint also works well on the tiny split shots. The white paint will also help you find your swinging line in the darkness.

Tempering the Handpole

A cane pole may have a sluggish, damp feel to it because it may have been cured for only a minimum length of time before it was shipped. These poles can be heat tempered, and if tempered properly can be made to feel stiffer and crisp. Tempering a bamboo pole is a very simple procedure. All you need is a source of steady heat and some cold water close at hand. The steady heat can be provided by a regular kitchen stove (if your wife will let you in the house with the pole), a portable torch, or a Coleman stove. Simply turn the pole over your heat source as you would a pig roasting on a spit. Never heat one portion for too long. If you do, you'll have a nicely charcoal-broiled bamboo pole.

Once the bamboo is too hot to touch, take a wet rag and swab it until steam rises from the stalk. Repeat this process until the pole turns an orange brown. Then flex the rod. It will have a steely feel to it and may seem a little lighter than before. You'll find the stiffer the rod, the more sensitive the feel. So temper the pole until it acquires the desired stiffness. One word of caution: The tip will get hot faster than the rest of the pole. It will be a very simple matter to overtemper the tip and burn it right off, so go very easy when you're close to the tip.

Fiberglass Extension Poles

Fiberglass extension poles are truly a blessing for those of us who fish with long, long poles. As do the bamboo models, these poles come in an incredible assortment of lengths. However, these poles also have the ability to telescope out and become even longer. When retracted, the rods usually stand a short three or four feet. They are short enough to stuff in the back seat or trunk of a car. These poles can be extended from five feet to twenty-six feet, the desired length for fishing from high cliffs or piers. The longer the pole, the more extension links it will have.

Fortunately, the tips, as well as other parts of the pole, are all replaceable. Again, coating the tip with white paint is a blessing when

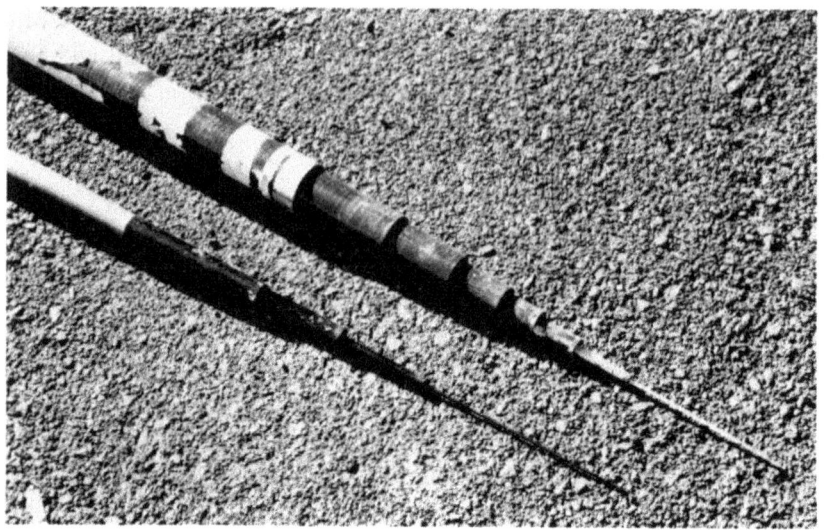

Fiberglass Extension Poles

fishing in the dark of the night. All of these poles generally come with a tip loop attached to them. If the tip should get broken, simply follow the directions for installing a new bamboo tip loop and you're all set.

Most people cut off their lines and retract the extensions after they're through fishing for the day. Some fiberglass models come with a snap on the butt section of the pole. The line is wrapped around the snap to keep it out of the way when the extensions are retracted. If your pole doesn't have this feature, then the next best thing is to wrap some rubberbands or electrician's black tape to the butt. Wrap the line around the pole shaft until you've taken up all the slack line. Secure the hook to the rubberband or black tape. By making these preparations, on your next trip, once you unhook and unwind the monofilament you'll be ready to go fishing.

Using the Right Monofilament and Hooks

Monofilament is a wonderful invention. It stretches, bends, has good shock strength, and retains good knot strength. But once it's nicked, burned, or abraded, the strength noted on its label may be reduced by 50 percent.

A good quality monofilament is one of the most important components you'll ever purchase for the handpole. It's also one of the most inexpensive items in your tackle box. If you figure cost per foot, you'll find that monofilament costs very, very little. So don't waste time with old, brittle, bargain basement brands—buy a good, brand-name, proven monofilament.

You won't be very successful if you try to catch 'oama with 80-pound-test monofilament. The line is just too big. The fish will glance up and see what probably looks to him like three-inch steel cable and then swim away. Besides, you just can't get 80-pound monofilament into the eye of a #20 Mustad hook. So if you're going after relatively small reef fish, use the thinnest monofilament possible and the smallest hook.

When a small fish like the 'oama swims up to a well-baited hook, it likes to nibble and pull at the bait. The fish will take the bait into his mouth and blow it out several times, and each time break off small bits and pieces of it. If the hook is too big, the fish won't be able to take the hook into its mouth. As a result, you'll have a lot of nibble but no fish. So make the hook small and the bait of an edible size for

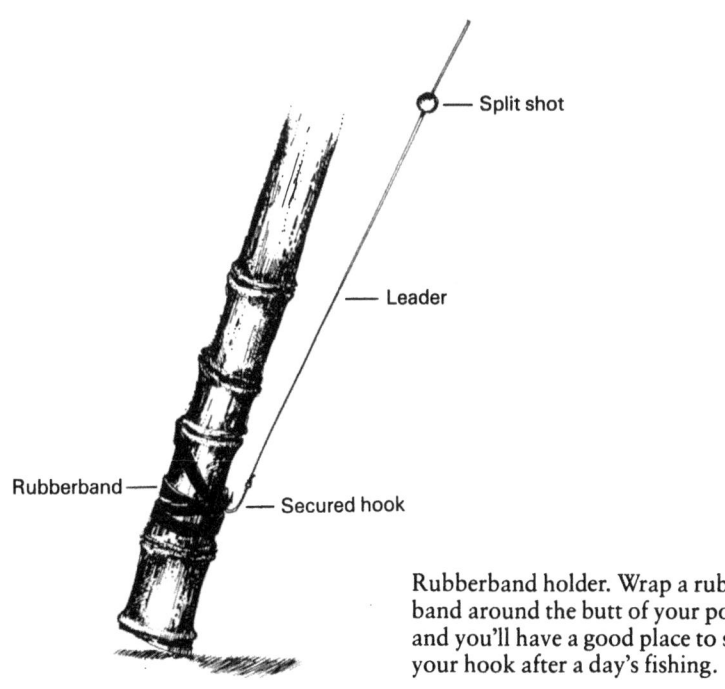

Rubberband holder. Wrap a rubberband around the butt of your pole and you'll have a good place to secure your hook after a day's fishing.

the fish. With a small hook, you can also use a line with a small diameter.

Also remember that the more free swinging the bait is, the more natural the bait will look in the water. The split shot should be as far from the bait as possible (at least eight inches) but still be able to take the bait down fast. If the hook's too close, you'll lose the drifting effect and your percentage of hook-ups will fall.

A lot of times the shore fisherman will *palu* the waters he wishes to fish; that is, he will toss ground up fish or crab into the water to stimulate the fish's appetite. If the bait looks rigid and stiff, the fish, able to see the difference, will bypass your bait and head for the easier free-drifting pickings. So the lightest monofilament is best. Don't be afraid to go down to 1- and 2-pound test. Monofilament is very durable and can withstand a lot of pulling, so use whatever weight line you can get away with. The lighter the line, the more hook-ups you'll get.

Again, have the baits as free swinging as possible. Some people like to use a small snap swivel and then a lead (see "Swivels," Chapter 9); they feel that it keeps the line from tangling and aids in the natural swing of the bait. Unfortunately, the shiny quality of the swivel has also been known to scare away more fish than it helps to bring up. Swivels, therefore, have no place in a handpole fisherman's arsenal.

The following are approximate monofilament sizes for specific fish:

	pound test
āholehole (Hawaiian flagfish)	1–4
'āweoweo (Schneider's bigeye fish)	4–8
halalū (*hahalalū*; bigeyed scad)	4–6
kūmū or *moano* (goatfish)	4–8
mamo (damselfish) and other reef fish	1–4
menpachi (*mempachi*; squirrelfish)	4–8
moi-li'i (threadfin)	1–4
mullet	4–8
'oama (juvenile goatfish)	1–4
'ōpelu (mackerel scad)	4–6
palani (surgeonfish) and *enenue* (rudderfish)	6–15
pāpio (juvenile jack) and *ulua* (trevally jack)	6–20
ta'ape (blue-lined snapper)	1–6
to'au (red and green snapper)	1–6

Knots for the Handpole Fisherman

Several fishing knots meet the total requirements of the handpole fisherman, but if you learn just one—the Improved Clinch Knot—then you are pretty much covered. This one knot is sufficient for tying the monofilament to the rod tip; and for tying the hook to the line and even to the swivel, if you decide that you would like to use one. If you have the time, learn to tie as many monofilament knots as you can. They're easy to learn. All you need is some discarded line and some spare time. Take the time to learn to tie knots correctly. (See Chapter 4 for a discussion of individual knots to use with handpole.)

Floaters

The technique of using a small bobber or floater is as old as the Uncle Remus tales of the Mississippi. All you do is place an old cork stopper above the bait and you're in business. The floater acts as a signal that lets you know if a fish is biting. Nowadays floaters come in a limitless assortment. They can be made of plastic, cork, wood, styrofoam, and of other materials that I can't pronounce much less spell. But they all float and, if taken care of, will last for years.

One of the most important things to consider about floaters is their visibility. You'll find a lot of them painted fluorescent colors in some weird combinations and with weird designs. Some people purchase unpainted floaters, take them home, and paint them bright color combinations to make it easier to tell their floaters from the many that usually crowd in a small area.

Mullet fishermen, notorious for fishing in a small circular group, rely heavily on floaters. Each fisherman will sit in his small dinghy or on a small wooden carpenter horse seat with his eyes glued to his floater and with his nerves wire tight. The floater is like a hair trigger on a target pistol; it is the fisherman's signal that the mullet is nibbling on his bait. Most mullet floaters are homemade and become favorites, which is why their construction is judiciously kept a guarded secret.

So when using a floater, you can't be looking all around or telling your favorite fishing story to the guy next to you. You've got to keep your eyes on your floater. If the mullet nibbles lightly at the bait, the floater will twitch. If the mullet takes the bait, the floater will quickly tilt up. This is when you haul back and set the hook. Sometimes the

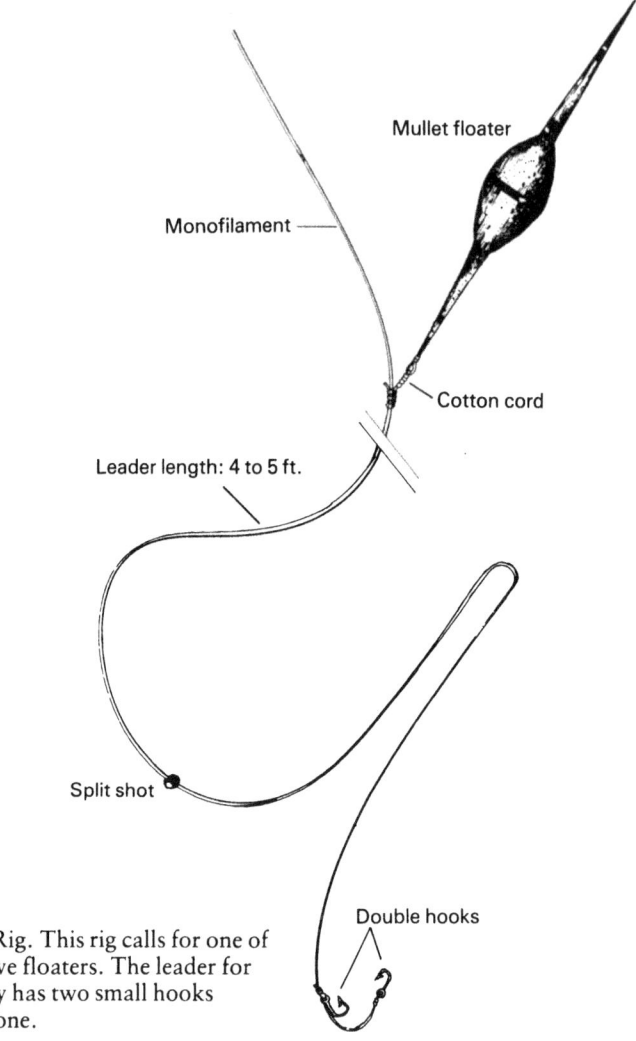

Mullet Floater Rig. This rig calls for one of the most sensitive floaters. The leader for this rig normally has two small hooks instead of only one.

floater will just disappear entirely and you won't know what happened. When this happens, haul back for all you're worth and, with luck, you'll have a fish on and not some other guy's line.

When fishing the open ocean's white water, never, never use a white floater; you'll go stir crazy trying to find your floater. Use a bright red or orange floater that will stand out like a rose in the desert. The length of your leader is also a very important consideration when you're out on the open ocean. You've got to get the bait down to the fish or else you won't catch anything but a cold. You must have a long or extra-long handpole. Keep adjusting the bait and

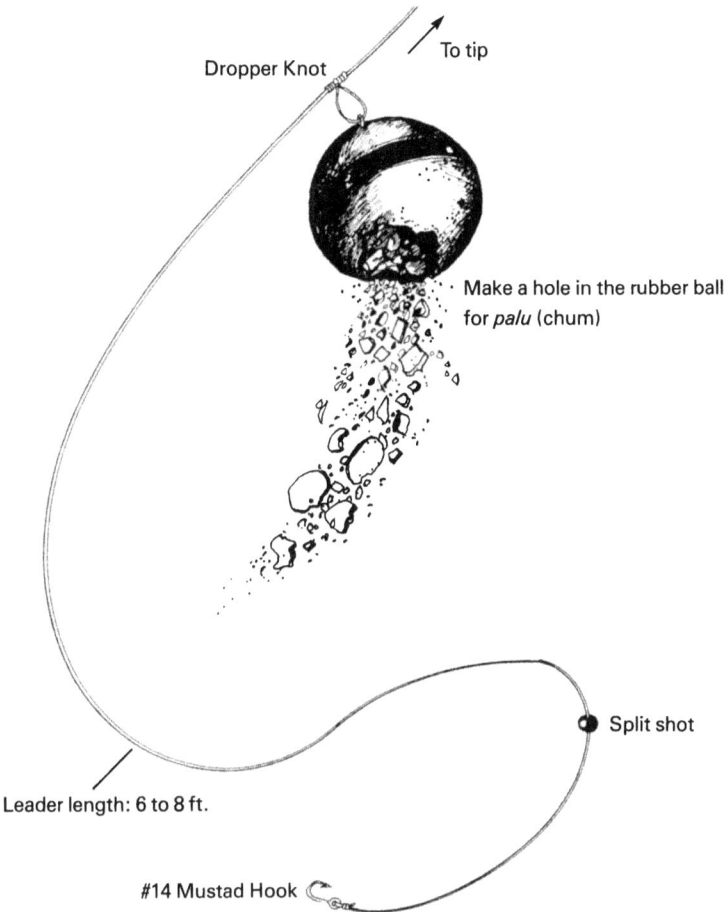

Rubber Ball Floater. This floater carries its own chum, which is tucked into a hole dug in the ball. While the ball floats, chum is dispersed around the bait that hangs below it.

the leader length until you start getting bites, and then keep your leader at that length all the time.

Sometimes when you're using a floater and the ocean is really rough, it can be hard to know when the fish has taken your bait. You may even see the floater simply go under the surface for an inch or two and quickly come back up. If this happens, just pull your handpole up until all the slack is out of the line; then, if the floater goes under the surface, you should be able to feel if it's a fish or not.

If you've got nerves like a steel spring and you respond to any sudden movement with a vicious, hook-setting yank, you'll often find a fish on the line for only a second or so. What will happen is the hook will penetrate the lip or jaw of the fish and create a keyhole. The hook rattles in the large hole as you fight the fish and eventually comes loose. So the best methods of setting the hook with a handpole are to tug the line with a quick snap of the wrist or to pull slowly when you see the floater dip under. The tension from the pole bending and the fish pulling the other way is sufficient to set the hook. At this point, if you're still unsure of whether the fish is hooked or not, just give the pole a light jerk and continue to fight the fish.

The dream of every fisherman is to fight and successfully land a trophy fish, a real monster that would make any fisherman proud. For the handpoler, it is no different. The only problem is that the handpoler is handicapped: He has a limited length of line and no way of following his fleeing prey. He doesn't have a reel and therefore no adjustable drag system and hundreds of yards of line. All the fisherman has is a good bamboo pole and an incredible desire to eventually land a big fish. And more often than not, he'll lose the powerful running fish to a broken line or even to a broken hook. But he still has some chance and one method of successfully landing a big fish on a handpole.

To land a big fish with a handpole, bow with the run as you continue to maintain some resistance on the pole. Above all, don't try to haul up the fish on the first run. The idea is to try to follow the mad dash, especially if the run is parallel to the pier or shoreline. If he runs out to sea—you've had it. The line will whine as it cuts the surface of the water, and this usually makes most anglers panic and haul back with all their might. The end result is usually a lost fish. When you hear the line whine, ease off and let the fish pull and work against the tension of the pole.

The idea is to keep the fish for the first ten to thirty seconds as you try to play the fish as best you can. This may seem like a long time to you but it's a whole lot longer for the fish. As you become knowledgeable about handpole fishing, you'll find that most of the big fish are lost within the first five seconds of battle. If you can hold or follow the fish for a short time, the odds will rapidly increase in your favor.

It's a funny thing but a lot of anglers don't like to get the tip of the rod in the water. They will frantically try to hold the rod tip up against the panic-stricken fish. But when a large fish is on, the rod tip can give you an edge. When the fish lunges downward, you should let him pull the rod tip into the water. Don't fight him. If need be, let him take most of the rod into the water. As long as you can hold the fish as you buffer some of the hard and fast runs by bowing and following, you can work the fish back up. As you bow and follow, you'll find that the lunges will get shorter and shorter and eventually the fish will become very tired. Once he's pretty tired, start looking for a place to land him. A beach, a low rocky point, or a half-submerged pier tire will all do in a pinch. The best thing to use to land the fish is a net. If you don't have one, try to drag the fish up onto the shore.

The worst thing you can do when a fish is on his first and most powerful run is haul back. Play him, don't rush him. You'll find that during the first two to five seconds, the fish will panic and expel most of its energy trying to get away. So follow the lunge. Let the fish burn up its energy and eventually you'll get the trophy you have been wishing for.

Other Techniques for the Handpole Fisherman

When handpole fishing in an area that has a sandy bottom, you will sometimes find that although you can see the fish swimming around, they just won't bite, and praying just won't seem to help. When you begin to feel like a Class A-1 fool, try this trick: Let your bait sink completely to the ocean bottom and let it lie there for awhile. Then pull the handpole to the side of your body. This will cause the bait to drag or bounce on the bottom. Drag it for two seconds and then stop. Then drag and stop again. The bait and split shot will make a scraping noise on the bottom and will attract the fish. Fish are naturally curious creatures and will investigate any movement or sound. This dragging technique will get the fish to at least take a look at the bait; the smell and movement will do the rest.

Another trick very similar to the one just mentioned involves dropping the same bait and letting it settle completely on the bottom. Leave it there for awhile and then lift the bait, stopping about a foot or so from the bottom. This sudden movement will attract the fish's attention and will draw some spontaneous strikes.

This method is also good for deep-water (thirty feet or more) fishing. Let the bait down and if nothing happens, give your bait some quick, snappy jerks. First, this will give some added action to the bait and will attract some quick responses. Second, it will tear off some of the bait and give the fish some chum or free samples. Third, it will cause a fish that is reluctant to take the bait to strike on reflex; it'll think the bait is getting away and will hit it. These techniques don't always work, but if the fish aren't biting, it sure can't hurt to try them.

A lot of times you will find yourself fishing right next to someone who is catching all the fish. You won't seem to have any of his luck and the more he catches, the more frustrated you become. You have three options: (1) ask him about his technique—what he uses for bait, his line size, and so on—and then adjust to his specifications and suggestions; (2) watch his style of fishing—is his method such that he varies his bait depth? or does he bounce or drag his bait; (3) quietly move to another spot and look the other way.

Try the first two options. Also try varying your hook, the fishing depth, and your bait size. One very obvious reason for your being fishless is your bait size. In fishing, bigger bait doesn't necessarily mean bigger or more fish. Many times a handpoler will put a big glob of bait on his hook and just sit there grinning and dreaming of the gorilla fish he's going to catch. Usually his hook will be too small for a fish able to take bait that size; or the bait will be too big for a smaller fish, which just wouldn't be able to get its mouth around even half of the bait. The small fish will simply peck at the bait, which will probably look like a fifty-pound New York cut steak to it. Therefore, if you keep the hook small and use just enough bait to cover the hook, you'll have a lot more strikes and more fish in the bucket. Stay away from big baits and use baits that are a reasonable size for the fish you're after.

Another cause for slow action is fishing at the wrong depth. Try various depths and see which gives you the most action. Sometimes small fish won't go very far from their homes and will stick to the security of the rocks; therefore, unless the bait is very close, they won't venture toward it. The idea is to fish right in the area of their homes, where they feel confident and territorial. By experimenting, you'll eventually find the right depth. Once you do, stick to it and you'll get all the fun and action you desire.

As you can see, the person who is adaptable and innovative and who experiments will eventually find the technique that is working for the day. Fish don't bite the same way every day and for this reason you must change techniques until you find the combination that is working for the day. Also let your friends in on your secret and you'll all have fun. And that's what it's all about.

Catching Bait

Knowing how to use a bamboo pole can be a great asset to you. With this pole you can get all the live bait you could possibly use, and even catch bait for your friends when they need it. Live bait that was just caught is the best in the world.

One of the best baits for the shore fisherman is the common goby, also called 'o'opu nākea (brackish to saltwater fish) and 'o'opu 'akupa (freshwater fish). It is a very hearty fish and will keep well on a hook, as well as overnight in a well-aerated bucket. This fish has a short, stout, blunt head and is usually dark grey in color. It lives almost exclusively in small shoreline ponds, brackish inlets, and estuaries. Sometimes it is a light color and blends in with the sand very well.

The best way to catch goby is with shrimp and a handpole. If you don't have shrimp, use small snails, which you can find in abundance along rocky shorelines. Just crush the shellfish with a rock and use the meaty portion for bait. Most people set up a standard handpole rig with the lead far from the hook; but the best way to rig your line is to slide the splitshot all the way down to the hook eye. (This rig is very similar to a jig, which has the lead head with hook embedded.)

Now look for a small, shallow pond with lots and lots of round boulders. Put the tiny jig next to some boulders and bounce, twitch,

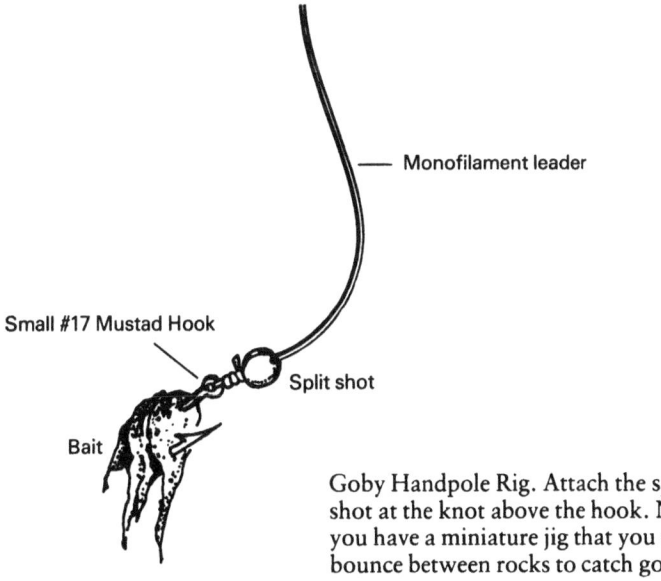

Goby Handpole Rig. Attach the split shot at the knot above the hook. Now you have a miniature jig that you can bounce between rocks to catch gobies.

and dance the tiny bait on the bottom. Keep working the bait all around the rocks and watch for some sort of movement. If there is a goby under a rock, he'll see the dancing bait and rush out from hiding and take it. Simply give the line a light twitch and pull the goby out and unhook it. Treat the goby as gently as you possibly can; it's tough but can get crushed in your hand. You'll find that this technique is pretty reliable, and that catching bait does not have to be a hit-or-miss chore.

The Zebra Blenny fish—more commonly called skipjack or jumping jack, or *paoʻo* in Hawaiian—is also a very, very good bait. The skipjack will rarely take bait, mainly because it feeds on algae and minute organisms. The best time to catch it is during a dark night. If you go when a full moon is out, the skipjack will be skittish and hard to find and catch. Take along a pair of *tabi*s or sneakers, a strong headlight, and a deep scoop net. Slowly put the net over the skipjack as it sits on a rock, or grab it if you're fast enough. It'll be slippery and very fast, so if you decide to catch one with your hands, I suggest you use black cotton gloves. These gloves will be harder to see at night, and with them you can make closer approaches and get more bait in the bucket.

Handle the bait with great care. Small baitfish don't take to rough treatment and will die very quickly. Always keep the bucket very well aerated when catching bait and once you've hooked the bait. It's also a good idea to unhook the baitfish in a water-filled bucket so that the amount of time that the fish is out of the water is kept to a minimum. Change the water often and add some big leaves to give the baitfish cover. Skipjack and other baitfish seem to calm down faster if they can find some cover. Rocks should not be used since they tend to crush baits against the sides of the bucket when it is in transit.

Battery-operated aerators are good for on-the-field use. If you have to keep a bunch of bait overnight at your house, then an electric 120-volt aerator is the best bet. Battery-operated aerators aren't very dependable after many hours of use. Often the batteries will run down or the motor will burn out and leave you with some smelly dead fish.

2
Reels for the Shore Fisherman

The Evolution of the Reel

During the pre-war years, a reel was a very poorly handmade contrivance that often sounded like the proverbial coffee grinder. It was basically a "direct-drive" creation, that is, spool and handle were turned together at a 1 to 1 ratio. It was dangerous to the fingers and knuckles because whenever a scrappy fish grabbed a well-presented bait and headed for the horizon, the spool would turn at an incredible rate and the handle would become a blur. Any attempt to grab the whirling knob would mean terrible bruises, torn fingernails, and several badly damaged fingers. This did not stop many careful and determined anglers from developing a newer and better-built reel, however.

The "adjustable drag mechanism" was invented by a Californian named William Boschen, and it did away with the dreaded spinning handle. After working on the drag mechanism for several years, Boschen took his new invention to a well-known pair, machinist Julius Vom Hofe of Brooklyn and craftsman Joe A. Coxe of Catalina. Together they created a revolutionary fishing reel that permitted the spool to turn against an adjustable three-plate, multiple-disk clutch system. The system consisted of multiple washers, some fixed metal washers with slots that wouldn't turn and some soft washers that would turn. This combination created the right amount of drag or resistance. Being that it was fully adjustable, you could also set the drag to the tension you wanted. In 1913 the idea was so original that it wasn't accepted. When Boschen landed a 335-pound broadbill with his new reel, however, manufacturers soon began to use his creation as a model. Later a company by the name of Hardy Brothers Company of England designed the "star drag turning knob," which is now a standard part in all conventional and trolling reels.

An Englishman named Holden Illingworth, another trail blazer, created the "fixed-spool reel" in 1920. Illingworth actually combined several ideas, one of which came from a Scotsman, Peter Mallock of Perth. In 1884 Mallock invented a fixed-spool reel that was a totally confusing apparatus. Illingworth redesigned the innovative invention and made it a more functional fishing machine. The reel later got the popular name "spinning reel" because of the spinning turntable that wrapped the line onto the fixed or stationary spool.

Soon the Vom Hofe and Illingworth reels had to make way for the more sophisticated reels of today. Reels now boast magnetic casting control devices. This device, if adjusted properly, will guarantee a trouble-free cast. Reels are also becoming so well machined that baitcasting reels can handle small-diameter lines (i.e., 6- to 8-pound test) without the line sneaking between the spool and the side plate. And casting is truly an ease when one of these new casting marvels is properly broken in. Never to be seen again will be the huge blisters a heavy spool that overruns at the drop of a hat leaves. Today we have spools made of aluminum alloys and incredibly strong plastic that make a spool simply float on the stainless steel ball bearings. These spools are a far cry from the brass spools and the crank-at-your-own-risk direct drive reels that left white calkline burns on the thumbs.

Truly, fishing reels have come a long way. The reel manufacturers of today compete in a huge multimillion-dollar angling market—a market that wants higher capacity, finely tuned, highly durable, and smoother performing reels. Thus reels can no longer host jerky, unreliable drags; small, narrow spools; and weak, brittle gears. The drag disk has to be able to dissipate heat very quickly. The spool has to be able to withstand the enormous pulling force from deep-sea fighting fish and still remain fully intact to catch fish another day. This may be a tall order, for some of the deep-sea dwellers that prowl the shoreline at night can cause so much damage that any reel may be literally turned into a pile of useless junk.

Today it's a fairly common thing to go fishing for big game on small, light tackle because today's tackle is better and more dependable. Dependable reels will land giant fish when used with finely tuned angling skills. Veteran angler Stu Apte didn't land an eighty-two-pound sailfish on 8-pound test by selecting poorly made reels. Anglers like Apte select the best reels they can find and maintain them so that no point can be charged against them when they finally hook-up with that record-setting fish.

The evolution of the reel has not yet reached its zenith, for the demand is still on for more sophisticated and finely tuned fishing reels. The search will go on and, we hope, never end.

How to Choose a Reel

The simplest way to choose a reel is to determine first, your line class or pound test; second, the conditions in which you will fish; and third, the size and strength of the fish that you will be presenting bait and lures to. All of these major points will help you select the reel that will more likely serve you in the best way possible.

When purchasing a reel remember not to settle for second best. Cosmetics and flashy advertisements do not mean smooth drags and dependable gears. Check the specifications of the reels that are on your list of potential choices, then go to the store and take a look at them. Pick the reel up and look at its construction, design, and ease of operation. Does it seem like a few parts are loose or poorly

Spinning Reels *(right to left):* Daiwa D2600, Penn #550, Daiwa BG#90, Daiwa Mini-Mite.

machined? If it's a spinning reel, check whether it has a skirted spool (a device that keeps the line from dropping under the spool) and a roller guide that actually rolls. Does it have unnecessary protruding contraptions, such as extra-long bail screws, which have the potential to cause failures or to entangle fragile monofilament when in constant use? Also look for good, salt-resistant frames and parts. Freshwater reels have no place in very corrosive salt environments. And last of all, does it feel right in your hand? Compare its feel with that of the rod you either own or wish to purchase. Attaching an ultralight spinning reel to a heavy surf-casting rod wouldn't make much sense. Think about balance and comfort. Remember, you'll be fishing with the reel for many hours in a day and comfort will make the fishing more enjoyable.

Consider also the reel's line capacity in relation to the size line you'll be using. Be sure it will hold the hundreds of yards of line that you will require when you hook that monster of your dreams. Putting 100-pound-test monofilament in an ultralight reel will get you very few yards. But don't second guess the fish by thinking that it will never strip your spool clean. Eventually the day will come when you'll get a chance at a big fish, and when that day comes, you'll want to have as many chips stacked on your side of the rod as possible. Large trophy fish don't come from fishing luck but from finely tuned, well-selected, and lavishly pampered tackle. Saltwater fish aren't like most freshwater dwellers. They don't rush for tree stumps or brush piles but look for deep water and head straight for it by taking the fastest path possible. For instance, a bonefish or trevally *(ulua)* can beeline out and straight down the side of a coral reef and disappear into the blue abyss before you realize your first hundred yards have disappeared.

Once you've determined how much line you'll be needing for that long running fish, you've got to find a reel with a smooth and dependable drag system. Nothing is more important than a smooth drag. A reel that merely looks sharp and classy doesn't always contain a well-engineered drag system. Look for a reel that has a wide adjustment range on the drag tension knob, that is, don't select a drag that goes from ultra-light to rock bottom in half a turn.

One way to test a reel is to put some line on the spool and hold the line up against the weight of the reel. Let the reel fall while holding the line. The reel should fall against the drag at a smooth, constant rate. If the reel doesn't fall unless you give the line a good jerk, then look for another reel.

If you have a chance, look inside the reel to check the drag disk placement and size. If that's not possible, look at the parts diagram, which is usually tucked away in the box with the reel. It should tell you if the parts are made of good material, such as high-grade steel for gears and not soft brass, which tends to break quickly when you're fighting a big fish; or if the manufacturer is hiding some potential problems. Be sure to purchase a reel that you can get parts for. Reels break down, and they seem to break down most often at the beach. When this happens, you don't want to be having to go to the store to buy another reel and cannibalize parts from it. Look for a reel that has replaceable parts and that is backed by repair services and a good reputation.

Another good thing to do is check with a lot of good fishermen. See what kind of reel they prefer. They've been around for a long time and usually will have tried all the lemons and settled on a reel that they can depend on. If asked, they will usually tell you all the good and bad points of all the reels they have tried. They'll also tell you how to improve on the ones that suit your type of fishing.

Unfortunately, all reels don't come tailored to fit your unique fishing needs exactly. Although they try to design and engineer the best reel they can, manufacturers must cater to a mass market. This is why conversion kits were invented. These kits were designed to fine tune or adjust your reels to better suit your personal fishing needs.

Spinning Reels

Of all the reels used by shore fishermen, the spinning reel reigns supreme. The reason for its popularity is its obvious ease of operation. But the greatest attribute of the spinning reel is that you don't have to worry about horrible backlash problems or getting a red hot casting thumb. Just about any beginner or eager child can learn to cast a spinning reel. All it takes is a few minutes of good tutoring, a very attentive person, and good tackle.

To use a spinning reel, hook the line in the crease of the forefinger of your right hand, flip the bail, and with a slow flip of your wrist make your cast. Once the plug hits the water, turn the handle and engage the automatic bail. After the bail is secure, all you have to do is crank the handle and take up the line. It's simple and yet very, very efficient.

Spinning reels are ideal for the shore whipper primarily because of

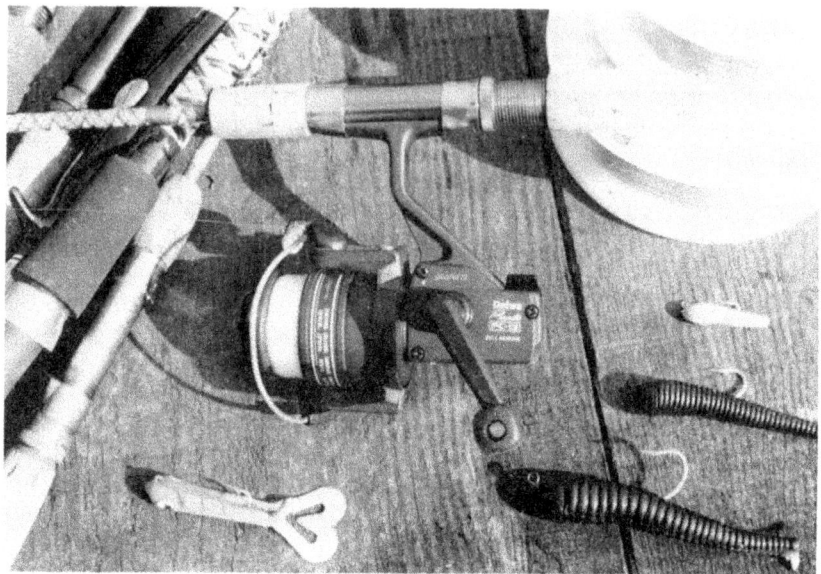

Spinning Reel

their 5 to 1, 4.5 to 1, and other high-speed ratios required for fast retrieve patterns. The high-speed retrieve enables the fisherman to work plugs and lures at various speeds that will literally drive gamefish wild. With a spinning reel you can skip plugs, make them dodge, dart, and dive; you can even jig the bottom with great effectiveness. And all this can be achieved without worrying about line being wound improperly. The up and down movement of the reel spindle and the spinning bail will automatically wind the line on the reel spool in an orderly manner.

As for maintenance, the spinning reel requires very little care. Actually the bail spring is the most troublesome of all the parts of the spinning reel. If you use some foresight and purchase an extra spring when you're at the fishing store or when you're buying the spinner, then you will have an extra bail spring in your tackle box when you need it.

Periodically spinners need lubricating. Just clean out all the old grease and pack in new grease. Before every trip lightly grease the bail spring to ensure that you have a snappy tripping of the bail. Some anglers also give their reels a good spray with a high-grade lubricant such as WD-40 or LPS after every trip. This prevents corrosion of body casings and, with luck, extends the life span of the spinner. The major external areas to lubricate on a spinner are usually the handles and bail spring. Give the bail and reel handle a tiny drop of 3-in-1 oil before the day's fishing begins and you're all set. The bail must be able to spring back with some authority, and without a liberal dose of oil, the bail will flip back like a rusty door. It's also a good idea to take a small screwdriver and check for loose screws, sometimes the result of constant shore spinning.

For the fisherman who does constant shoreline whipping and who uses the walking technique, a spare spool or spools of line is really a must. Most well-prepared spincasters keep several loaded spools in separate cloth sacks and secure the line onto the extra spools with rubberbands. When that big fish strips your spool clean, it's usually a long walk back to the car to get more line. It's also hard to walk straight after your reel has been stripped clean and you have a bad case of wobbly knees.

With the advent of the skirted spool the old problem of line getting caught inside the internal windings of the reel has been virtually eliminated. (In the old days, you had to stop spinning, handline in the already cast line, and unscrew the spool to get the coiled line off the spindle.) But this doesn't mean you should throw away your skirtless spinning reel. If it suits your needs and doesn't give you a hard time, keep it and use it until the end of its days. Most skirted spools also come with a quick release button located on the top of the spool. With this device, you can quickly change spools without going through all sorts of unscrewing. A good thing to do is purchase several spare spools and then rebuild the drag system for each spool to specific line sizes: a spool for 6-pound test, for 12-pound test, and for 20-pound test, for example. Then when you're fishing and need to change line sizes, you can switch spools and already have the drag system for that specific line size. You can rebuild the drag system by taking out all of the soft and hard washers and checking if any of the other parts, such as the springs and spreader washers, should be replaced with more soft and hard washers. The more of these washers you use, the smoother your drag system will be.

Another obvious feature of the spinning reel is the ease with which it can cast light to ultralight lines. Although the new generation of bait-casting reels are becoming so well tuned that they can cast light lines, 4- to 6-pound test, it is the ultralight spinning reels that efficiently cast the 1- to 4-pound test. These small jewels are really miniature versions of larger, heavy-duty spinners and not little, poorly built toys that are used for catching minnows. They now support very well engineered drag systems and have superfast, high-speed gear ratios.

They also have the capability to fight and land some fairly large fish, ones that tip the scales over the twenty-pound mark. With these reels you can easily cast tiny $1/16$-ounce jigs and plugs that would normally prove difficult for larger reels. Since the tackle is scaled down for small catches, you can hook more fish, as your arms won't tire out as easily.

Every so often you tangle into a big one that seems to really rattle your knees and stop your heart. When you're going after fairly large gamefish that will run like blazes and you're using ultrathin line, the drag will have to be velvet smooth. If you're serious about successfully landing large gamefish with this reel, then purchase the best reel with the best engineered drag. If that's not possible, then look for a system that will be easy to tailor to your specific needs.

Another good thing about the spinning reel is its cost. It is relatively inexpensive in comparison to some of the bait-casting reels on the market. This does not mean spinners are poorly made but that they are more popular and thus the competition in that market is stiffer. The spinner varies in cost and quality. No matter what type of spin-fisherman you are, there will be a spinner you can afford.

Although a lot of today's reels look like computerized contraptions, with their sleek lines, numbered plates, shiny handles, and complicated-looking bail systems, the best reel is the one that is strong and dependable. A lot of fishing is done on some rough terrain and reels do fall or get accidently dropped. A strong, well-built reel will weather all this abuse and still come back fighting. Brittle handles and soft bail wire just don't stand up to the true harshness of the saltwater environment.

Bait-Casting Reels

What scares most fishermen about bait-casting reels (also called plug-casting reels) are the constant hassles with backlash, that is, a spool overrunning during or just after a cast. This annoying malfunction that leaves a badly tangled mess of line was a problem with most bait-casting reels of the early 1800s. These reels had as standard equipment a direct drive cranking system, heavy brass spools, and a poor tolerance between spool and side plates. With these reels it was only after countless months of casting practice and nerve-wracking fishing trips that the thumb could successfully make a cast that went further without mishap. The bait-casting reels of today, however, are literally casting marvels. They flaunt centrifugal brakes, or magnetic brakes that make bait casting almost totally backlash free. With the centrifugal tension knob, a device on the left of the reel (or on the right side if the reel is for left-handed fishermen) that regulates the speed and tension applied to the spool, you can set the reel for trouble-free casting and use just about any size plug. The bait-casting reel can cast anything from the two-ounce heavies to the quarter-ounce miniature plugs. Gone are the direct drive bait-casting reels that limited casting distance to under twenty feet. Bait-casting reels boast as standard equipment superlight spools, beefed-up drag systems, and a high gear-return ratio (4.7 to 1, 4.8 to 1, 5 to 1, and others).

From an angling standpoint, the bait-casting reel is superior to the spinner when you're after big husky gamefish. The drag systems of most of these reels have proven to be very dependable and can withstand extremely long "hot" runs. Many of the fish that seem to give the spinning reel a hard time are quickly controlled because of the bulldog characteristics of the bait-casting reel. It's truly the work horse of small casting reels. Team this reel with a 7½- to 8-foot glass or graphite rod with a fast taper and you'll be able to lick just about any gamefish with incredible regularity.

Using one for shoreline whipping is a unique experience. The spinner has been the accepted standard for so long that it is really unusual

Bait-Casting Reel

to see a bait-casting outfit along the shoreline. Its compactness and lightness makes it seem out of place on the rough lava shoreline, but it casts just as far as a good spinner and will retrieve a plug with more dexterity because of its compactness. However, it still seems that it would be more suitable for the quiet work of fishing for panfish in some weed bed of a placid lily pond than for *ulua* on some lava-strewn shoreline. But the bait-casting reel handles the severity of the strong, determined runs of big shoreline game well and has never come up lacking.

Although the spinner can cast light line a great distance and with great ease, it has one limitation: the spinner cannot handle heavy line for casting. With a light spinning outfit, the quality of heavy line (20- to 30-pound test) capable of being spooled in a spinning reel is minimal. During an average cast, the line uncoils off the spool against the resistance, and as the line gets closer to the spool's center, distance casting suffers considerably. The line seems to come off the spool in a clattering flutter and the plug goes nowhere. So, the only way to make a good long cast is to use an extra-heavy plug. On a bait-casting reel, however, the line comes off directly from the spool and therefore the cast is very long and graceful.

When you look at what's available in bait-casting reels, you'll find a very wide and varied selection. Although the selection may seem endless, there are only a very few reels that will fit your needs. What you'll need for shoreline fishing is a reel that has a good drag, large line capacity (approximately 250 yards of 15-pound test), and a set of ball bearings on each side of the reel. Now, with this reel you have the ability to reach the far reef and the line capacity to fight long-running saltwater fish. Abu-Garcia reels meet these needs, as do other brands such as Daiwa and Shimano. Garcia's #6500C or, even better, the #6500CA both do the job very well, have all the above features, and are well built.

Surf Casting Reels

In the old days, if you wanted to go surf casting for big game, you had a very small selection of conventional reels to choose from. The selection ranged from Ocean City's to Pflueger-Templars and Atlapacs, and later to Penn Senators. Today's conventional reels come in all shapes, forms, and makes, and they vary in price range. Obviously, reel manufacturers saw that the conventional reel market was not being capitalized upon enough. They saw a demand for a new line of reel and also for improvements for existing reels. Now we have Daiwa's Sealine series, Garcia's surf casting line of Ambassadeurs, and Carl Newell's ultrasmooth surf casting reels. These reels are basically lighter, smoother on the cast, and are able to hold up to strong, determined runs. They flaunt lighter spools, stronger brace bars, and a relatively low selling price.

The Penn Senators have been the standard for shore casters for many a generation and will forever be known for bringing up some huge gamefish. Penn Senator is really a household word when it comes to shore fishing. The Penn Senator reel is popular because it is simple in design, easy to maintain, dependable, and able to take punishment from the harshest of environments. The second best thing about the Senators is that you can extend them with Carl Newell extension kits for more line capacity. This capability greatly expanded the range of ways in which the Senators could be and still are used.

Because the contours of the ocean bottom and fringing reefs are different around each island, you'll find a different selection of standard reels in use on each island. On the Big Island you'll see the #6/0 (114H) Senator, the Daiwa #600H, the rare Pflueger #400 (1419 $3/4$) and the #500 (1420 $1/4$), and sometimes even the Atlapac reel, being used pretty much everywhere, although not all of these reels are still

Surf Casting Reels

being manufactured, namely the Pfluegers and the Atlapac. At times you'll find the Penn International #50W in use, but the cost and weight being what it is, you won't find very many. In each of these reels you'll find mostly 80-pound-test Maxima monofilament from top to bottom. Some very resourceful individuals will use 100 yards of 60-pound Maxima on the bottom and 150 to 175 yards of 80-pound Maxima on the top. (Maxima is a standard brand of monofilament in Hawaii because of its great resistance to abrasion and its overall strength.) After the top 80-pound mono has taken a lot of beating and the time comes to replace it, only the top 150 yards is changed. The use of the 60-pound test adds more line to the reel that has a one hundred-pounder on the other end looking for the horizon. Most of the time the 60-pound mono isn't used, but when it is, it handles most fish very, very well. Besides, most of the abrasion from fishing around coral and rocks occurs on the first 50 yards of line; therefore, the bottom 60-pound test is rarely damaged when fighting shoreline gamefish.

Maui's shoreline anglers have the Penn #3/0 Senator as their standard, a far cry from the standard #6/0 Senator used by the Big Islanders. Although their reel is much smaller, it can be extended to a maximum line capacity by using the Carl Newell extension kit. With the bottom terrain being mostly pebbles and sand, their main concern is line capacity and not line strength. For this reason their line size is anywhere from 30- to 50-pound-test Maxima. Both Honolulu and Kauai fishermen use smaller reels like the ones Maui anglers use. They too are more concerned with line capacity than with line strength, and therefore their line class falls between 30- and 50-pound test.

So, each island's fishermen use a different line size for their standard type of shore fishing. Each environment or terrain also requires a particular line as well as size reel. There is really no sense in purchasing a #9/0 or #10/0 Penn Senator for fishing from a small sandy point that has a sandy bottom. If the bottom terrain enables you to let a fish run to its heart's content without your having to worry about a severe drop-off or a coral abyss, then line capacity should be your primary concern.

Rarely will you find shore casters using reels over the #6/0 size. Only a select few have gone not only to #9/0 Senators but on to #10/0 Penn Senators, and have loaded their reels with 130-pound-test monofilament. This is extreme and reduces the sport to a full-time job. The weight of the reels alone will astonish most average-muscled fishermen. When clamped onto a thirteen-foot rod and loaded with fourteen- to sixteen-ounce lead, this reel makes throwing your back out a simple matter. So, ultralarge reels and lines are for the heavy-set soul who doesn't ever want to lose the fish that has taken his bait. One good consolation about using heavy lines and reels that imitate winches is you can literally crank up a fish from the water's edge without a gaff. With 130-pound test on your spool, it's a small matter to crank up a twenty-five-pound fish and flip it onto the shore as if it were a small *menpachi*.

Prior to the creation of extension kits, the standard procedure for a fisherman was to take his fishing reel to a very expensive machinist and have his spool cut and extended. The job also entailed having the reel bars and reel seat extended. As a result, the fee for this precision work would total up to twice what the fisherman paid for his mortgage. A lot of times he would also have to wait for the machinist to make time for his job. And quite often the machinist would make mistakes, or have some kind of misunderstanding with the angler and either make the bars too short or the spool too long. Because of this the fisherman would have to have available more parts and extra spools just in case the machinist flubbed it.

But once the adjustments were made and if the fisherman was lucky enough to get the spool machined right, he had a reel that could very easily hold 300-plus yards of 60- or 80-pound test. He'd never have to worry about a big fish spooling him or cleaning him out. But human nature being what it is, when an angler had a strike he'd invariably put a lot of pressure on the initial run which would collapse the spool during the strike. This caused a severe bend in the spool shank; the flanges of the spool would bind; and the spool would cease to turn. The extended spool has what is called "memory," which enables line stretched thin by a stubborn fish to expand back to its original size. It is important that you relieve some of the internal tension created by the expanding monofilament by recasting it because the line will exert incredible pressure on the side plates of the spool. The spool will then pull the extended center apart and lodge itself against the side plates. Once this happens the reel will be totally out of commission and cranking will be out of the question. If this happens during a difficult battle, your only alternative is to handline the fish in and hope the fish won't make a determined run against the locked spool.

With this kind of thing happening, a very clever individual by the name of Carl W. Newell (940 Allen Avenue, Glendale, California,

91201) provided the angling market with well-designed cast aluminum spools and specially designed reel support posts and reel frame bases. The wider and more solid reel support and modified reel seat transformed the Penn Senators into more solid and wobble-free reels. With lighter spools and stronger posts, the Senators acquired a brand new face and longer fishing life. Today these adaptor kits do cost a considerable sum, but they eliminate the more costly and time-consuming process of having a machinist do the job.

Basic conventional reels will have a fairly low gear ratio because this ensures greater fish-fighting power and control in playing a monster fish. The average ratio is 2 to 1 and on up to 2.5 to 1. The Newells of today have gear ratios that are over 5 to 1, but these tend to be smaller than the standard surf casting heavies. They are tailored more for whipping and not the dunk-and-wait style of the average big-game fisherman.

Drags on conventional reels are of two basic types. The multiple-disk star—pretty much standard on all Penn Senators, Daiwas, and Newells—is a simple, starlike mechanism situated directly under the crank of most reels. A simple turn of the star drag will either loosen or tighten down on the drag disk. The second type of drag is the finely adjusted, lever-operated single-disk drag. This is more common on highly priced, big game trolling reels, such as the Fin Nor and Penn International reels.

One item that is usually used by offshore trollers but that plays an important role in the shore caster's reel is the harness lug. The lug is used with a harness belt when the fisherman is fighting large offshore fish. The harness lugs are usually situated on the top of both of the reel's end plates. Surf casters don't normally use a harness during an all-out battle, although it is not a bad idea; still lugs play a very important part in shoreline fishing. In shoreline fishing the lugs hold all the safety lines, which in turn keep the entire outfit from flying into the ocean during a vicious strike. The lines are usually secured to the lugs with either a slip knot or a brass clip. The other end of the safety line is tied to a railroad spike or any kind of pin that can be pounded into the shoreline. Sometimes an *ulua* strike can be quite powerful and rods and rodstands have been known to break or be ripped right out of the lava cracks they were embedded in. Some anglers don't trust the side lugs and connect the safety lines to the rod itself. In this way if the reel lugs don't hold up to the tremendous stress exerted on the tackle, the outfit is still kept on shore. The safety lines can also be attached to the rod and sometimes to the cross bars.

The cross bars have a tendency to bend and pull the side plates in and immobilize the reel's spool, so stick to either connecting the safety lines to the rod or reel lugs. Sometimes it may just seem like extra work, but when your strike comes you'll appreciate the extra time and effort you invested in taking precautions.

Maintaining Your Reels

One of the chief reasons big fish are lost on light tackle is poor equipment maintenance. All too often a trip will go completely bad and become unpleasant for everyone because of equipment that had been neglected. It all goes back to how you took care of your tackle during the last fishing trip at the beach, as well as after you came back. Even if the fishing tackle of today is of high quality, it still requires constant upkeep or else it will fall into disrepair, when even cleaning or lubricating will not restore the tackle to fair working condition. All too often you'll see someone who has gone through all the trouble of planning a long trip and who has spent untold amounts of money get to the shoreline only to find that the handle on the spinning reel refuses to turn. Or the bail spring is broken. Or the handle squeaks badly. Or the drag mechanism doesn't work because it was locked down tightly for the last two months. A lot of times valuable fishing time is wasted making repairs. A lot of this type of grief can easily be avoided if you take the time to at least loosen the drag tension knob or star drag and relieve some of the tension on the soft washers. If you simply rinse all of the moving parts with fresh water, the bail spring will not be left to collect salt crystals. Careless fishermen will always wonder why some people catch all the fish and why they always seem to have bad luck. But the same people who land a great quantity of fish keep the quality of their tackle up to high standards. They go to the trouble of cleaning and lubricating all the moving parts of their equipment, and they check troublesome parts that have the potential to break down on succeeding trips. It's also very curious but those who maintain their drags and gear always seem to land fish that are bigger and tougher than the fish a guy who doesn't maintain his gear lands. So, good fishing is relative to the amount of care you give to your tackle.

At one time people thought that you didn't have to take the time to repair gear: if something broke, you simply went out and bought a new one. Today this idea still seems to persist to some extent. However, because the prices of fishing tackle has drastically gone up (some prices look more like mortgage payment figures) people are becoming more selective when they purchase tackle. Yet many still neglect to maintain a $100 reel. It seems that today one must fix equipment and maintain it or do without.

Oiling up a reel to keep it working up to par is really an easy matter. Most manufacturers provide a complimentary tube or squeeze bottle of high-grade lubricating oil for just this purpose. Once a bottle is empty, it's a small price to pay to have it refilled, or to purchase another from the local fishing store. Tube lubricants are very inexpensive and will last for many, many trips. And because reels are much more intricately designed and their construction is much more complex than before, manufacturers have made it easier for the angler to lubricate his reel by labeling those spots that require it. To make things even simpler, you'll often find a maintenance guide with most reels. This guide is usually thrown away and forgotten about until a specific part is needed and must be ordered, or until the angler needs to know if the gear for the rotating whatchamacallit goes before the thingamawhatsit. These small booklets are tiny enough to keep in a small drawer or shoe box until you need them. When the time comes that you need the booklet, it will seem worth its weight in gold.

Fortunately for us, manufacturers maintain factory service centers throughout the country. Others have training programs for independent tackle repairmen who do repairs on a part-time basis. Companies of today also maintain a direct ordering service outlet and will send you any part you need as long as you give them the right parts number and reel model. It's comforting to know that you can send your reel away to have it fixed and restored to near perfect working condition, but it is far easier to keep your tackle in good working condition through constant maintenance.

A large repair job often centers around a small, easily maintained component; so if you take care of the small problems, you will most likely eliminate the possibility of a large one cropping up. For instance, if a bail spring is encrusted with salt and refuses to flip up, chances are that you will try to force it up and down until it gives and slowly becomes easier to flip. If the bail refuses to flip, you will most likely bend the bail bar or tear it off the bail mechanism. If you don't force the bail but try to unscrew the bail screw—also frozen shut—with an extra-large screwdriver, you may break the screw off completely or crack the spindle housing. If you break the screw off, your fishing for the day will be over, and chances are you will have to buy a totally new housing or new reel. All this can easily be avoided if you simply wash the reel prior to storage and give it a small dab of light oil.

Well-made reels are like carefully engineered cars: they need a regular oil change and lube job every so many miles. Without this constant care and feeding, the reel's life span will be greatly shortened. Fishermen who travel a great deal recognize the importance of constant maintenance. They know they have to keep their gear in tip-top working condition because at some time they may be far from any parts store. This requires constant vigilance and stocking of spare parts, if not carrying a spare reel. All this boils down to the fact that proper planning and constant maintenance usually culminates into a wonderfully enjoyable fishing experience.

Improving Your Drag System

The drag is the most important component of the reel. Its level of efficiency determines whether you land a fish or lose it. Very simply, what it does is it feeds out line when the fish runs and permits you to take up line when the fish stops. Prior to the creation of the adjustable multiple-disk drag system, the angler had to create drag with his thumb and a leather tab connected to one of the cross bars on the reel. Invariably the angler would very quickly get a blister the size of a nickel or a snow white crease on his thumb that would hurt like the devil. While the fish is running, ideally pressure is applied on the side plates or flange of the spool; but if the reel is full and the fish is running full-on, the only place to apply pressure is, unfortunately, on the line surface.

The drag disk surface has almost the same function as a car's brakes: it applies braking pressure to the spinning spool. The only difference is that the resistance is internally applied. If you take apart a reel, whether it be a spinner or conventional reel, you'll find basically two types of washer disk, hard and soft. The metal washers are stationary disks and the soft washers are moveable or rotating disks. When line is pulled from a spool, the spool turns and the soft disk and hard disk rub against each other. Because the more drag surface the better, it is preferable to have more or larger disks. The drag will slow the fish, which can run an average-sized reel up to 3500 rpm as it makes its all out run for Timbuktu. By utilizing the star drag as an adjustable turning knob, you can vary the amount of friction placed on the disk surface and increase or decrease the applied drag. It should be noted that it takes more force to get a drag moving, or to overcome the inertia of the spool (also called the starting drag).

When tested a good drag should make the rod tip bend radically on the first pull and then rise and level off into an even arc. If the rod bends and bounces like a jumping bean, then the drag is binding, a signal that you'll quickly lose the fish because the line is about to cut. If the line doesn't cut, internal damage to the gears will undoubtedly occur. As was noted earlier, one good way to test a drag is to adjust it to a little less than the reel's weight, then pull out line. While holding the line, let the reel fall against the drag resistance. The reel should fall smoothly. If it takes a small jerk to get the reel started on its way, and if it jerks as it falls, then the drag either needs adjusting or needs a new soft disk.

In actuality the ideal way to test a drag is to apply prolonged pressure on the drag disk and thereby simulate as closely as possible the true fishing event. To do this, pull line from the reel until you have about a hundred yards or more of line. This can be accomplished by pulling the line with an electric motor that has a winding drum; or by connecting your line to a car, bicycle, or fast-running kid. The test should be done several times to get a true reading of the drag's performance. The heat within the reel plates will build up and give the drag system the acid test.

Heat is one of the leading causes of drags becoming erratic, which in turn can cause you to lose your fish. Soft disk washers quickly get glazed, teflon turns back into a powder, leather roasts like a side of beef, and felt starts to burn. Most fishermen at some time have witnessed someone pouring water over a reel to keep it cool. The metal stationary disk heats up against the induced friction to the point that the side plates get hot to the touch and the drag slowly loses its smoothness. For this reason metal disk washers that dissipate heat very quickly and efficiently are necessary, otherwise the internal and chemical properties of the soft disk washers begin to change dramatically. The most efficient metals for drag material are brass and aluminum. They dissipate heat very quickly and do not rust. Stainless steel seems like a good choice but it doesn't dissipate heat as freely or as quickly. It works well with lubricated leather and felt, but on a long run will quickly glaze the surface of the soft washers.

Another thing to look for is a drag adjustment that has a lot of latitude for tightening. Don't select the reel that boasts of a drag system that goes from ultralight to full lock in a quarter turn. The drag should have a working setting of approximately 2 pounds resistance, and with at least a 360-degree turn to spare before a full lock. More then 360 degrees is even better.

Although the drag is the most important part of the reel, unfortunately it is also the part least checked by anglers. The drag should be released to zero tension immediately after a day's fishing to ensure that the soft washers have a chance to expand back to their full size. If not, the washers will retain their compactness and your drag will eventually go bad after repeated use and will have to be replaced. Should this happen, go back to the retailer or manufacturer and purchase a new set of drag disks (soft) and install them. Sometimes this cannot be done because your reel has become obsolete and its parts just aren't available. But if the reel is still working well and you'd like to continue using it, then the next best thing to do is to make your own drag washers out of material you can easily obtain.

Drag washer materials come in a wide selection, but only a few are worth mentioning. Manufacturers have made washers of leather, felt, teflon, delrin, asbestos, cork, brake-lining material, and other space age materials; but the most easily obtainable and reliable are felt and leather. Chrome tanned leather is best, and its optimum thickness should be about that of a dime. Oiled leather is the best material for washers, and oiled felt material the second best. Both are easily purchased at either a well-stocked leather shop or hobby shop. The cost is minimal and the results are fantastic. Simply remove the washers that need to be replaced and trace their shape on the leather or felt material. Next, cut the washer out using a gasket cutter or a sharp pair of scissors.

When the same leather or felt washer is lubricated its coefficient of friction will change greatly. Adding selected oils to the felt and leather increases the slippage and permits you to add more pressure on the soft washers, which in turn allows for more direct contact with the reel surface. This enlarged surface area greatly increases the smoothness of the drag system. One of the favorite lubricants of top anglers like Mark Sosin and Bob Stearns is a combination of top-grade machine oil and Never-Seez, a compound designed to prevent metals from corroding and binding together (obtainable at plumbing supply stores or by writing Never-Seez Compound Corporation, Broadview, Illinois, 60153). Another good lubricant now on fishing supply store shelves is #0025 Special Lubricant with teflon (marketed by Roy Dean Products Co., 23440 Kean, Dearborn, Michigan 48124; or by J. Lee Cuddy Assoc., 8255 N. E. Second Avenue, Miami, Florida 33138).

Once the new leather washers are installed you'll find you have a remarkably smoother drag system and better chances of stopping that fast-running fish. But leather is not a cure-all for drag systems, mainly because it requires lots of care and maintenance to keep up its super performance. Thus constant checking and changing of washers are part of keeping the reel's drag in top shape. This is not to say that you'll be changing them every other day, but several times a year is about right, depending on the extent of use.

It's a good idea to precut lots of extra washers and keep them handy in the tackle box or repair kit that you should carry. You should also have extra sheets of washer material handy for people who need help changing their washers. Half the fun of fishing is watching a good friend catch fish and cheering him on.

Teflon washers come with many of the new reels and can be purchased in fishing supply stores to replace old, worn ones. It is a good washer material and doesn't require much maintenance; however, it doesn't take to high-speed runs and has a tendency to increase drag tension, which can be dangerous in battles with strong, long-running fish. So if you use teflon, be sure to loosen the drag tension knob during an extended run. Teflon is good for fishing reels that don't have drags that require frequent tightening. Although they are easier to use and cleaner to install, they have more drawbacks than benefits for the light tackle angler.

As you can see, the way to a smooth drag is to maintain the gear and to take the time and effort necessary for replacing its parts with tried-and-true components. Although these components may seem extremely inexpensive, the results speak for themselves. And that is what you want—results. Tackle, no matter how sophisticated and innovative, has to be maintained well and at times pampered.

Your Emergency Repair Kit

Even if you maintain your gear properly, there is always the possibility that something will break; or, even if the reel is in good shape, things still may need tightening or adjusting. And it always seems that you never have the proper tool for making the necessary repairs. A lot of times using the wrong tool will lead to more problems or never really restore the reel's full potential.

You need a small but well-supplied repair kit. Fortunately, these kits are easy to assemble and relatively inexpensive. First of all you need a container that is water resistant, rustproof, and able to hold an adequate supply of tools. You can purchase small, crushproof plastic containers from any store that stocks a fairly large inventory of school supplies. Pencil cases, utility boxes, or old discarded Tupperware sandwich containers all work very well.

Tools with specific functions such as reel wrenches should be kept in these containers. Small booklets that give a rundown on reel parts can be placed in plastic bags and kept at the bottom of the container or taped to its cover. Most reel wrenches come with screwdrivers and heads that fit specific nuts or screws on the reel. A good selection of these types of wrenches will greatly enhance your tackle tool box. Small kits that carry a good selection of tools, such as ratchet sets and screwdrivers that are interchangeable, are a good choice. These tools have multiple functions and don't take up too much space. Other tools such as small, well-made wrenches, channel locks, and vise grips are valuable additions to the tool kit. They cost quite a bit, but good quality tools that are dependable usually do. Cheap tools don't do the job and only lead to added frustration.

Good quality oils can be quite easily obtained either from well-stocked fishing supply stores or from hardware stores. WD-40, LPS, and Wonder Mist lubricating oils now come in small spray containers and are ideal for small tool kits. The old standby, 3-in-1 oil (sewing machine oil) is an old favorite of mine and it too comes in small metal containers that fit nicely in the kit box. Add to this the small squeeze tube containers that come with your reel and you're pretty much set for any kind of lubricating job necessary. One tip: If you don't have any oil and need a small amount to keep the reel handle from squeaking, or if you need to keep the bail springy, use the oil from your car's motor. Simply take the dip stick and dab a little drop on the spot needing the oil. The oil isn't top quality but at least it's something.

If you check with some well-stocked hobby stores, you may find a small propane torch the size of a Bic lighter. These small torches do a wonderful job on tip guides or regular rod guides and are a valuable addition to the kit. In a pinch, a torch will start signal fires, weld back broken bail springs, and weld split rings completely closed on plugs that tend to open up during heavy strikes.

Another thing to keep in your repair kit is an assortment of drag washer materials. A small section of thin leather (a dime's thickness) and some good quality felt are easy to keep, and when used with high-grade oils will give you a top-quality drag. Naturally you can't carry around a gasket cutter for cutting all these washers, but you can carry a pair of small fold-away scissors, which will very easily do the same job.

Also, reserve a spot for spare parts in the repair kit. Keep whatever you can stock, short of reel housings, and store items in small plastic zip-lock bags. Ask politely at the nearest jewelers for a small handful of tiny zip-locks, which are usually used for rings and such.

Other miscellaneous items that should be kept in the kit but that are not mandatory are things like small squeeze tubes of epoxy, electrical tape, a small roll of nylon rod-wrapping thread, ferrule cement, and a pair of hemostats (a surgical tool). Another good item to have is a small quantity of telephone copper wire for speedy repairs and even some sewing chores. Dental floss is good for sewing chores and can be wrapped around a loose guide in nothing flat. It's strong and easy to tie. Keep a supply of needles tucked away in the dental floss container.

Other miscellaneous items are pretty much personal items. Some people carry emergency rescue supplies in the same tool kit: a signal mirror, flare kit, fire starter, signal smoke, waterproof matches, compass, and smelling salt. These are all good kit items for the guy who's going to be far from home and at times far from civilization.

3
Fishing Rods

"God made poles and men made rods" is an old saying that goes back a long ways, but it is still true today. The old Mississippi cane pole has evolved drastically from the days of cotton cords, whiskey bottle cork floaters, and catfishing in freshwater rivers. The evolution of rods began back in the ninth century, with the Chinese leading this development with their rods made of bamboo and hand-crafted reels. During the thirteenth century, men in Europe were starting to build rods. This was not surprising since these craftsmen knew how to build long bows, many of the skills and materials for which were appropriate for the fashioning of crude fish poles.

Actually the craft of rod making is generally traced back as far as 1496 to a book entitled *The Book of Saint Albans* by Juliana Berners. This enterprising book details the process of constructing one's own rod with hazel, willow, or ash. The book also explains the processes of curing, drying, straightening, and even tapering rods. The common rod of this era usually ranged anywhere from ten to eighteen feet in total length. The main reason rods were so long was the reel hadn't been invented yet and casting far out in the river demanded longer rods.

In 1660, a French book entitled *Les Ruse Innocentes* by Frère Francois Fortin appeared. It included articles about constructing rods out of hollowed-out holly or hornbeam with the tip of a whalebone. Iziak Walton's book, *The Compleat Angler* (1676), contains descriptions of rods constructed of hazel, and it also recommends using fir.

Most of these rods were basically of solid construction and were very heavy. Rods that were over twelve feet were especially heavy and limber. It wasn't until the late 1600s that rods were constructed by gluing strips of fir or hazelwood together. Soon a group of expert craftsmen graced the scene with more sophisticated rods which eventually created a huge market and made rod building a profession.

Calcutta bamboo, which is still in use today, was popular and in general use in the 1600s. Poles made of the bamboo consisted of solid pieces instead of beveled strips. Other rod-building materials of this time, including hickory from America and lansewood, were greatly cherished. Although they took a set quickly, they were handled with great care and handed down to succeeding generations.

By the 1800s, the split-bamboo rods came into general use, but they were primarily used only for their tips. As a result split and beveled sections of bamboo were being glued together in three- and four-strip tips in the 1840s by British rod makers such as Bernard, Aldren, and a Mr. Farlow. These great rods with butts of ash and tips of bamboo were eventually put on exhibit in 1851 in a craftsman's show. Although splitting the bamboo was apparently thought up by the British, using six pieces of 60-degree-beveled split-bamboo segments was a totally American idea. This revolutionary six-sided bamboo rod was to become the forerunner of the traditional split-cane fly rods that are still professionally built today.

If any one person should be credited with the creation of the six-sided (hexagonal) bamboo fly rod it should be Samuel Phillippe of Eastern Pennsylvania (1855). But many rod builders followed. These craftsmen included Charles F. Murphy of Newark, J. E. Green, also of New Jersey, and William Mitchell of New York City. It is recorded that Mr. Green built the first four-sided, complete bamboo rod in 1860.

Eventually the split-cane rod found its way to the ocean. It did not, however, have the solid backbone needed for the strong saltwater species. The cane took a set very quickly, but the salt ate into the varnish and totally ruined many a great bamboo rod. The bamboo rod was more suited for freshwater fishing and a great amount of pampering. This is not to say that rods of cane didn't still defeat a lot of saltwater fishes; many rods of split cane were used on the ocean and defeated many a marlin and other deep-sea gamefish.

Fiberglass was one of the many by-products of the Second World War, and it was just the material anglers were looking for. It fit the bill with its responsiveness, durability, lightness, and strength. Although the first fiberglass rods were hastily contrived staffs, they were the first of many to be made. Some were solid, others were hollow. The hollow staffs were made by wrapping a fiberglass sheet around a tube or mandrel.

Today's glass cloth is made of fine, ultrathin, unidirectional fibers (i.e., fibers that run the length of the rod and to some degree perpendicular to the blank). The glass fibers are saturated with a special resin. After the resin dries, the blank is carefully wrapped with cellophane to provide high-pressure lamination. After the blank is allowed to cure, the cellophane is carefully removed, and, as a final touch, another coat of resin is applied to the rod blank.

A Rod for Every Job

The value of a rod blank often depends on the grade of the materials used to construct the blank and the amount of quality control maintained during its manufacture. Proportioning rod wall thickness with the blank's strength is a prime factor with rod builders because a lighter rod is easier to fish with all day than one that is heavy and cumbersome. And because everything must be taken into careful consideration, by the time the rod makes it to local fishing supply store shelves, it will have gone through many checks.

But there are many kinds of blanks. If you look at fishing catalogs and blank catalogs, you'll find a vast array of them—blanks as short as 4½ feet and as long as 16 feet. Each has its own job and will do it efficiently. Your job is selecting the rod that suits your needs.

Important questions to ask when you make your selection include: Is casting your primary concern? or is fish fighting the most important criterion? Will you be going after big fish with light tackle and need a rod that has the forgiveness required to land fairly giant gamefish? Are you looking for a rod with which you can feel every bit of the cast, such as a slow taper rod? or are you looking for a rod that only requires a quick flip of the wrist to make the plug fly? The possible requirements are endless.

So how do you select a rod blank? First of all, consider its taper. Will you be fighting a fish that you will need to power out of the weeds? Is stopping the fish very important? If so, then you're probably looking for a rod that has a very fast taper. What is a fast taper? The speed of the taper is determined by the speed of recoil and recovery. A slow taper rod recovers slowly and has a full bend that nor-

An assortment of rods *(left to right):* Fiberglass casting rod, #1084 spinning rod, graphite surf casting rod, 16-foot *menpachi* whipping rod, #1082 spinning rod, ultralight spinning rod, triggerless bait-casting rod, bait-casting rod.

mally goes all the way down to the butt. Rods such as this have very poor lifting power and are more suited to landing fish with light tackle. For this reason slow taper rods make better ultralight rods than fast taper rods. These rods have a lot of forgiveness and can cast relatively light lures a great distance.

The fast and extra-fast taper rods have very stiff and heavy butts. They require more casting expertise, and their bending to recoil time is much less than that of the slow taper rod. These rods make great fishing sticks and yet still allow for some degree of forgiveness in their tips. Their lifting power is phenomenal and if used properly, they can land extremely large fish on light tackle. The fast taper rod is not really meant for ultrasmooth casts. It is basically a fish-fighting tool and only requires a quick flick of the wrist to make a plug fly.

The best all-around rod is the medium taper. It has all the qualities of a good casting rod, and it has fish-fighting capabilities. When ordering a rod, check to see what the rod's taper is. Most catalogs will make it clear what the taper is and ninty-nine percent of them will have more than their share of medium taper rods.

Once you've decided upon the rod's taper, then all you've got to look for is line weight and overall length. If you're looking for a rod that will handle 12-pound test as its standard, then look for the rod with that qualification. Rods can take lines from 8- to 20-pound test or 10- to 15-pound test. The one that comes closest to the test you want is the one you should choose.

The rod's length is the next consideration. If you expect to be fishing from high cliffs and making extra-long casts, then look for a rod that is a little on the long side. A 4½-foot blank is a waste of time for this type of fishing; so take the rod that is from 9 to 13 feet long. Nine feet is a good all-around size: it has the length, yet is stout enough to stop a lot of reef fishes.

If you go to a fishing supply store and are astonished by the selection of rods, the quickest way to cut through the crop is to look at the label above each rod's stock or grip. There you'll find the information that you're looking for: the rod's make, length, taper, suggested line weight, and lure weight.

Next, look at the reel seat and rod guides. The guides should be of good quality and condition, not half corroded on the stand. Ceramic guides and others, such as silicon carbide guides, are good. Plain stainless steel grooves quickly. With these guides, before you know it you'll have to change them—it's either that or continue to lose fish. Some rods come with single- or double-foot guides, also a major consideration. The single-foot guides permit a lot of flexing of the rod yet guide the lines with great efficiency.

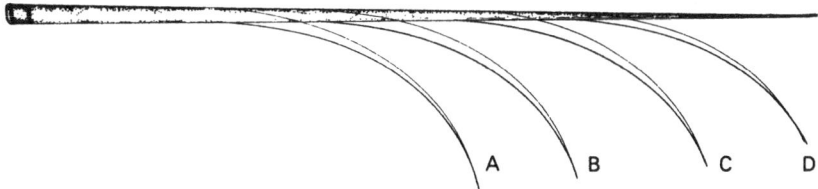

Rod tapers: slow (A), medium (B), fast (C), extra-fast (D).

The reel seat is the next thing to consider. A plain, shelf rod normally comes with a reel seat that is soft aluminum. This seat is a poor buy and will only be more trouble and hardly worth the savings in money. Good, solid, stainless-steel seats or graphite reel seats make the best buy. They are strong and really lock the reel's foot solidly. Check to see if the reel seat has one or two locking rings. The double lock is without a doubt the best. If the seat's shoe is large and bulky, then it too will cause a lot of trouble later. A reel that constantly comes lose is a pain in the neck because you'll find yourself constantly checking to see if the reel is seated properly. Eventually it will cost you a large fish.

The distance between the reel seat and the butt of the rod will also make a tremendous difference. The farther the reel is from the butt, the harder it will be for you to fight the fish. If you have to really reach for the reel when you have the butt of the rod tucked in your belly button, then the reel is too far from the butt. The closer the reel is to the body, the more control you'll have on the reel, on its drag, and on the fish. If the rod begins to get top heavy during the battle, then quickly grab far up the rod and battle with one hand high and one hand on the reel. Some fishermen feel the reel should be far from the body for proper casting. To some extent this is true. But don't have it so far that you won't be able to reach the reel.

Nowadays cork has given way to a new material called hypolon, although some angler's still prefer cork because it affords them greater sensitivity in the grip. This soft rubber material takes very little care and is just as light as cork. If the hypolon grip gets dirty, simply rinse it down and scrub it if you have to. It is easier to hold than the cork grip and has an overall better feel to it. If you ever make your own rod, you'll find that hypolon is much easier to use than cork. It now comes in such a wide assortment of colors and shapes that you can get almost anything your heart desires.

The most important single component on a rod is the tip top guide. This is the guide that takes all the punishment and abuse. Most people will poke the tip top guide into the ceiling or the ground, or jam fish—not to mention swivels, plugs, and jigs—into it by cranking too far. If the tip top is soft and made of cheap metal, you'll quickly have problems. My best advice is to use some other kind of guide, such as a ceramic guide or one made of a harder substance. Changing a tip top guide is a simple matter. It involves melting the ferrule cement with a light flame, pulling it off, reapplying more ferrule cement and replacing the tip top guide with a new one. If you have a hard time with things such as this, then I'd advise you to take the guide down to your local fishing supply store and have them put it on for you. Many stores will gladly do this small favor as part of their service and not charge you anything for it.

One of the things that almost always goes unnoticed is the manner in which a rod is wrapped. I don't mean the colors and patterns of the diamond wrap but the fact that some rods are wrapped with the guide's foot secured directly to the rod blank. Underwrapping the blank—that is, wrapping the blank once and then seating the guide on this prepared cushion—is best. This stops the guide from eventually digging into the blank. With the amount of flexing and unflexing the rod undergoes, the guides very quickly begin to dig into the blank and eventually leave several very weak points in the rod. So if you have the chance, select a rod with the double-wrap cushion and not the fancy single wrap.

Ultralight Rod

The ultralight rod is really just a lightweight fishing tool. It will add a whole lot of excitement to your fishing mainly because of its size and feel. Any fish landed with this type of rod will seem like a real monster and you'll sweat out every minute of the battle.

The proper line sizes to use in ultralight tackle range from 1- to 6-pound test. For this reason the rods that are used are built to be forgiving and to bend quickly when stressed. The best type of rod to use actually would be a fiberglass rod, the reason being that fiberglass is a little more flexible and has a deeper bend. Since the rods are all so tiny, there is hardly any difference in rod weight and casting performance. Graphite or boron, however, are usually stiff to the feel and therefore more apt to cause premature break-offs with lines in the 1 and 2 pound range. Manufacturers of graphite rods agree that graphite tends to be rather stiff, and are designing graphite ultralight models that are perfect for the angler after large game with light lines.

To me one of the best things about ultralight fishing is the ease with which it can be done. Everything is so light and compact that you can very easily grab a handful of lures, leader material, swivels, and an extra spool and be off whipping the shoreline in no time at all. Whereas when whipping with heavy gear, you need a pack to carry all

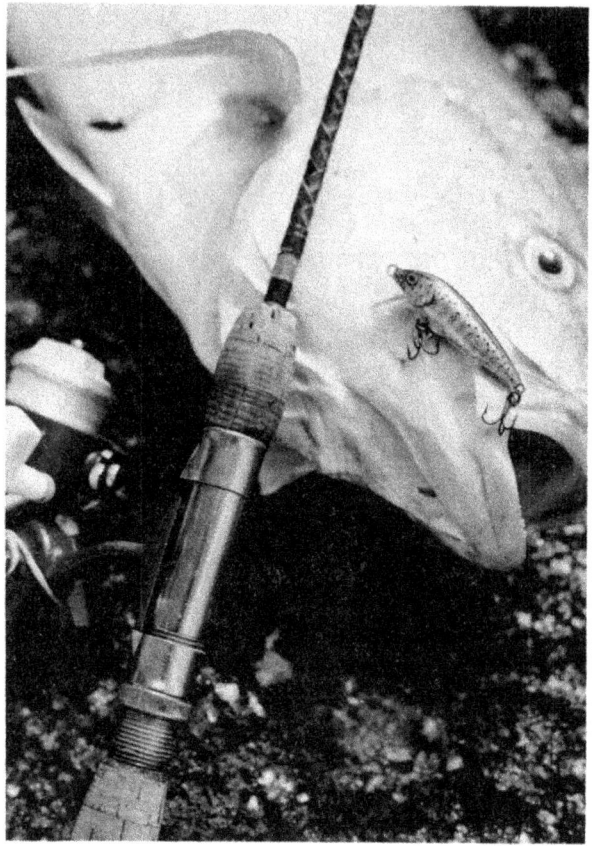

Ultralight Rod

the lures, leaders, crimping tools, and slide gaffs you'll need; and to top it off, you'll have to carry a rod and reel that will make your arms ache within an hour. I remember once while on Christmas Island Stan Wright showed me his tackle box which he was able to stuff neatly into his wading shorts. It was a Fuji Film canister, with his hooks, glitter strips, swivels, and leads. It was cheap enough and water-tight too. With just these little items, Stan was able to go wherever he wanted and wasn't hindered by a large, bulky tackle box or cumbersome backpack.

Also, everything in the ultralight tackle except the rod and reel are really inexpensive. As Stan also proved, you can use household items to make the fishing game even cheaper yet. Cutting one's own glitter strips adds to the savings. One block of glitter strips, which normally runs you approximately 60 cents, can be made into sixty to a hundred individual strips. Simply buy or find a sharp GEM single-edged razor blade and carefully begin cutting the block up. You'll be surprised to find how many strips can be cut if you take your time and do it right.

Other necessary items in ultralight tackle fishing are line and lures. The monofilament that is used in ultralight is so inexpensive that the angler who doesn't change his line during or before every trip is a fool. Since the line is web thin, the monofilament will not be able to take much abuse. Small nicks and scratches made by constant casting or jagged rocks take fast toll on thin lines. This and the fact that a bulk spool of 2-pound test is hardly a dent in one's fishing budget is reason enough to keep changing your line.

The lures used in ultralight fishing are nothing in comparison to those used in heavy shoreline whipping. The cost of one large Rapala for big game can buy you enough jigs and glitter strips to last you several months if not half a year. If you're fortunate enough, you may even purchase for yourself a lead melting pot and some jig molds (a very good investment), and make your own lures for pennies and save even more money. There is really no joy like the joy of catching fish consistently on lures that you've made with your own hands.

I recall one trip that I took with Ernie Theodore. He had flown into Hilo and I picked him up at the airport. Straightaway we were off and running to the nearest fishing hole. His rod, reel, and tackle were all in one small pile in my station wagon. His tackle box was a small six-compartment box, and it had everything he needed for a full day of fishing.

Ernie's favorite line class is 1-pound test, and he used it with quite a bit of confidence. I stuck to my "heavy" 4-pound-test line. All of his tackle was mostly homemade: he melted his own egg sinkers; cut his own glitter strips; and tied his own mini-jigs, which weighed about $1/16$ and $1/32$ of an ounce.

During the day's fishing he hooked and released many small *pāpio*. I learned what it was like to fish with real ultralight line when I watched him go through his steps. He soon hooked into a *pāpio* that was fully a match for his tackle. The fish stripped line from his spinner like a hundred-pound *ulua* on its way to the horizon. Ernie held on and let the fish run till it turned to the left. He then began working and putting full stress on the fragile 1-pound test. With nerves on the very edge, wrist kept limp, and concentration held steady, he eventually landed the one-pound-plus 'ōmilu. I would never have believed it if I wasn't there to watch the twenty-minute battle. The landing of a small *pāpio* suddenly became the biggest thing since Earl Matsui of Maui landed his 150-pounder. That small fish made everyone cheer and shout like it was a true trophy. And in truth it really was—on 1-pound-test line? I should say so!

This is what ultralight tackle fishing is all about. The small *pāpio* on 15-pound test is no challenge at all; but hook the same fish on a tiny rod and spiderweb-like line and you'll find yourself digging deep in your memory for all tricks and experiences.

Some people think ultralight tackle fishing is for the beginner. Nothing is further from the truth. Ultralight tackle fishing demands the most from the angler and from his experience. The beginner will get very frustrated very quickly, especially if he is lucky enough to hook a lot of good-sized fish early in the game. If the angler is willing to accept this, then he'll eventually find himself learning the rudiments of fishing and fighting fish very quickly. With ultralight tackle fishing you get many more strikes per day than you do slide-bait fishing, which is why you will learn fish fighting techniques right away.

In ultralight tackle fishing, you will find that the angler who catches the most fish is the one who knows what his tackle can take and how much it can dish out. This is only learned through experience and by knowing your tackle. Your tackle has to be in super shape, so keep your equipment performing up to its utmost by maintaining it (see "Maintaining Your Reels," Chapter 2).

The normal length of the ultralight rod is anywhere from $4\frac{1}{2}$ to 6 feet. Most rod manufacturers have a fairly good selection of rods in this length range and line weight. But this is not to say that the ultralight rod need only be this length: some rods measure up to 11 feet from tip to butt. The ideal rod should be soft and long. The reason for this is that the rod, if tapered right, will still have the ability to cast the ultralight lures and the super small lines. The added length will simply give the angler more forgiveness and a higher line-to-water angle, and thus the line will be kept off of the rocks and weeds, and the angler will be kept from running headlong into the water as he chases the fast running fish.

The ultralight rod should also be proportionate in size to the reel that you'll be using. Most ultralight enthusiasts use tiny reels with fine lines and velvet smooth drags. If the reel vastly outweighs the rod, your fishing will be awkward and clumsy.

Mighty Midget Rod

Ever since I learned to tie a decent fishing knot, which was when I was about ten years old, I have had a compulsion to battle fish with small, compact tackle. The fish I encountered in Nuuanu Stream during those years of my youth were usually small, scrappy tilapia and ʻoʻopu. Hooking and landing a quarter-pound tilapia on 15-pound test with a Daiwa BG90 spinning reel was just not my idea of fishing fun.

For this reason I used as tiny a tackle as was obtainable with my miniscule income. All I could afford was a ten-cent bamboo pole, a cardboard roll of Mason monofilament, split shot lead, and ten cents worth of Mustad #12 hooks. With these basic materials, I later constructed a tiny, tiny ten-inch-high bamboo rod complete with reel seat, guide, tip top, and small, functional reel made of a redwood spool and sheet metal sideplates. In this reel I loaded about three cardboard spools of Mason 1-pound-test monofilament line which came to about thirty yards of line—not very much line for ocean fish but plenty for tilapia. With this mini rod-and-reel combination, I hooked, fought, and lost many a good fish. The fun was back in fishing with this tackle and I never got over the need to make fishing more and more fun by making my tackle smaller and smaller.

And so ultralight tackle has always captured my fancy. Hooking, fighting, and landing a two-pound *pāpio* on 80-pound test is nothing to brag about, but the same two-pounder becomes a real prize on 1-pound test. However, even ultralight tackle has its drawbacks, primarily in that a lot of the rods are too soft to really work a fish in a long battle. Granted, an ultralight rod should bend to relieve the strain on the 1-pound-test line, but a big fish and a soft rod make for battles that are sometimes too long and frustrating, especially when the fish is lost.

Aware of these problems, I scouted around town and looked through rod-building catalogs for a rod that was short and small and that had the guts I needed a rod to have. The investigation eventually led me to Tokunaga Fishing Supply in Hilo, which just by sheer coincidence had the blank I was looking for, a Fenglass #CA-557. The blank stood 56.5 inches tall, had a fast taper, and was rated for lines up to 20-pound test. I found the tip to be soft enough to cast small $\frac{1}{8}$- to $\frac{3}{8}$-pound jigs, the jig sizes I preferred. It also had a tremendous amount of reserve power in the butt section, and this gave the rod an enormous amount of lifting power, important when you're fighting good-sized fish away from rocks or coral.

Although a rod of this stiffness is not really an ultralight rod, using lines down to 4-pound test is not unrealistic. The angler should always be aware of the rod's stiffness and make adjustments in his fighting techniques. The fish should be allowed to take all the line it needs on the first run. Any attempt to stop it with this rod may very well end in a lost fish. But once the fish has stopped its run, the rod will prove itself to be truly gutsy. Pulling on a fish that is stubborn with a rod like this will have instant results. The angler does not have a worry about the rod collapsing on him during a battle; instead he has to worry about fighting the fish with a limp or soft wrist. Being aware of these things will compensate for the rod's stiffness.

The cost of the blank ranges from $9 to $10. The total cost after the rod is built will come to approximately $25. This amount makes using on the same trip several rods loaded with different reels and different line classes feasible. Since the rod can accommodate up to 20-pound-test line, it can also accommodate lures heavier than $3/8$ ounce with no problem at all. And with its great lifting power it can battle fish far up into the thirty pound range.

Without a doubt the rod is small and light, but it occurred to me when I first found the blank that if it were made of graphite it could be even lighter. And Fenwick does have a graphite equivalent. However, fiberglass has proven to be the best material for this type of rod. Graphite, with its lightness and sensitivity, does not have the smooth flexibility and deep lifting power that fiberglass has. It also seems that graphite is not able to handle as wide a range of lures and line as fiberglass can. But if graphite is the route you would like to go then the equivalent rod blank is the Fenwick HMG Iron Hawk series. The blank is coded HCA-557. Other blanks that should be considered are the HCA-107 and the HCA-105. Both are excellent rod blanks from which tough, small rods can be constructed. They both are sixty-three inches long and have fast to extra-fast tapers.

For the angler who wants to get the most enjoyment out of working the shoreline for hours on end, the Midget Rod is perfect. The rod is very small and compact, and working a lure and flexing your wrist for a full day takes so little effort that it isn't even worth worrying about. Other rods, like the larger surf rods, really wear an angler out and very quickly make fishing a mental chore and physical effort. Also, due to the CA-557's stiffness, working action into the lure by twitching the rod tip as you retrieve is extremely effective. Every movement of the rod tip is instantly telegraphed to the lure and the lure will move like the fish seducer it should be.

Another feature of the CA-557 is the rod's stiffness. When a fish strikes, there is no problem in detecting a strike. The strike will feel like a sudden jolt, which will quickly run down the rod. For this reason the hook should be set into a fish's jaw instantly and decisively. Once the angler feels the jolt and hauls back, there will be no doubt that the hook has been driven home.

The list of this rod's features can get longer and longer, but it should not be overlooked that the short, stout rod is just plain fun to use. The fish, whether it be large or small, now is a match for the tackle, even though the tackle has been scaled down to the ultralight category. The angler now has the reserve power to battle as hard as his arms will let him, and yet the ultralight qualities of the small tackle are not diminished. With this small tackle all your fishes will become trophies and you'll be able to land more fish per day and get less tired per hour.

Bait-Casting Rod

This rod, also called a plugging rod, stands anywhere from $6\frac{1}{2}$ to $7\frac{1}{2}$ feet tall. It has a fast taper and is known for its stubborn backbone and power to pull those hard-headed fish that eventually tangle you up.

Principally the bait-casting rod was used for "worm fishing" in the bayous by fishermen after largemouth bass. The bait-casting rod of days long past and rods of today have basically the same features. The rod's handle usually has a pistol grip and a submerged reel seat, which is intended to enhance the capability of the rod. The reel stays or sits a little low and thus makes it easier to control the spinning spool.

Now more and more anglers are finding out that the bait-casting rod is a great casting rod and also a superior fish-fighting tool. The rod that is ideal for the shore fisherman should stand anywhere from $7\frac{1}{2}$ to 8 feet, as the length aids in the casting of plugs from shore or from high cliffs. The rod should have a fast to an extra-fast taper. The tip should be a little on the soft side because if worked right, it will be able to cast even light plugs and jigs. If the uppermost portion of the rod—the tip section—were sawed off, the rod would be much stiffer and would loose much of its ability to cast light plugs and jigs.

The ideal distance between the reel seat and the butt is approxi-

Bait-Casting Rod

mately eight to ten inches. When the reel is closer to the angler, it is more effective as a fish-fighting tool. Using a short handle takes some getting used to, but after repeated practice, you'll slowly get the knack of snapping your wrist to get the plug out. Once you get used to the rod, you'll be able to feel how the upper portion of it does all the work. But once the fish is on, you'll be amazed at how fast you can lick a tough fish. The rod's lower butt has fantastic lifting powers and will lift many a strong fish off of the bottom and into the boat.

Combined with a good, high-speed bait-casting reel and some 12- or 15-pound-test tournament line, the rod will be a true terror of the shoreline. Even light lines such as 12-pound test, when teamed with a rod that has a light forgiving tip, will be able to hold any fish for a long time.

As for plugs, I have found that the best plug to work with a bait-casting rod is one that has a plastic or metal lip. If you're shoreline whipping, the plug's action, coupled with a stabbing rod tip action, will make the plug look like an injured minnow (see "Skipping the Plug," Chapter 7). The action of the rod tip should be very carefully monitored until the plug does just the right kind of jigging and dancing. At the same time you twitch the rod tip you should make a quick crank of the reel. This is when a fast or high-speed reel is so important. So, again, the action is: take up line . . . twitch the rod . . .

take up line . . . twitch the rod, and so on. Every so often I will make a sweeping drag to the left or right of my body. This will make the plug dash a good ways suddenly and then stop. Because of its fast taper, the rod will make the plug respond very quickly.

The best type of reel seat for a rod of this type would without a doubt be the graphite grip. It seats a reel solidly and will not come loose during the rod action. The guides should be the best you can find and staggered on the rod, so that it will maintain its original arc as much as possible.

As for cushioning material, the best grips to use would be the light hypolon stocks. This material will add to the rod's longevity and efficiency. A good thing about the bait-casting rod is that you don't have to purchase too much hypolon for it; the stocks are so short that it only takes a single piece to complete the rod.

The blank should be a single piece. This may be hard if you do a lot of traveling in a Volkswagen, but it'll be worth the hardship once you get a reel on the rod and start casting. The single-piece bait-casting rod can handle so much more stress and will really work for you when the need arises.

Even with the advent of graphite and boron as rod-building materials, fiberglass seems to make the best bait-casting rod. It seems, to me anyway, that glass can stand up to so much more full bending and lifting. The fiberglass blank that I normally choose has a thin wall and is one solid piece. The 540 Sabre is this kind of blank.

Some people think that a bait-casting rod isn't made for long and graceful casts. With a rod that is stiff as a cue stick and only $6\frac{1}{2}$ feet long that may very well be true. But a well-designed, $7\frac{1}{2}$-foot rod with just the right tip can throw a plug an incredible distance. Although graceful casts depend on the education of the thumb, a rod as long as $7\frac{1}{2}$ feet has a lot of its own smoothness.

One of these days you should give it a try. I think you'll like it. Hook a fish and fight it to a frazzle and I think that you'll like it even more.

Medium-Action Spinning Rod

The medium-action spinning rod is probably the most popular of spinning rods. It does just about anything, and when teamed with a good, smooth, well-maintained spinning reel, will be able to take on all comers.

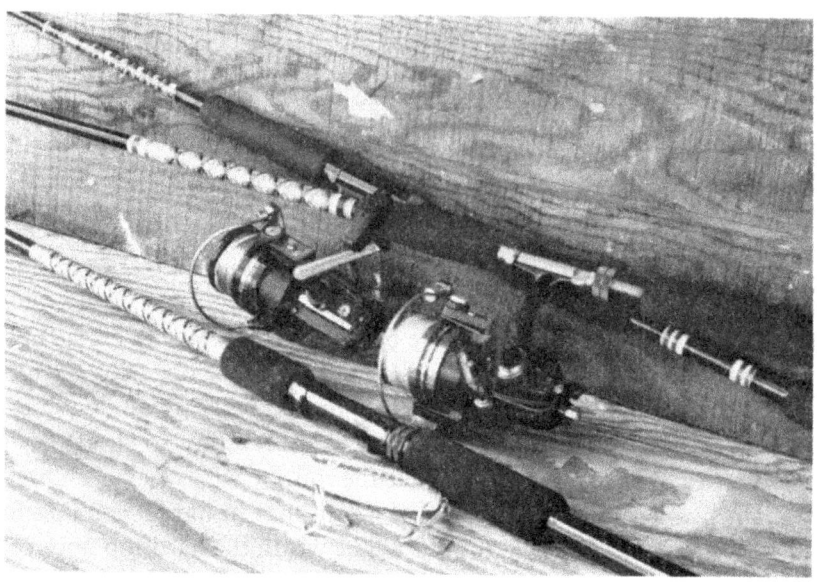

Medium-Action Spinning Rods

The Fenwick #GSP 1084 and the stiffer #GSP 1082 are two of the best blanks made. They have a smooth taper and can use a vast assortment of line classes. It is best to carry extra spools of line for these rods. I normally carry spools with lines that range from 6- to 15-pound test. The rod will handle both very nicely. With its gently tapering butt, it has a lot of reserve lifting power and can cast light lines with no effort whatsoever. This is the magic of the medium-action rod.

This rod's length is normally about $8\frac{1}{2}$ to $9\frac{1}{2}$ feet and it has a medium to fast taper. Usually it is two pieces and glass or graphite ferruled.

The nice thing about medium-action and weight spinning rods is that you can fish with them all day long and not feel the strain. A rod made of graphite is even better. The lightness of graphite, coupled with the sensitivity of the material, makes the medium-action spinning rod a joy to use. You will be able to spin the surface waters with great efficiency and with almost no effort. The action of the plug in the water will become one with the action of the rod. The plug will literally dance for you when you wish it to.

Switch to heavy plugs and heavy line and the rod will not suffer too badly. Then switch from heavy to light lines and the rod will still give

Heavy-Weight Spinning Rods

you the delicateness and the sensitivity you'll need to work small to very small plugs and jigs along reeflines. The best guides that a medium-action rod can have are single-foot guides. Reel seats should be made totally of graphite and should match the rod's diameter neatly. The handle should be hypolon, and you should have a smooth rubber cap on the end.

Even if spinning rods normally have long butts, a short butt is not ridiculous. Butts that measure about sixteen to eighteen inches work well with medium-action spinning rods. When it comes time to stick the butt into your navel and really work a fish, you'll find that a short butt makes it easier to fight a fish and to get at the handle of the reel. Once again, this fish fighting tool can still have the finesse and taper to handle smaller fish and give you great enjoyment.

Heavy-Weight Spinning Rod

This rod is the heaviest of the spinning rods, especially compared to the ultralight graphite or glass rod. It normally is used with a heavier line class, stands approximately 12 to 13 feet, and has a long butt section. It is usually of two pieces and glass or graphite ferruled.

The primary function of this rod is shoreline bait "dunking." The bait is either attached to the line, which is cast out, or it is slid down after the cast. It is a very good bait-casting rod, and because of its overall height, it has the clearance to hold the line over oncoming waves. If rock or sand spikes are used, it will have even more clearance for the high waves. The rod's overall height also affords it the ability to cast a long anchorline if need be. This aids in keeping the bait off the bottom and away from some of the prowling eels that feast on the free baits.

As a heavy-duty spinning or whipping rod, this rod is second to none. Teamed up with a very large spinning reel, heavy line, and super-large plugs, this rod can handle just about any large shoreline predator. The guides should be large agate or ceramic guides, or made of some of the new guide materials now on the market. This type of spinning rod should have the best components you can get. The reason for this is that the fish you will be seeking will normally be over the forty pound mark.

The rod will have to have guides, reel seats, and butts that can withstand tremendous strain and pressure because in shoreline whipping, the strike will come with tremendous force in a very short span of time. This must be considered especially if the reel's drag is in poor condition. Many custommade rods have been broken because the reel's drag refused to function properly and the rod had to take the brunt of the strike's impact. Guides have often been ripped off a rod, or guide rings torn away from the bridge.

The tip top should be constantly checked for deep grooves and rust. Sometimes it may be loose and will need to be cemented back on. At other times the tip may be broken on only one bridge and thus appear to be functioning properly. But once you hook into a big fish, the ring may come flying off and leave you in some deep trouble.

Being that the rod tip is the most important section of the rod, extra tips should be kept in your plug bag or backpack. It is a good idea to keep a single-foot guide a little bigger than the tip top guide. If the tip should be broken off, this single-foot guide will work great. You may find that the slip-on type of tip top guide won't fit because it's either too big or too small. So a single-foot, ceramic guide is the best bet. It can be wrapped right onto the broken tip with dental floss and coated with nail polish.

Rods such as these should all have a double-wrapped (underwrap) guide, or a base-wrapped guide. Guides that have only a single wrap tend to scar the glass or graphite quickly, and they eventually leave the rod with a severely weakened area. The rod's job is to take tremendous amounts of strain and for this reason the guide base is an important component.

Ulua Pole

The *ulua* pole or shore casting rod is one of the unique creations of the Hawaiian shore fisherman. It was designed for big game, long casts, and durability. It has undergone an amazing amount of change over many generations and I seriously believe that it will continue to evolve with coming generations.

Not surprisingly, the *ulua* pole looks very different from all other rods. The difference is most evident from island to island. Maui's standard *ulua* pole is of a different length, made of different materials, and has a taper different from the rods of, say, the Big Island. Likewise, the rods of Oahu differ from those of Maui; Kauai's differ from Oahu's. The differences may be barely noticeable to one who isn't a very serious *ulua* fisherman, but to one who seeks the *ulua,* the differences are very apparent.

Ulua Pole

Originally the *ulua* pole was a standard staff made of bamboo. The bamboo was Calcutta bamboo and could be purchased from many of the local fishing stores of the day. The bamboo had a very slow taper and was known to take a set (permanent bend) quickly. The bamboo rod was very long (approximately 14 to 15 feet in length), and its guides were either purchased or homemade. The rod was neatly wrapped with standard cords, and the butt section was wrapped with standard cotton cord. Several coats of varnish were applied to the rod and allowed to dry thoroughly.

Bamboo was also imported from Japan (as it still is today), and this type was a favorite among *ulua* fishermen. A rod made of this bamboo had a better taper and didn't take as much of a set as did the Calcutta bamboo rod. It was also much lighter and relatively inexpensive. The fishing supply stores kept a fairly good stock of bamboo so that you could go into the stores and select the bamboo stalk that suited your fancy.

Hawaii as well was found to have a lot of bamboo. Probably brought in with the first Chinese or Japanese immigrants, bamboo flourished as it does today in Hawaii's tropical climate. This bamboo was found to make some excellent *ulua* poles, and when treated and tempered with care, the bamboo rods would provide years of successful service. They also made great pole gaffs and tent poles.

The bamboo blanks were all cut green and transported to the garage of the angler. There, each was carefully burned and straightened. It was also checked for wormholes, dry rot, and other common bamboo ailments. The rods that couldn't be straightened to satisfaction were used for firewood or tent poles, or just thrown away.

Usually the angler would cut himself a great many butts and hope that many of them would be usable. At times, only a very small percentage of the bamboo would make it through the aging process, which lasts over a year or two. Because of this the bamboo was labeled and dated. The location was written on the blank as was the date cut. Knowing where the blank came from was of primary importance. Some areas on the Big Island, for example, had a tendency to yield bamboo that was much wetter and that took longer to dry. In other areas, the bamboo was denser and stronger because the power fibers were closer together. This was easy to inspect. The butt section of the bamboo was simply cut to expose the fiber construction. The power fibers are the darker fibers close to the skin of the bamboo. They get farther apart and less dense near the core of the blank. The denser the power fibers are near the core, the stronger the blank.

Once the bamboo was selected and cut, it was then tempered a light coat. Some anglers used gasoline or kerosene to take off all of the rod's outer oils and powder. This left a bright luster on the blank and allowed the bamboo to breathe. The bamboo blanks were then stored away and periodically taken down and tempered again. This would go on for months and months. Meanwhile, the blanks that were not up to par were thrown out.

After twelve to fifteen months, the bamboo blank was ready to be made into a rod. It was hoped that by then the rod blank hadn't become termite-ridden or acquired severe cracks, which commonly happens when the rod dries too fast. The knuckles or bamboo dams were then shaved off with a bastard file and some fine sandpaper. Once these were removed, the guides were wound onto the rod and lacquered or varnished.

Each individual had his own favorite colors and type of basic construction technique. With the coming of the newer resins, the lacquers and varnishes were gradually replaced. However, the resins made the rods heavy and ponderous to use, so most anglers simply stuck with varnishes and periodically varnished the rods to keep out the moisture and mildew.

What to Look For in an Ulua *Pole*

The right overall length for the *ulua* pole is, as was stated earlier, determined by the terrain of the fishing spot. Because the terrain is different on each island, the rods that are used on each island are also different. On some islands where the beaches are low and very sandy, the breakers are close to shore. This means that if your *ulua* pole is short, the bait will be hard to sink. I know of people who used coconut trees to hoist their line. In much the way a flag is raised up a flagpole, the line was taken up with a trolley. A rubberband was used to allow it to break away when there was a strike. But you can't depend on finding a coconut tree wherever you go, and you definitely cannot bring one along with you. Most of the sandy shore anglers just use rods that are relatively long.

Other terrains, such as those on the Kalapana coastline of the Big Island, are the complete opposite. The cliffs stand over fifty feet high with the water directly below. You don't need a long rod here because of the height. The boulder-strewn bottom and the sudden drop-off, however, means you have to have a rod that is short and fairly stout. The idea here is to stop the fish before it gets too far out and over the drop. So Big Islanders choose to use rods that are much shorter and stouter than the rods sandy beach anglers use.

Each angler chooses the rod that suits his own basic needs. Some like the longer rod because casting with one is easier; others like the short, "lead pipe" rod that has a slow taper and resembles a trolling rod. Many individuals who look at the shorter version of the *ulua* pole think that it would be impossible to cast, especially with a ten-foot anchorline attached to it. But surprisingly enough, if the rod is well designed and well made, it will cast very, very easily and not require superhuman strength.

Usually the rod has a slow taper. The rod's butt diameter is very small and feels much like a small toy. But load up the rod with a reel and the proper size lead, and you'll be in for quite a surprise.

Most *ulua* poles have a dowel placed in the butt section of the rod. This was commonly done with half-and-half rods (half bamboo and half fiberglass) because of the tremendous strength the *ulua* has during an initial strike. Without this dowel, the rod would bend in the stand and eventually snap at the point of the most stress, the butt. The newer, all-fiberglass model also should have a wooden dowel set neatly in the butt. Over this butt section should be a shiny stainless steel or chrome butt cap. This cap will reinforce the bamboo butt, keep it from splintering and absorbing water, and also protect it from general wear and tear at the shoreline. All of these things are crucial for an *ulua* pole. Make sure that the rod has these features when you purchase or make one.

The reflective tape (night shining tape) that is placed on the *ulua* pole should be of a color that is easy to see at night. Blue doesn't work too well, and neither does red. These colors make for a pretty rod but are hard to see in the middle of the night among a dozen rods. White is the best all-time color. If you're worried that someone else's rod has the same color as yours, then change the stripping pattern and you'll

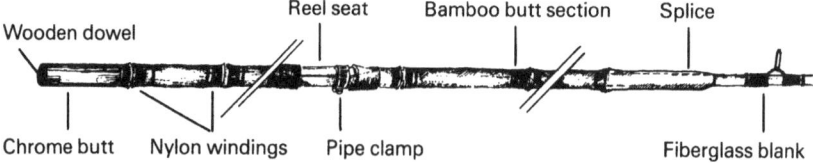

Popular Half-and-Half Rod. This type is still used extensively on many islands of Hawaii.

be okay. Don't scrimp on the reflective tape; use it liberally because it makes finding the rod much easier when it's pitch dark.

Most anglers wind a small little fiberglass or brass tube a little above the reel seat. It doesn't have to be wound high on the rod, about three feet above the reel seat is fine. To this attach a bell. The bell should have a tough, straight wire (normally stainless steel), which should be passed directly through it. The best thing about the bell holder is that it doesn't get in the way and is very light. Plus that, it works great. Once the bell wire is in the tubing, the bell won't come off, even during the most vicious strikes.

As with most rods, the amount of decoration you want to put on the rod is purely up to you. A lot of the store-bought *ulua* poles are wrapped to catch the angler first and then the fish. You'll find that the most serious anglers will have very simple-looking rods. They are looking for performance, not aesthetics. Also, you'll find that most of the simple rods tend to be much lighter, and when they're much lighter they're easier to use and less liable to tire you out during an extended trip. So, the *ulua* pole that looks plain and simple may be a streamlined version of a fancy-laced, store-bought rod. It won't look very fancy but it'll catch fish first.

As with all rods, the tip top section or guide is the most important section of the *ulua* pole. Through this single component will go all your line and hopes, so select the tip top that is ceramic and fairly large. The larger the tip top's opening, the easier it will be to cast the leader. Also, when fighting fish, you'll find that a double-line knot or other large knot will get hung up on the way back to the reel. The larger the guide, the easier the reentry. No one likes to put a rod down and walk to the front of it to help force a knot through a guide.

In summary, the *ulua* pole has undergone some drastic changes over the years and it is different on every island and for every type of shore. There is no perfect rod. There is only the rod that works for you and for your type of fishing environment, so adapt your equipment and techniques to your type of terrain and you'll find yourself catching more fish.

Fiberglass *Ulua* Rod

The all-glass *ulua* rod has been around for quite sometime. Because it does not have a bamboo butt section as does the half-and-half rod, the fiberglass rod is much easier to maintain and lighter in weight. It is a better rod and has a cleaner bend to it mainly because it is not spliced like the bamboo and fiberglass rod is. Although the cost of an all-glass rod is greater in the long run, it is a much better rod to invest in if you intend to be fishing for many, many years. Bamboo, on the other hand, has to be changed every so many years because of the bamboo's tendency to keep the bend created by excessive flexing in one direction. If the cost of replacing the bamboo butt constantly is taken into consideration, a fiberglass rod will seem even more economical. Naturally, the strength of the rod should also be a factor when comparing rods, but making a comparison is relatively hard to do since *ulua* fishermen who splice bamboo to fiberglass all seem to have different ideas about how it should or should not be done.

As for durability, I have seen many *ulua* rods of the half-and-half construction that have landed many huge *ulua* and they are still in very good shape. Granted, they are pampered darlings, but then this just goes to show that with proper care the bamboo rod can last for an incredibly long time. If the same rod were left out in the sun for days on end, it would quickly deteriorate: the wrapping would change color, the varnish crack and peel, and the bamboo start to change from a nice orange brown color to a pale, drab brown. Once this happens the rod is useless and it will take a set quickly if it is not split on the first series of flexing. If left out in the rain, the bamboo would quickly rot, as the weathering makes the bamboo lose its resiliency and flexing qualities and renders it useless for fishing for big *ulua*. Unfortunately, bamboo is also eaten by termites and once you get several termite holes in a blank, it's time to take it up to Boot Hill and bury it.

There are several fiberglass blanks on the market today. One very popular blank is the #540 Sabre. It comes with a tip and straight butt section that has to be spliced to increase its overall length. The splicing is very simple to do, especially since it comes with a fiberglass dowel that helps in the splicing process. Some anglers glue the joints together with epoxy and wrap strong nylon cord around it to reinforce the spliced section. Once this is done the rod is ready for cutting and wrapping.

The angler should select a rod length that suits his fish-fighting needs, as well as that matches his physical strength. The best way to find the rod length that suits you is to keep trying several *ulua* rods that are already finished. Try as many as you can get your hands on and once you find the rod that you feel comfortable with, copy it point for point. Most anglers are not stingy about sharing rod dimensions and construction components, so copying a rod is nothing to worry about.

One rod that is becoming increasingly popular with Big Island *ulua* fishermen is the Lamiglass blank #SB160-6M or the #SB162-5M. Both rods stand 13 feet 6 inches. Barry and Pauline Sugimoto use this type of rod and no other, mainly because of its narrow outside diameter, which makes gripping the rod easy and comfortable. They also add crystal particles around the grip section and use varnish as an adhesive; this way even if Barry's hands get slimy from handling *puhi* baits, there is no chance of him losing his grip on a hard cast.

Barry cuts his rod down to an amazingly short 10 feet 5 inches, and he uses a #32 tip top guide. Since the rod's outside diameter is so small, the Sugimotos found they could use a #28 Fuji graphite reel seat. Compared to this set-up, the standard pipe clamp securing the reel seems obsolete. Barry also does not use stainless steel guides; instead, he wraps on three bridge ceramic guides. These guides hold up very well considering the abuse the *ulua* leader inflicts on them when *ulua* fishermen make their casts. Some anglers also feel that the smoother ceramic guides help them make longer casts; but, even better, they find that the ceramic guides do not groove and tear up the monofilament the way stainless steel guides do.

The narrow butt section notwithstanding, the rod has thick fiberglass walls that give the rod its lifting power. The rod's stoutness and its shortness both help to make the rod surprisingly easy to cast and also make battling a fish quicker and more challenging. The Lamiglass 6M's slow taper makes for good lifting power; yet it has the forgiving qualities of fiberglass that are needed when lighter lines are used.

The comfort of the narrow grip plus the lack of extra weight enables the fisherman to put all his power into the cast. The rod will throw an eight-ounce sinker with no trouble at all. Since the rod has a slow taper, the casting time is slowed down a bit to compensate for the rod's bend and push; but once the cast is made you'll find that the rod has the umph! that is required to throw the lead and leader a good hundred yards.

All in all, the best thing about the Lamiglass 6M is that is is easy to use and consequently fun to fish with. Whether you clamp on a #6/0 Penn Senator or a #4/0 Senator, you will find that the rod will perform to its utmost. Next trip to the fishing supply store, take a good look at the Lamiglass SB160-6M; you'll be surprised at its qualities.

Graphite and Boron Rods

Usually graphite rods are lighter and stiffer when first taken off of the shelves. Compared to fiberglass these rods seem to be considerably stiffer until loaded up with some line and a reel. Many fiberglass rod manufacturers have gone into the graphite rod–making business and construct rods with very little graphite in them. What you find is that these rods have graphite mostly in the butt section and not throughout the entire blank. If you buy one of these, you will be paying for a high-priced rod that has the same performance as a very well built fiberglass rod. So hefting a rod from a rod rack and wiggling it around is a poor way to determine if the rod's action will suit your needs or not.

The best way to check out a graphite rod is to inspect its standard features. Bits of information about lure size, line class, and rod length all should help you determine the right rod for you. Most dependable rod manufacturers will have much of this needed information where the grip meets the rod. If nothing is printed there but the company name, be suspicious of the rod.

When selecting any rod, you have to determine your specific needs. First of all, the rod should be able to cast the lure or bait with efficiency; second, it should have the sensitivity to detect a strike; and

Graphite and boron rods

third, it should be tough enough to handle the fish that you're looking for. If the rod doesn't meet any of these requirements, then it is useless to you.

Due to the stiffness of the rod, the angler who is whipping plugs or lures will actually work the lure better and detect strikes better. If the rod is soft and yielding, it makes the lure action very poor. Also, if you're into deep jigging the lure, a soft rod will perform very, very poorly.

But the most important attribute of the graphite rod is its lightness. Being an avid shoreline whipper, I make hundreds if not thousands of casts in a day. I feel the more casts I make, the better my chances of hooking a decent-sized fish. This being the case, a heavy fiberglass rod will take all the starch out of me by midafternoon—either that or I'll have to take quite a few breaks during the day and pace myself. But with the graphite, I can fire-cast all day long and not get tired out. The rod weighs so little that it feels like a little toy in the hand.

Like all well-made rods, the graphite rod requires care during handling. It tends to be a little more brittle and thus can't take as much abuse as the fiberglass rod. Also, you really have to hold back the tears that suddenly come welling up when you break one because of their cost. So the best place for a graphite rod after a day's fishing is in its rod case. I quickly put my rod back into the rod sack and out of harm's way.

The reason for the high cost of the graphite rod blank is that the space age material it is made of costs about $30 per pound (fiberglass costs $6 per pound). It comes in an epoxy tape form ready to use for rod building. Boron is even more expensive—costing about $225 per pound—but it is a much better rod material because it is light and recovers from a bend much faster. It is for these two attributes that you pay a much higher price. But whether graphite or fiberglass, performance boils down to how the rod is constructed. A good or well-constructed fiberglass rod can be just as good as or better than a poorly made graphite rod. Therefore, an extremely well designed and well constructed graphite rod will be better than a boron rod. It all hinges on good quality control.

What do you look for then in a graphite or a boron rod? There are at this time no regulations concerning rod construction. You buy what you get and sometimes the situation can be summed up in the phrase Let the buyer beware! My only recommendation is to buy from a reputable manufacturer and check the warranty and standard features of the rod. If the company doesn't believe in the rod, it will offer a very weak warranty, which should quickly give it away. Afterall, if you're coughing up $200 to $250 for a rod, I think you'd better check to see what you'll be getting.

Half-and-Half Rod

Although most of today's *ulua* fishermen use all-fiberglass rods for any kind of *ulua* fishing, there still are a few individuals who like to fish with the half-and-half rod. Their reasons for doing so are many, and it is not for anyone to question their judgment.

The half-and-half rod is a very inexpensive rod, when you really get down to it. If you cure your own bamboo, it becomes even cheaper yet. You can purchase bamboo for splicing, if you wish; just go down to the local fishing supply and select one that is straight and without any cracks, blemishes, and termite holes.

Take the fiberglass rod tip and measure the butt section for mating. Hollow the bamboo until you have the right inside diameter for the fiberglass. Next, taper the outside of the bamboo until it is pencil-shaped. Once this is done split the bamboo to the bamboo knuckle and drill the inside section of the knuckle and punch through. Take a bastard drill and roughen up the outside section of the fiberglass that will be spliced with the bamboo. This will ensure a solid glue-up and not allow the tip section to slip out.

Acquire a set of reel or pipe clamps and a large tube of two-part

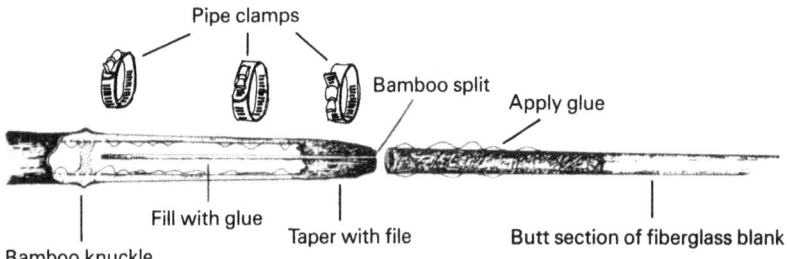

Splicing the fiberglass blank to the bamboo butt. First taper the bamboo tip with a bastard file and sandpaper. Saw-cut the stalk so that the fiberglass butt section can be inserted into it. Roughen the fiberglass butt to allow for better adhesion. Drill out the bamboo knuckle to allow for the fiberglass butt section. Once all this is completed apply epoxy on the fiberglass blank and inside the bamboo. Clamp the bamboo around the blank. Make sure the butt section of the fiberglass blank extends beyond the bamboo knuckle. Let the splice dry for several days at least.

epoxy cement. Mix the cement and apply to the inside of the bamboo and the outside of the fiberglass blank. Force the fiberglass blank into the bamboo and set the butt of the fiberglass just past the drilled out dam or bamboo knuckle. The fiberglass will be surrounded by a solid section of bamboo. Twist the blank until you are sure that the glue has been distributed over all parts and then secure with the rod clamps. So the glue won't get into the clamps and make them impossible to unclamp later, place paper under the rod clamps before securing them.

Allow the rod to cure for at least twenty-four hours. Unclamp it and file down all the burrs left by the hardened glue. Next, wrap a layer of nylon cord tightly around the entire spliced area to make sure that it is solid. Coat with varnish or paint for a permanent seal.

That's really all there is to it. There are other variations to this splice that probably work just as well, but this is one you can try.

Rod Cases

Rod cases come in many different styles and designs. One type is simply a section of PVC (polyvinylchloride) plastic conduit with a cap on each end. Another is a custom-made spun aluminum tubing with

Rod cases and sacks

threaded brass caps and sealed butts. Both function the same and both protect rods from rough luggage carriers.

The most inexpensive of the two types is the PVC conduit model. The PVC comes in several different types including the EB and DB conduits. The EB (Encased Buried) conduit is the lighter and also the cheaper of the two. It tends to get brittle with age, however, and can't stand up to much abuse. But the price is right for a short trip, that is, a trip that does not involve traveling over rough terrain.

The DB (Direct Buried) conduit is a little stronger and just as light weight as the EB. This is the best of the two and is still lighter than the PVC schedule 40 conduit. The DB conduit will hold up under a lot of stress and is relatively inexpensive as compared to the PVC schedule 40 conduit. It is also easy to cut to make rod cases.

The PVC schedule 40 conduit is the toughest of the plastic pipes. It is a heavy-duty case and weighs a lot. If you have a rod that can't take any punishment in cases, then this is the case for you. This conduit is easy to obtain, but is also more expensive than the DB or EB conduit. I think it is stronger than aluminum cases, although one has to contend with its weight. The bigger the size conduit, the more the tubing weighs. Thus a four-inch conduit can become a real chore to lug around; a five-inch conduit is almost impossible; and a six-inch con-

Aluminum rod cases are strong and relatively light for the amount of protection they provide. However, these cases are expensive and they don't come in the larger sizes.

duit unthinkable. But if it's indestructibility you want, then you have to use the schedule 40 conduit.

Aluminum cases are a sight to behold. They are real treasures and normally come with any expensive bamboo rod or custom-made graphite rod. The inside diameter (ID) of those cases normally measure about $1\frac{1}{2}$ inches. They are hardly found in larger sizes, such as 4 and 5 inches. Although they are light and easy to carry, they don't take to severe punishment and tend to get crushed under heavy luggage or during heavy use. No matter how nice the case, if it doesn't protect the rod inside, it is of little use. So if it's not aesthetics that you want but performance, then select the PVC-DB conduit rod case.

How to Make Your Own PVC Case

The best way to make a rod case out of PVC-DB is to measure your rods and cut the conduit to the desired length with a common carpenter's saw. (You'll have a neater cut fast.) Allow several inches for the padding material and for unforeseen mistakes. Once the conduit is cut, make sure all the edges and burrs are smoothed. Swab the inside of the conduit to clean out dirt and dust. You'll be amazed at how much dirt and gunk you'll find.

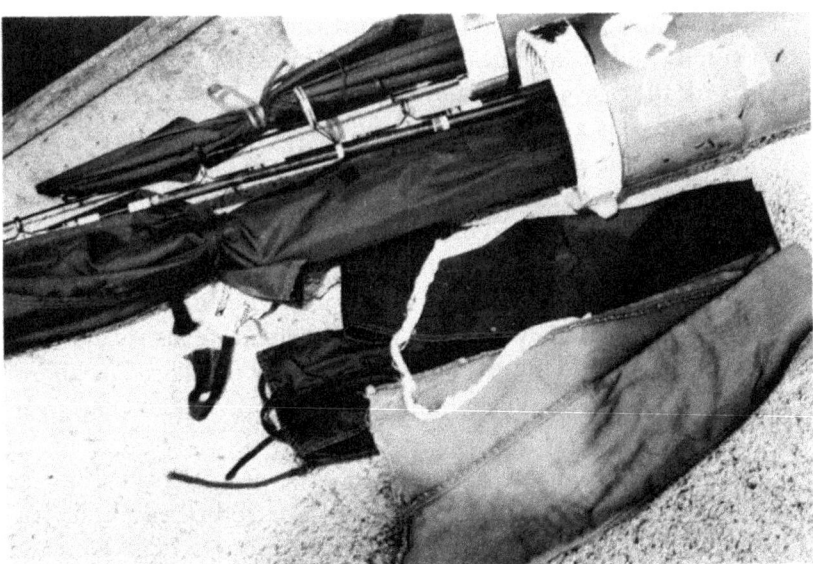

PVC case

The best caps are the heavy-duty schedule 80 type. They can be purchased at any plumbing retailer, and with them you can purchase the PVC glue. (The glue is really powerful, so keep it out in the open and try not to sniff too much of it.) The bottom cap should be the type that can be permanently glued in place and that is without thread. The top cap should have two sections: the bottom section with the thread and the top section for the cap, threaded also.

To attach the top cap, glue in the bottom threaded portion and allow it to dry until the section is glued solidly. Make sure that the threaded portion is set good and tight because some threaded plugs will screw in very tight and if the glue isn't set right, you can uncap everything with all the turning you'll be doing. Once the bottom section is set, you have a rod case. These cases are super easy to make. If you want you can add some handles to the center of the case. Find the exact middle and then attach your handles. A short section of rope either taped or tied to the center of the case will do fine.

The best thing to look for in padding is foam, which can be obtained in an electronic parts shop. Foam padding is extra soft, light, and will protect any rod. Stuff the bottom and top sections of the case with foam before you screw on the top.

The way to test a rod case is to shake it to and fro. If the rods inside slide up and down the case, then you're in for trouble. The rods shouldn't move at all. If they do, by the time you reach your destination you'll wind up with neatly broken off tips. To really protect your rods, stuff the case with extra foam.

Once the rods are in the cases and padded so they aren't rattling around, tape the caps shut. That way, even if the caps or plugs get loose, the tape will hold them securely during the flight and during handling. The best tape to use is fiber tape which is strong and can't be broken by hand. Wrapping the caps will discourage most baggage thieves and ensure your tackle's arrival at the fishing destination. "Gaffer's tape" works well too. It is relatively inexpensive and can be reused if taken off with care. The tape can be purchased in big rolls and will repair just about anything you can think of, including an arm or a leg.

Labeling your rod cases is a good idea. Some anglers purchase and label brass dog tags and attach them to their rod cases and luggage. The most secure way to attach them is with a section of Sevalon and a brass sleeve. These materials also prevent corrosion due to salt water. Dog tags can also be rivetted to the side of the plastic conduit.

A good, felt-tipped indelible ink pen will also put a good label on a rod case. Make the lettering big and broad and easy to see. Write your social security number on the rod case and anything else that will help your case find you if it gets lost.

Reflective tape is another good choice. A large section of this tape wrapped around the rod case will make it easy for the luggage handler to find your case in the cargo hold in the dark. If reflective tape is not available, then shiny sparkling tape is a good second choice.

If you go on a trip with friends and you all have the same type of rod case, then the best thing to do is to use a little extra colored tape on your case. A bright orange or red tape will quickly distinguish your case from all the others. These small little tricks will help you keep your sanity on some long and tiring trip.

Rod Sacks

Rod sacks are only cloth tubes and can be made on the sewing machine. The sacks keep the rods from getting nicked everywhere and the tips from getting broken in rod cases during long trips. The easiest way to make a rod sack is to politely ask your wife to make one. Look around for some old curtains, sheets, pillow cases, or some old, discarded sections of cloth. It doesn't take a genius to figure out a pattern for a rod sack. After you've looked at a lot of other anglers' sacks, you'll be able to figure out a style of your own that you'll feel comfortable with. If you don't have a wife or if she's all thumbs and hates to get stuck with a needle, then have a dressmaker sew one for you. Or sew one yourself. You could also buy one from any rod or custom rod shop. Just let them know the dimensions of the rod or rods and they'll take it from there.

Some anglers go have their names embroidered on the rod sack. This is nice and makes the sack easier to locate if you lose it in the shuffle. If this isn't possible, write your name in indelible ink on the cloth in big bold letters. It'll take a little time but it'll be worth it.

One thing about rod sacks is that they tend to get wet and soggy. It is important to dry out the rods after they have been in the sack because the moisture will get under the varnish and eventually rot the wrappings of the rod. So even if the rod sacks protect rods, they can also cause some serious problems. They should be washed and dried periodically, especially if they've been subjected to a lot of handling and exposure to salt water.

4
Monofilament and Monofilament Knots

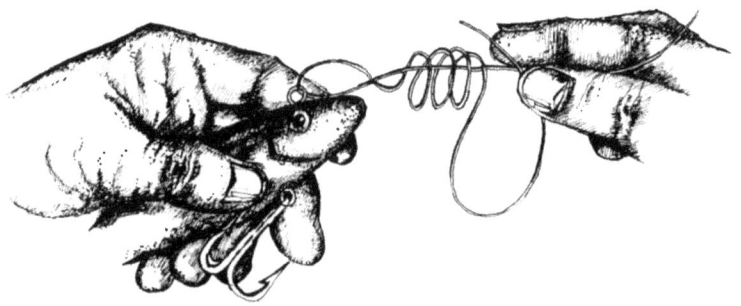

Monofilament is one of the greatest inventions since the wheel. Monofilament stretches, has good line to diameter strength, is abrasion resistant (to a point), and can have either the limpness or the stiffness (whichever quality you prefer) for long, determined casts. Because it stretches, it apparently has forgiveness. Whereas with dacron, which tends to have much less stretch than monofilament, you'll find very little forgiveness in the line. Any quick and unexpected lunge or jerk on the dacron line could mean immediate termination of the battle.

This is not to say that monofilament doesn't have its own set of problems. Monofilament can be made to have a great deal of impact strength, but like all other lines, sudden jerks can break the line. So, the better the quality of monofilament you purchase, the better the line will stand up to abuse.

At present there are over 250 formulas to create monofilament and over 100 different types of resins with which to make monofilament. Naturally, then, you'll find monofilament of the so-called bargain basement brands. These low quality lines are products of manufacturing shortcuts or essentially of poor base materials. Technically they are a very poor buy and any serious angler should avoid them.

Unfortunately, there is no real way of distinguishing the good line from the junk, except by looking at the product price in relation to the amount of line in the spool. You could also simply talk to others and learn whether a particular brand has a good or terrible reputation. The reputation of the company that makes the brand will follow it all over the fishing industry. Bargain- or basement-brand monofilament does have its uses, however: it makes good anchorline and is great for starting-off kids in the fishing field. Because the cost is minimal, it's no problem if the line gets caught and must be cut.

As I mentioned earlier, quality control for monofilament is very poor. You will be purchasing monofilament strictly on the basis of the product's reputation and your past experiences. Labels may be misleading and a strong line isn't necessarily a better line. There is no regulation that says the line has to break at the test specified. Some lines break far from the specified weight, and if the line should class over the labeled test, it may cost you a world-class fish.

Even the line diameters in the bulk spools will vary greatly. At the beginning of the bulk spool you may have very thin line for its line class; in the middle the line may have a very large diameter; and at the end you may once again find line that has a small diameter.

This is not to say that there are no really great lines, but that the lines that meet high quality standards are the basic tournament-grade lines. These lines are pretested and are supposed to break below the line class specified. Line such as the 20-pound test should break at 18- or 19-pound test, not at 23- or 24-pound test. These are the better

Monofilament is sold in various spool sizes. The best way to buy monofilament is on large bulk spools.

grade lines and therefore at times they may cost you quite a bit more; but if you're after large fish with light line, then this is the line class you want or should be looking for.

The quality of the monofilament is diminished not only by poor production and lax quality control but also by the water itself. Monofilament loses about 15 percent of its breaking strength once it becomes fully saturated with water. It absorbs moisture much like a sponge, though not quite as fast. Within twenty-four to forty-eight hours the line can become at least 9 percent water. So during storage line should be kept as dry and free of moisture as possible. Line that has been kept in constantly damp or wet spools will tend to be much weaker than line allowed to dry.

On the other extreme, monofilament is also affected by heat and ultraviolet and fluorescent lights. As you know, these lights will cause the line to fade and eventually to become very, very stiff and brittle. Reels left connected to the rods and stored in an open garage, for instance, will have lines that are weak and stiff as wire. The breaking and knot strength will be remarkably low. The line actually should be thrown away. It's really amazing how many people keep in their reels line that is years old. Line that has been left in a reel for months and months and that has lost all of its color will still be used, and the angler using it will wonder why he keeps losing fish.

Most anglers who fish a great deal and for fairly large fish don't hesitate to change lines before each major fishing trip. Some even go so far as to change their line after every major battle if they feel that the line has lost much of its strength, and especially if they're fishing for world-class fish. The last thing they want to compromise is the strength of the monofilament.

Another reason for changing line is the terrain of the area. Some areas have a lot of coral outcroppings or have bottoms that are heavily strewn with barnacle-covered rocks. During a battle, the fish-drawn line might scrape some rocks and suffer a severe nick. Sometimes a line can get tangled on the bottom during a heavy battle, and if the angler is lucky the line may suddenly come free. If the line is terribly frayed, however, it should be changed right away.

The best way to find out if your line is frayed is to run the line through your fingers and concentrate on the line's smoothness. As soon as the frayed portion hits the fingers, you'll feel it. Cut off the torn section and then some. I personally feel that monofilament is very inexpensive and should be changed often. The best way to purchase monofilament is by the bulk. At first the huge spools will seem to cost a great deal, but after you get used to filling reel after reel, you'll eventually learn how many reels or spools you can fill with one big bulk spool of line.

Since you'll be filling your own spools, you'll quickly learn that line becomes twisted if not spooled right. Spinning reels are especially prone to causing line twist. If your line is not spooled properly, you could lose a considerable number of fish, not to mention become frustrated when the cast line comes off in huge, messy clumps. Each cast that is messed up causes loss of valuable fishing time and may even lead to the loss of a potential strike.

These problems can be alleviated if line winders that conveniently clamp to the rod are used. Another solution is to wind your spinning reel spools on an electric drill. Construct your own spool holder with a set of common machine bolts and wing nuts. With a few extra pennies you will have an effective spool winder. You could also run down to the local fishing supply store and politely ask the clerk to wind it for you.

When winding the monofilament into the reel, don't overfill the spool. Overfilling a spinning reel tends to cause the line to leave the spool in large, tangled clumps, and should you manage to hook a fish, the tangles will quickly weaken the line and you may quickly lose the fish. Spinning reels should be filled about $1/8$ inch from the spool's edge. Conventional reels should be filled to the edge of the spool's lip, but not until the line hits the cross bars.

Once the reel is full of line you'll find that the line will have a tendency to spring forth and create a mess. This is especially true with spinning reels. The best way to secure the line is with a rubberband. Next, soak the line or the spool in some warm water for a few minutes; this will help to stop the memory in the line.

After a hard and determined battle with a stubborn fish, you should quickly take the line from the spool and crank it back in with less tension. The reason for this is that during the battle the line stretches a great deal and once it is cranked back into the spool it will start to regain its size and eventually split the spool. The best way to avoid this is to let the line out behind the boat on the trip back to the docks. Crank it back in at your leisure. If you're on the rocks, then have someone pull the line from the rod tip and let it lie on a tarp or poncho before you wind it back in. Another alternative is to simply take out the line and crank in fresh new line. The monofilament is the only thing that holds you and the fish together, so take care of it and it will take care of you.

Knots and the Leader

With the right combination of knots and good quality leader material, you will have yourself a strong and dependable leader that will last you through many battles. But before you have these battles, you should learn to tie monofilament knots consistently well. Like anything else in this world tying a good knot takes time and a lot of practice. There's really no shortcut to learning to tie solid knots.

The best time to practice knots is when you're in front of the TV set or at the beach, that is, when you've got a lot of free time. The key is to have the right frame of mind when you learn how to tie knots. It involves memorizing steps, which takes a lot of patience. Study your instructions and practice them well.

There are a lot of books out that show scores of monofilament knots. Track them down at the local library and sit down and try them out. I used to take a small roll of monofilament and try out some of the knots at the library. It's pretty crazy now that I think about it, but it really has paid off in spades. I never believe I know enough knots, and there always seems to be a knot that is better than the one I just learned. There are also a lot of knots that you will not find in books, knots that some oldtimer has been using for generations and that no one even thinks about anymore. Watch some of the veteran commercial fishermen and you may learn a few really neat tricks for tying knots.

But all knots have specific purposes. If you can't find a knot to suit your specific needs, then you have to either invent one or modify an existing one. These things take time and patience. Keep asking questions and you'll eventually find the knot that will meet your needs.

Knots that break alway slip first—this is a proven fact. It's also a really good reason for you to cinch down the knot as tightly as you possibly can. I use a lot of saliva, it's plentiful and it helps cinch down knots perfectly. Saliva also helps to keep the line from heating up during the final cinching moment. I am always very cautious during the final moments of cinching the knot tight. If it seems to sit wrong or I'm not quite feeling right about the knot, I retie it. The wrong time to retie a knot is after you lose a fish to a bad knot. Check and recheck until you are fully satisfied with your knot.

If you're going fishing on a boat and are after fairly big fish with light line, you should always do your leaders the night before you set foot on the boat. This is especially true with shore fishing. Tie all your knots the night before and you won't have to rush the knot when the fish are biting. Take the time to do a little preparation. Tie good knots and you'll never have to worry about losing fish to a bad knot and having only a fishing story instead of a fishing trophy.

After you've hooked and landed a big fish that has really dragged your lines and leaders over the hot coals, pull out about fifty feet of line and run it gently through your fingers. Find the bad spot, cut it off, retie the leader, and go back to fishing. If you find you have taken out too much line, splice in new line and crank it in until the reel is again full. Retie the leader and go back to fishing. The obvious alternative to this is to have a spare spool ready so you can simply replace the old spool. I normally rig up two complete outfits, with leaders. It is a fairly good idea to some anglers to replace only the first hundred yards of the line; this way cost is kept down and the angler still has the luxury of using new line at any time.

The Knots

The following knots and illustrations should cover all your needs when it comes to monofilament knots, braided wire knots, and wire leader knots. Not all of these knots will have multiple purposes; some will have very specific jobs and these should not be used for other purposes.

Basically two kinds of knots are described in this section: the Double Line Knot and the Straight Splice Knot. All a Double Line Knot is, is a single line doubled to increase the leader strength. It is tied where the line is frayed because of contact with a fish's abrasive body or with sharp coral, constant casting pressures, or because of the general abuse the line takes when a fish is being gaffed. To some degree, the Double Line also adds a little more spring to the leader. Examples of this knot are the Bimini Twist Knot and the Spider Hitch Knot.

Throughout a fisherman's life the need to splice two similar sized lines will come up time and time again, whether the reason be a backlash that has to be cut out, tangles that come up from kinked lines, or a badly nicked line that has to be spliced with some type of knot. The knot that you choose must be totally dependable and also easy to tie. This is the Straight Splice Knot. Examples of this knot are the Blood Knot and the Uni-Knot Splice and Double-Nail Knot Splice.

Again, follow knot-tying instructions when you have spare time and are in a good frame of mind. If you run into a new, very functional knot, feel free to share it with your buddies. We're always looking for more ways to catch and land fish.

Bimini Twist Knot

The Bimini Twist, or Twenty Times Knot, is normally used by offshore trollers who want a double line with 100 percent knot strength. Saltwater fly fishermen also use this knot for making a "shock tippet" on the fly leader. Other anglers, such as bait casters, use the double line as a leader to decrease the possibility of being cut off at the lure.

This is the granddaddy of complicated knots and most people will shy away from it; but once you have learned the rudiments of knot tying, it should be fairly simple. All it takes is a little more practice than usual. Once you have mastered this knot, you can beat the best of them.

This knot is very dependable. I use it in most of my leader constructions and it rarely lets me down. So if you want to learn to tie this knot, take some time off and practice until you have it right.

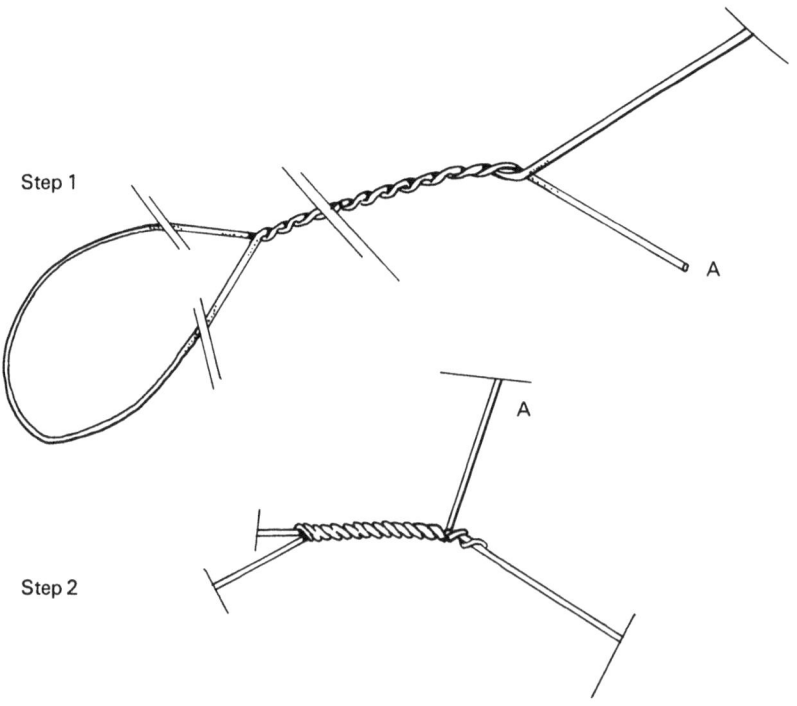

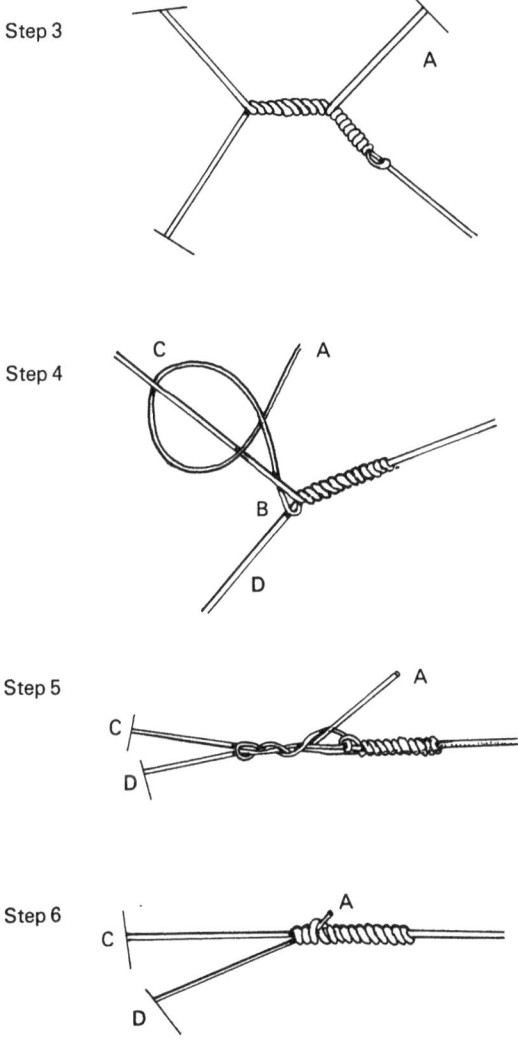

Bimini Twist Knot (100 percent breaking strength). *Step 1:* First double the mainline to the length you want and twist the line fifteen to twenty times. *Step 2:* By placing your feet into the loop and spreading the line apart you can tighten the twisted line. Grabbing the tag end (A), allow the line to hop over the coils and coil itself back down over the twisted line. *Step 3:* Allow the line to work its way down the entire length of the coil. Maintain the tension on the tight coils with your spread feet. *Step 4:* Once the coils have reached the bottom (B), apply the first half hitch to any of the two standing lines (C). This stops the knot and it will not come undone at this point. *Step 5:* Take the tag end (A) and make a half hitch around both standing lines (C,D). Make two or three more turns around both standing lines with the tag end and then draw it tight. *Step 6:* Secure hitches by adding saliva. Work the line with fingers until snug. Trim to about a quarter inch outside of the knot.

Spider's Hitch

This is one double-line knot that is fast to tie but that is not as strong as the Bimini Twist. If you have to make a relatively good double-line knot, then this could be one of your choices. I add a half hitch at the butt of the knot to make it a little more tapered and easier to thread through the guides. I also trim close to the hitch.

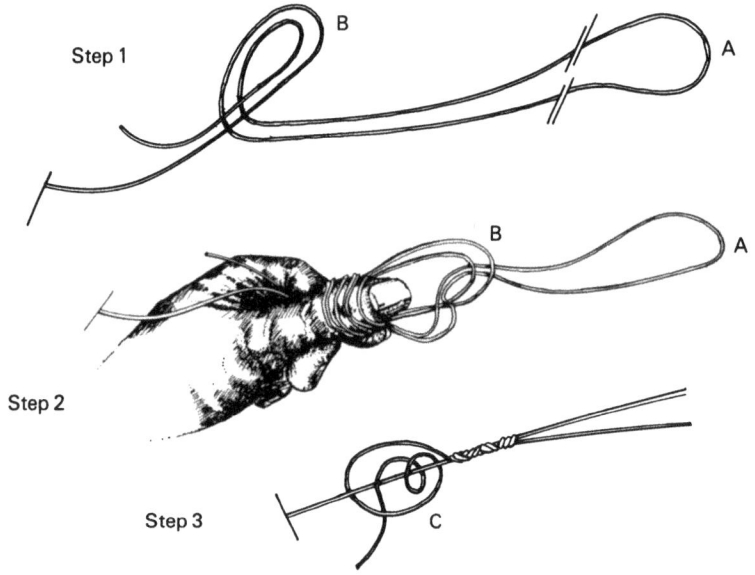

Spider's Hitch. *Step 1:* Double the line to the length that you want and then make a small reverse loop (B) with both lines. *Step 2:* While holding it with your thumb and index finger, wrap the double line five times around your thumb and the reverse loop. Pass the larger loop A through the small reverse loop B. *Step 3:* Pull slowly on loop A so that the line unwinds off of the thumb. Moisten with saliva and tighten. Add a double half hitch (C) at the base of the knot.

Surgeon's Knot

This is one of my favorite knots. It's so simple it sometimes makes me wonder if it can hold up under the stress I put it through. So far it has.

The Surgeon's Knot is most often used to knit two different sized lines: the mainline and a heavier leader for whipping, for instance, or a shock tippet and a fly leader. It is about a 95 percent knot and great because it can be cranked into the reel without creating too much resistance while going through the guides. To ensure easy threading, I put a half hitch at the end of the Surgeon's Knot. This way it also withstands abrasion better as it whips through the tip top guide.

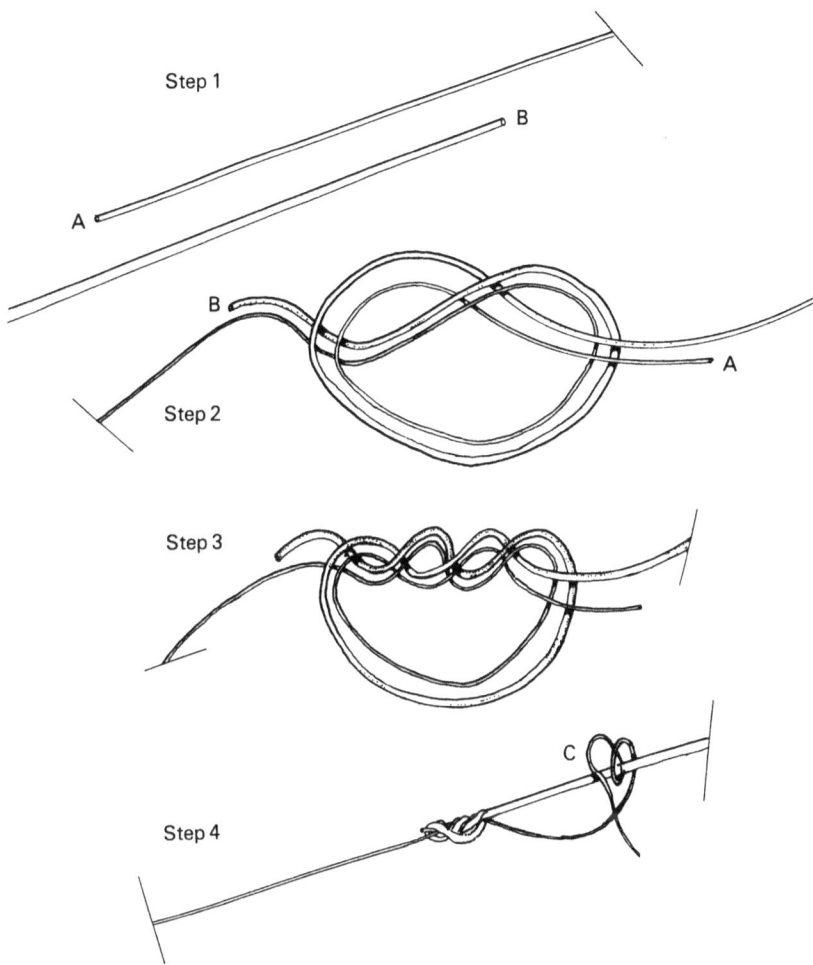

Surgeon's Knot. *Step 1:* Lay two lines (A,B) parallel to each other. *Step 2:* Using both lines, make an overhand knot. Both lines should be kept next to each other. *Step 3:* Make the same overhand knot once more. *Step 4:* Pull all four ends uniformly. Add saliva to secure knot. The optional double half hitch (C) is created with the lighter of the two lines (A). Trim close after the knot is completed.

Blood Knot

The Blood Knot is a basic splice knot and is a standard pretty much everywhere. It is very easy to learn to tie. Its breaking strength is around 90 to 95 percent. If you use a pair of cutting pliers, you will tend to leave some spurs and may get cut from them while doing some heavy shore casting with heavy lines. With this knot I clip very close to the tie with a pair of nail clippers.

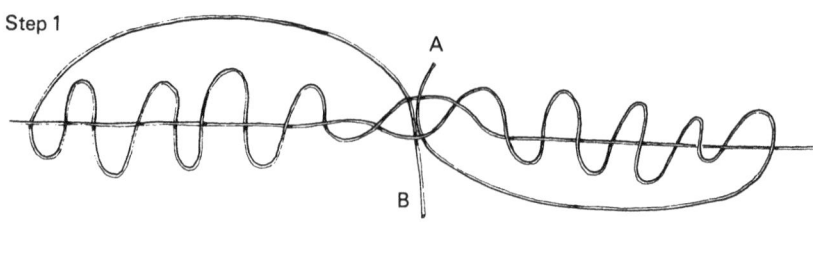

Blood Knot. *Step 1:* After laying both lines over each other, take a tag end (A) and make four or five turns around the standing line. Do this with the other tag end (B). Insert both tags into the opening loop that has been formed. *Step 2:* Wet with saliva and draw knot tight. Once the knot is completed, give it a quick jerk to help it seat correctly. Trim close with a nail clipper.

Uni-Knot Splice

This is a splice knot that my father taught me, and I have used it quite a bit since. I don't know what the breaking strength is but it's pretty darn tough. The knot seems to be a little smaller and a little more complicated than the Blood Knot but it's worth learning to tie.

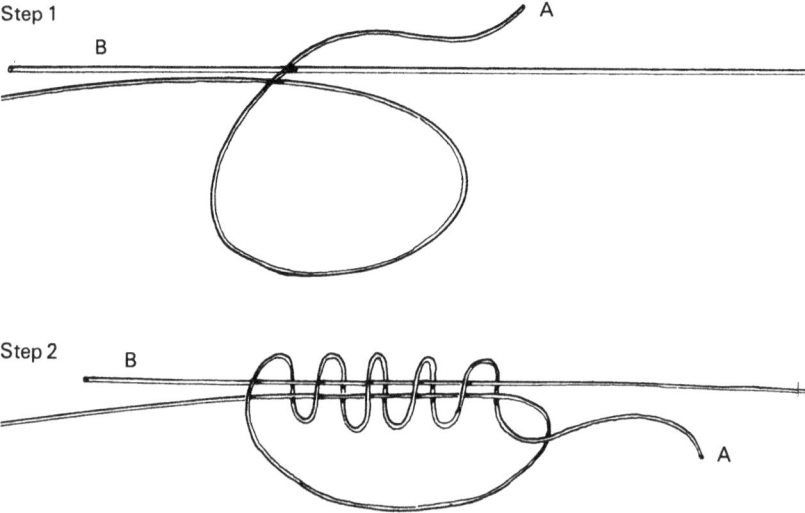

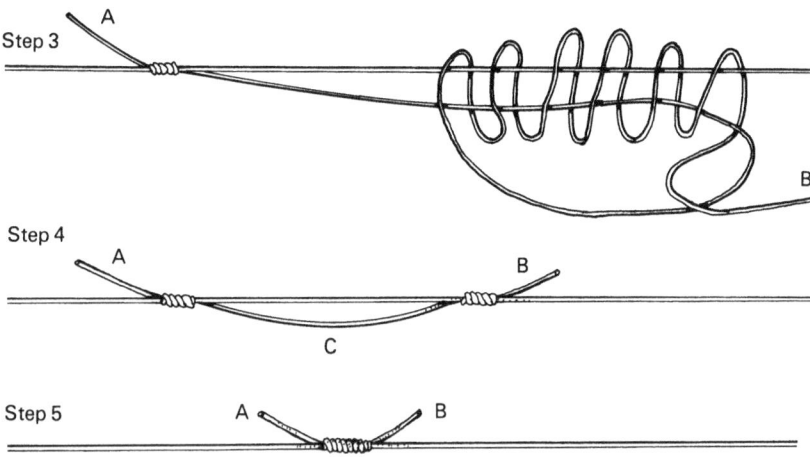

Uni-Knot Splice. *Steps 1 and 2:* Lay both lines parallel to each other. Take one tag end (A) and form an overhand loop. Wind the end four times around both lines and pull tight. *Step 3:* Repeat the last step with the other tag end (B) and pull tight. Add saliva to ensure a tight knot. *Step 4:* Once you have two knots on the two lines, add saliva to section C and pull both main lines so that the two knots slide toward each other. *Step 5:* Once both knots meet make sure they are snug. Trim at the tag ends (A,B).

Double Surgeon's Loop Knot

This loop is of the quickest ones to tie. Double the line, make a simple overhand knot twice, and draw it tight. You'll have a loop knot that is good on dropper lines, anchorlines, and various other leaders.

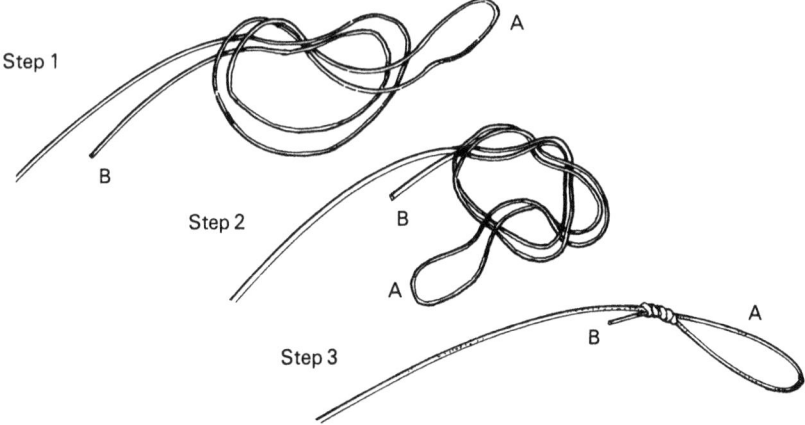

Double Surgeon's Loop. *Step 1:* Double the line and form a loop (A). Make an overhand knot with the loop. *Step 2:* Make a second overhand knot. Pull loop (A) tight while you pull tag end B to ensure a snug knot. Trim tag end off.

Double Nail Knot Splice

This knot is one of the best if you need to make a strong, straight splice. The only thing about this knot is that it takes time to tie and you'll need a nail or some kind of tool to make tying the knot easier. Other than that, the knot is very tough and will hold up under tremendous strain.

The best tool for tying this knot is a hollow brass tube or any kind of hollow object. Just slip the tag end into the tube after you've made the necessary turns and then slip the tube out. Make sure that the tube doesn't have a sharp edge on it. If it does, sand the edges so that it won't scratch the line.

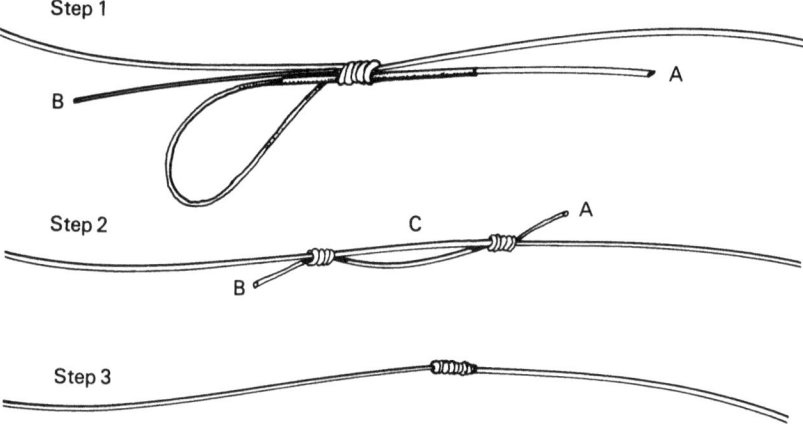

Double Nail Knot Splice. *Step 1:* Wrap a tag end four or five times around both line and a nail or a small brass tube about 4 inches long. Insert the tag end (A) into the tube and pull through. Once this is done pull the brass tube out to form the knot. *Step 2:* Apply some saliva to the knot and then pull tight. Repeat Step 1 with the other tag end (B). Add saliva to section C and pull both knots toward each other. *Step 3:* Snug both knots against each other and trim close.

Albright Knot

The Albright Knot is used mostly by *ulua* fishermen on the Big Island. Originally it was meant for offshore fishermen but has since been adopted by the big game shoreline caster. The knot is very dependable when it comes to joining two different sized lines together. It is especially great when used with a Bimini Twist for leaders and such. The knot is also 100 percent and has proven itself to many great *ulua* fishermen.

The knot is not that hard to tie and is relatively small considering the amount of work involved in tying it. As with all monofilament knots, the Albright Knot requires time and saliva. Once the line is ready to snug down tight, I add a lot of saliva to make it bind down tight. After that's done, I always trim with a sharp pair of nail clippers.

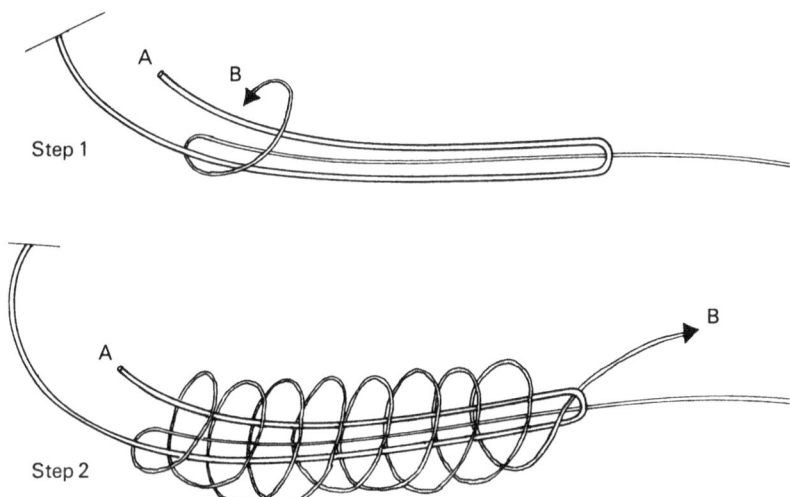

Albright Knot. *Step 1:* Take the larger line (A) and fold it in half. Lay the smaller line or double line (B) within the loop and make seven or eight turns around the leader line (A). *Step 2:* Pass the tag end (B) through the leader loop eye. Pull tight slowly, making sure that all the coils lay snugly and parallel to each other. Add saliva for a snug knot and trim close.

Perfection Loop Knot

The Perfection Loop Knot is another knot that is fast to tie. It is used a lot by fly fishermen for tying leader knots, but shore fishermen can find great use for it too.

A lot of times shore fishermen pre-tie a lot of their leaders, especially when fishing for *menpachi* (squirrel fish) and *ʻāweoweo* (redfish). They pre-tie all their hooks, and should one get cut off on the rocks, they simply pull out a new leader and connect it to the loop knot or lock the two loops together by weaving one into the other. This is easier and less time consuming than retying all the leaders.

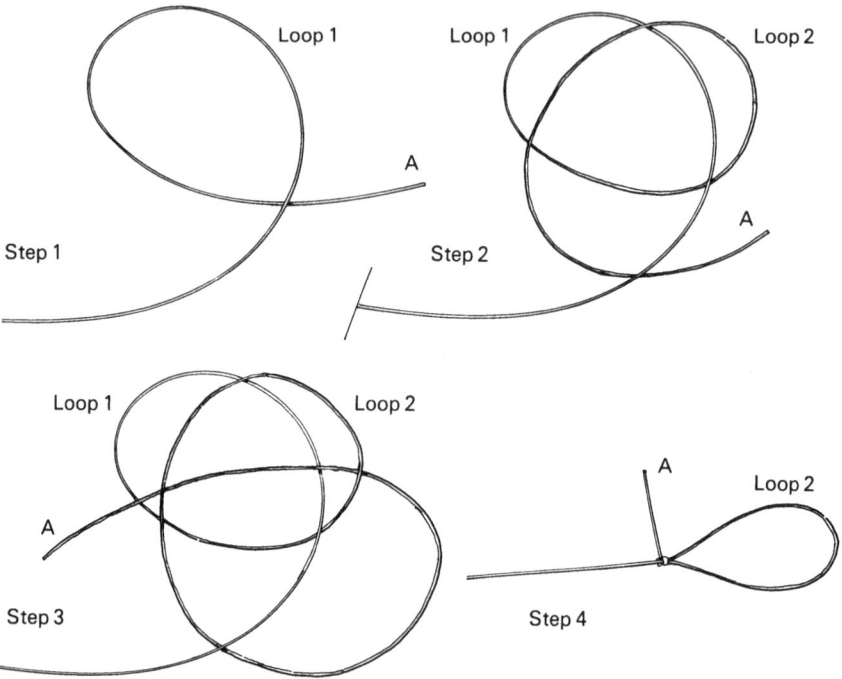

Perfection Loop Knot. *Step 1:* Form a back loop. *Step 2:* Form a second loose loop in front of the first loop. *Step 3:* Slide a tag end (A) between the first and second loops. Take the second loop, pass it over the tag end (A) and go through the first loop. *Step 4:* Draw tight and trim.

Dropper Knot

If you want to tie a loop at a right angle to the mainline or leader without using a simple square knot, then the Dropper Knot is for you. This knot is easy to tie, and once it is cinched tight it will perform well for you.

This type of knot eliminates the need for three-way swivels, and it is of course much cheaper. If you use stiff Mason lines for your leader and tie the Dropper Knot with a *menpachi* leader, you probably will get more strikes per cast. Swivels tend to scare fish away.

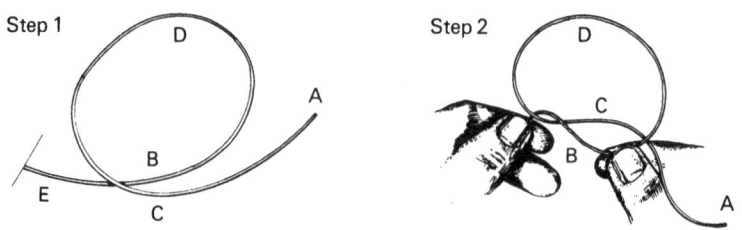

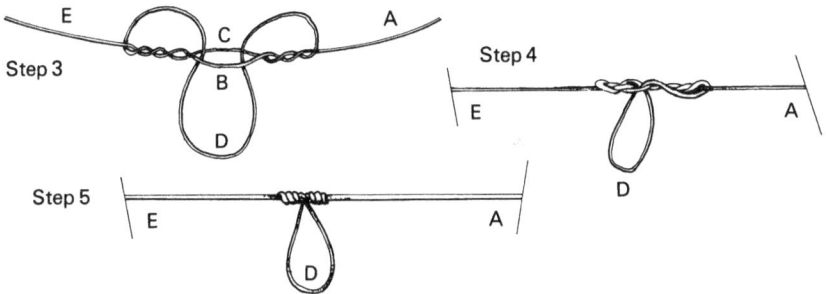

Dropper Knot. *Step 1:* Form a loop. *Step 2:* Pull section B of the loop over section C so that a gap in the line is formed. Twist sections C and B three or four times. *Step 3:* Pass section D through the gap in the twisted portion of the line. *Step 4:* Pull sections A and E to draw knot tight. Add saliva to set knot tight. *Step 5:* Finished knot.

Improved Clinch Knot

This is one of the easiest knots to learn to tie. I learned it by following pictures and simply practicing. With this knot you can tie hooks, swivels, and lures with great speed and can depend on the knot to do its job very well.

The Improved Clinch Knot is also one of the easiest to teach and to remember. It's so simple that it makes you wonder if the knot will hold. But it will hold and will prove itself to be at least a 95 percent knot. With this one knot you can do just about all the knot tying you'll ever need. It's just that dependable, so learn it well.

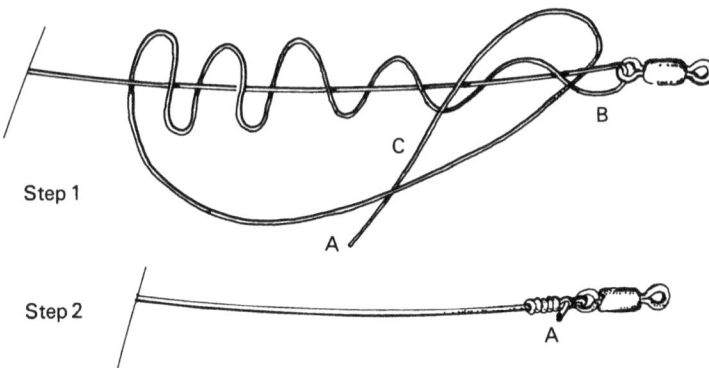

Improved Clinch Knot. *Step 1:* Take a tag end (A), pass it through the hook or swivel, and go around the mainline five times. Go through loop B and then through loop C. *Step 2:* Add saliva and pull both the mainline and the tag end (A). Secure knot and trim.

Three-and-a-Half-Turn Clinch Knot

This knot is very similar to the Improved Clinch Knot, except that the line is usually much bigger (such as leader material) and when tied the tag end doesn't go back into the second loop. For this knot, as with all knots, moisten with saliva when tying and pull the line until the knot is tightened snuggly.

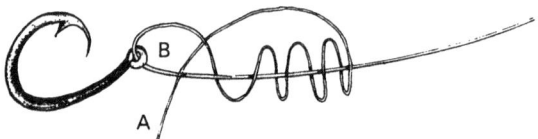

Three-and-a-Half-Turn Clinch Knot. Pass one end (A) through the eye of the hook, take three quick turns, and pass it through loop B. Add saliva and pull tight. Trim close.

Palomar Knot

The Palomar is another simple knot to learn. It has a 100 percent capability and, like the Improved Clinch Knot, it can be used on hooks and swivels.

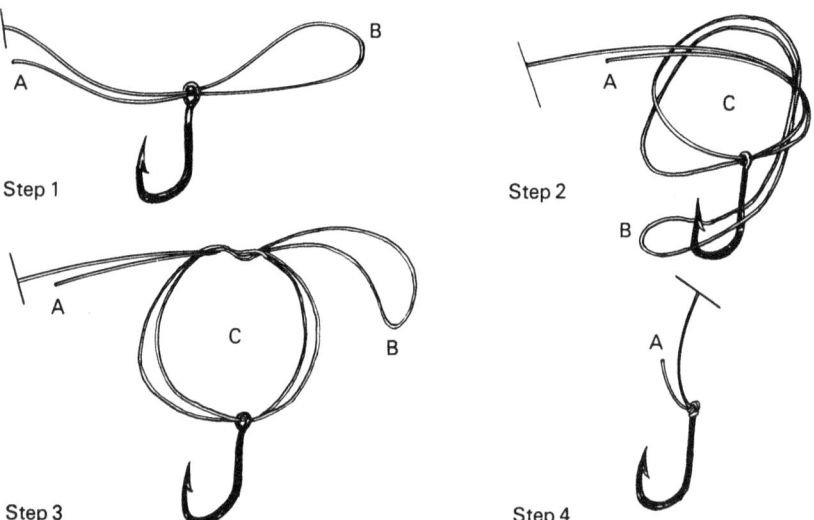

Palomar Knot. *Step 1:* Form a loop (B) and pass it through the hook's eye. *Step 2:* Form another loop (C) and make an overhand knot with loop B. *Step 3:* Pass the hook through loop B. *Step 4:* While holding the hook and mainline, pull tight. The line should be snug partly around the neck of the hook. Trim neatly.

Jansik Special

This was one of the knots my father taught me when I first started fishing, only he didn't call it the Jansik Special. In any case, it worked then and is still used today. It's a quick knot to tie and has a 95 to 100 percent capacity. It doesn't take too much time to learn and can be used to tie swivels, lures, and hooks.

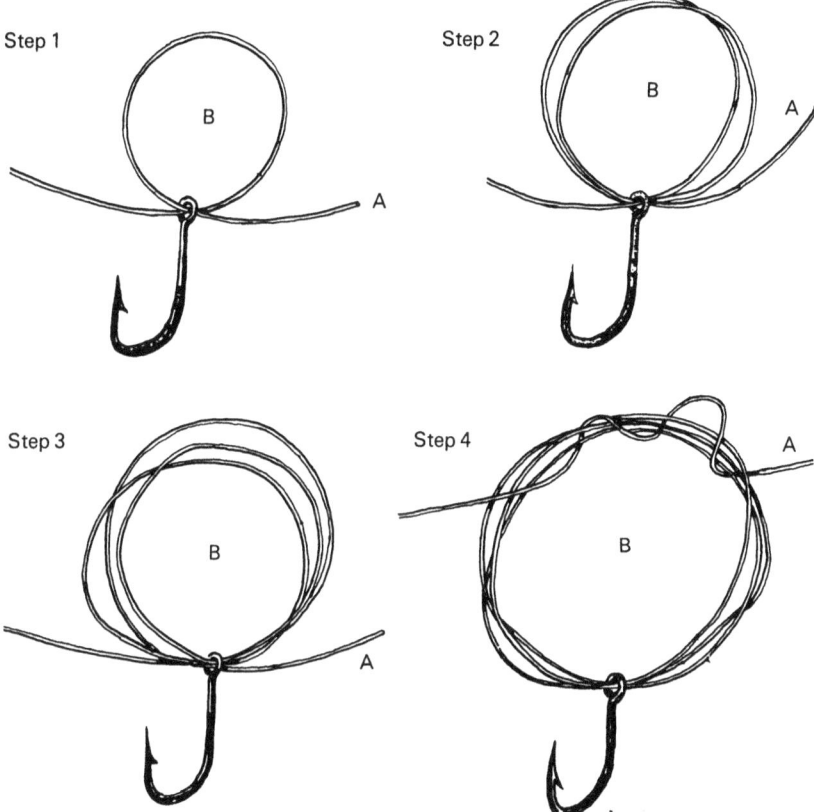

Jansik Special. *Step 1:* Pass the monofilament through the eye of the hook once and then a second time to form a loop (B). *Step 2:* Repeat Step 1 to form a second loop. *Step 3:* Once again make a loop. Slide the hook down onto the three loops so that the ends are free. *Step 4:* Using a tag end (A) make two overhand knots around all three loops. Hold the hook and mainline and pull tight after you add saliva. Trim close and then go and catch fish.

Homer Rhodes Loop Knot

This knot is one of my all-time favorites. I use it on all of my lures and have had wonderful results with it. The best thing about this knot is you can make a loop with it near the lure. This gives the lure much more action and with luck more strikes per day. It can also be tied very quickly, and when used with heavy leaders it will handle quite well.

One drawback with this knot is it tends to get banged up quite a bit and thus needs to be checked every so often. Once you see a small nick in it, you should retie the knot. Another thing that I do with the Homer Rhodes is add a half hitch to the knot. This cinches the knot and makes it even tighter, and it keeps the forward square knot from coming undone during fishing. Once the half hitch is on, I trim quite close to the knot.

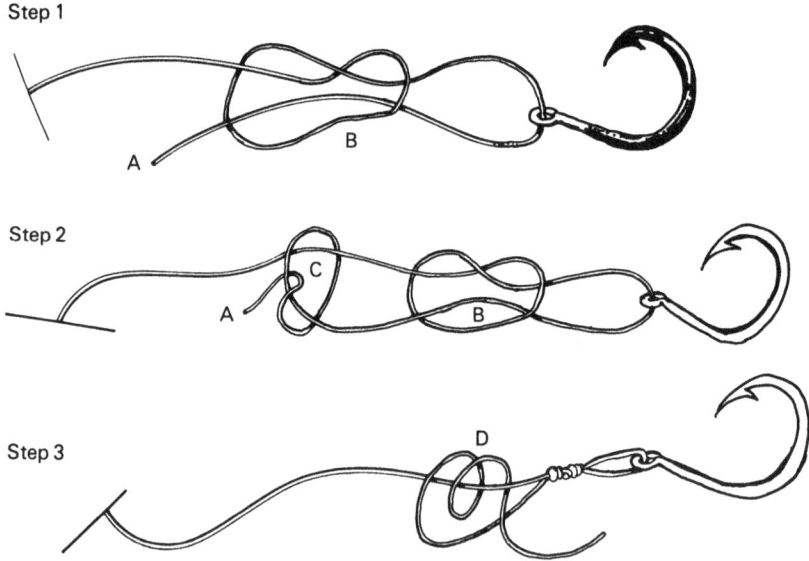

Homer Rhodes Knot. *Step 1:* Make a standard overhand knot. Feed a tag end (A) through the eye of the hook and then go back in the overhand knot loop (B). *Step 2:* Using only the tag end (A) make a second overhand knot (C) around the mainline. *Step 3:* Tighten both overhand knots and pull mainline to tighten further. Sometimes I add a double half hitch (D) to the end to close off the knot. Trim.

Japan Fishing Knot

This is another knot that was first introduced to me when I was knee-high to a cockroach. My father taught me this knot for 'o'opu (freshwater fish) fishing in streams and for catching 'oama (juvenile goatfish) down at the beaches. It's really a solid knot with good knot strength, and best of all, it's easy to learn.

One of the Japan Fishing Knot's greatest attributes is that the hook rides with the point sitting backwards. When the fish pushes downward, the hook springs back up. I don't know if it ever really landed more fish for me, but I've always used the knot and it has never let me down.

This knot is great for tying hooks to dropper lines and for meeting other bait-fishing rigging needs. The knot is very strong and will hold up under all kinds of bottom bumping and jostling. It's not very good for heavy lines, that is, 40-, 50-pound test, and up.

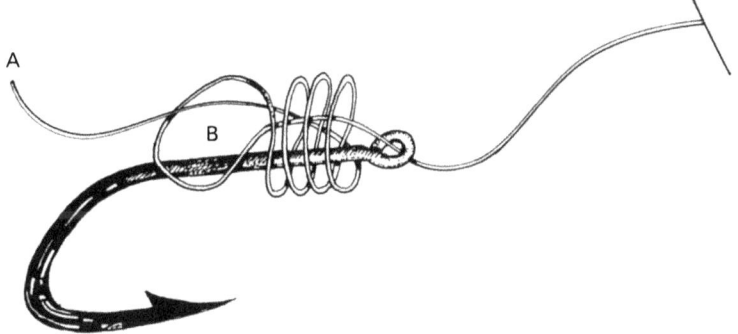

Japan Fishing Knot. Thread the line through the hook's eye, make a loop (B), and take three to four turns around the shank of the hook. Pass the tag end (A) through the loop and pull tight. Trim close neatly.

Figure 8 Knot

Ever been in a situation where you wanted or needed to use some braided wire for a leader? Maybe you suddenly saw a huge barracuda and figured on hooking it, but you suddenly found out that you were out of brass sleeves for the specific size wire you were using. Most anglers sit in despair at these times and think deep thoughts. But there is a knot for braided wires.

Although the Figure 8 Knot seems too simple to be strong, it is exceptionally effective. Tie one onto a hook and give it a good try.

Hitch a big hook onto a stationary object and pull until your arms are tired. I think you'll find that the knot is very tough. So follow the instructions for tying this knot and make use of it and get rid of all those sleeves.

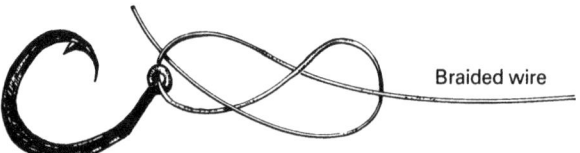

Figure 8 Knot. Pass one end through the eye of the hook, make a figure 8 with the braided wire, and pull snug. Trim clean with cutting pliers.

Trilene Knot

This is one knot I use when I feel the need for more cushion. The trilene has two loops that go into the hook's eye, and for this reason I like the double security. I apply a lot of saliva to this knot to make sure that it is snug.

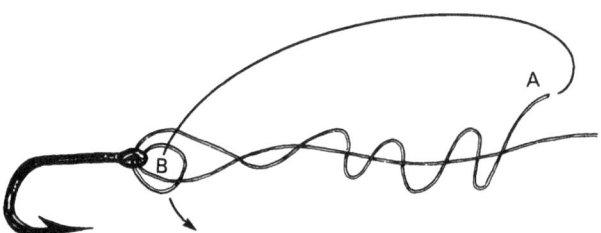

Trilene Knot. Go through the eye of the hook twice, take three to four turns around the mainline and go back into the loop (B) with the tag end (A). Moisten with saliva and tighten.

The Leaders

What exactly is a leader and what does it do? The basic function of a leader is to protect the mainline from abrasions caused by rocks, coral, sharp teeth of fish, and the rod's tip top guide. The leader is usually a much stronger length of monofilament, braided wire, or stainless steel wire. Its length is determined by the angler, and its breaking strength by the size of the mainline and the size of the fish the angler expects to encounter.

What type of leader material to use also depends on what kind of fish the fisherman wants to hook. Fish such as the barracuda will cut through heavy monofilament with great ease no matter how tough the monofilament is. So, fish like *ono* (wahoo) and barracuda really do require stainless steel leaders. If chances of the fish cutting through the monofilament leader are slim, then I suggest you stick to the clear monofilament. Your percentage of strikes will double and the lure's performance will be greatly improved.

The best leader is a long one. In my opinion, the longer the leader the better your chances of landing a fish. It also makes fishing much more efficient in that repairing a damaged section of the leader close to the hook is a simple matter of cutting it off and retying it above the torn section. Also, the longer the leader the less chance of losing a fish at the gaff or next to the cliff. Once the fish is tired and ready to be landed, all kinds of problems seem to crop up. More fish are lost at gaff than at any other time. With a strong leader, however, the fish can be manhandled and tossed around by waves, by poor gaffmen, and by overly excited fishermen.

On a trip to a place called Kalue in the Volcano National Park, Stan Wright and I walked for five and a half miles before we got to the fishing spot. It was important to travel light, so we didn't pack a slide gaff or pole gaff. To compensate for this, we used an extra-long leader of 30-pound-test Maxima. Once a fish was hooked and brought up to the edge of the cliff, we simply hauled it up hand over hand. We hauled the fish that weighed in at 10 to 12 pounds up fifteen- and twenty-foot cliffs without a problem. With the swinging and thrashing movements of the fish and the sharp rocks, the leaders got pretty well busted up; but they still held very well and we landed all of the fish we caught.

The best way to use a leader is to wind it into the reel. Since I make all my leaders long, they go into the reel and around the spool several times. For this reason, the leader cannot have a swivel attached to it. The swivel wouldn't be able to come up through the guides; swivels make casting impossible. All of my leaders are knotted together with a combination of knots (see "Knots and the Leader," this chapter). With this type of leader I can crank the lure or bait all the way up to the tip of the rod if I have to and make a pin point cast with a snap of my wrist.

The leader is of primary importance especially when it comes to whipping lures. Naturally, the leader and mainline sizes have to match properly for the entire rig to function at its best. With a leader and good snap casting, an angler will be able to make very deliberate casts to spots he thinks are holding fish. Without a leader the lure will probably snap off during the cast; or at the time of the strike the line will cut at its weakest point, the knot at the lure. A serious whipper will make hundreds of casts in a day and cause the line to suffer abuse from rocks, coral, poor knots, and a bad rod tip. This can ruin many lines and lose many fish. Therefore, using a leader is very important, especially if you want to land a trophy fish on light tackle.

The whipping leader takes the most punishment and for this reason it should be inspected more often than any other part of the rig. If the leader shows signs of wear and tear, it should be cut off and retied immediately. This may cost you some time, but it may mean one fish —probably the biggest fish of the day. Knots should be inspected and felt for minor abrasions. It's amazing how sensitive the fingers are: they can feel much more than the eyes can see when it comes to monofilament.

The slide-bait leader is one of the most bewildering of all leaders because it has undergone so much change in the years past. With the new generation of fishermen have come innovative ideas, theories, and styles of leaders tailored for a given area and terrain. The *ulua* slide-bait leader continues to change and will continue to evolve for many generations to come. But all in all the concept behind the leader is very basic: You slide your bait down the line after the lead has been cast and is secured to the bottom. If a fish comes along and takes the bait, the hook sets and the anchorline breaks. The fish pulls the slide-bait rig to the bottom of the leader and stops at the stop ring. The fish is now not hindered by the trailing lead and so must fight with the angler directly.

The system is great and works like a charm. What leader to use is determined by the terrain of the area you will be fishing. If the area has an abundance of rocks, then you'll need a leader that is tough and abrasion-resistant. It has to be long and its pound test has to be considerable.

Some areas have special problems—an overabundance of moray eels or sea worms and bugs that will eat bait in no time flat, for instance. The leader must be modified to survive all of these threats.

I have always believed that fishermen are very ingenious because they come up with some of the most interesting styles and techniques for fishing that you could ever imagine. The following leaders prove this.

MONOFILAMENT AND MONOFILAMENT KNOTS 95

Standard Big Island Leader

This basic leader is one of the most interesting of leaders and is also the most complicated to tie. But it works like a charm and has been proven successful beyond a shadow of a doubt. Although the leader is often modified, especially with regard to the type of leader material used and in the lengths of the double line and the leader, the knots used are usually all the same.

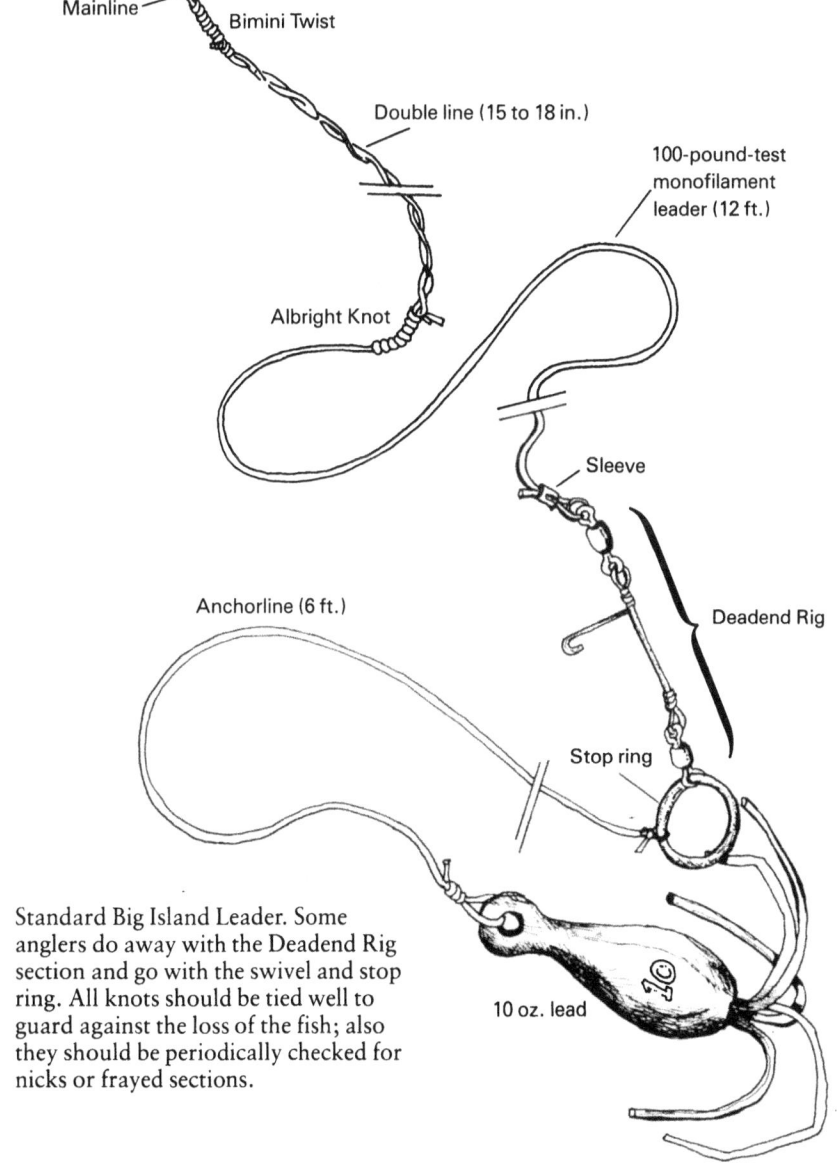

Standard Big Island Leader. Some anglers do away with the Deadend Rig section and go with the swivel and stop ring. All knots should be tied well to guard against the loss of the fish; also they should be periodically checked for nicks or frayed sections.

Deadend Rig

This rig has a stop ring section of the leader. The slide buckle is meant to stop at this section and not go any further. There are some crazy individuals who inadvertently forget to use stop rings and consequently lose fish because of this minor oversight. The type of stop ring used varies. Some are homemade with thick brazing rods that are bent into a ring and welded solid; others are simple steel split washers that are closed with pliers. Store-bought stop rings, however, still head the list of devices that stop the slide buckle. Although they have been known to split open under the strain of a tremendous strike, stop rings are easy to use and are very inexpensive.

A small section of stainless steel wire leader is used mainly to confine the hooked fish in one area of the leader. Some fish have been known to travel up the leader and cut themselves off on the mainline. This normally happens when the anchorline or the split ring is stuck on the ocean bottom. The fish will hit the bait and if it cannot break the anchorline or the entangled leader, it will travel up the line and cut it off when it runs perpendicular to the mainline. To prevent this from happening, the tip of the protruding wire is bent into a pigtail. This simple bend can end all the problems that a fish running back up the mainline can cause. The pigtail, then, is a very important feature of the Deadend Rig.

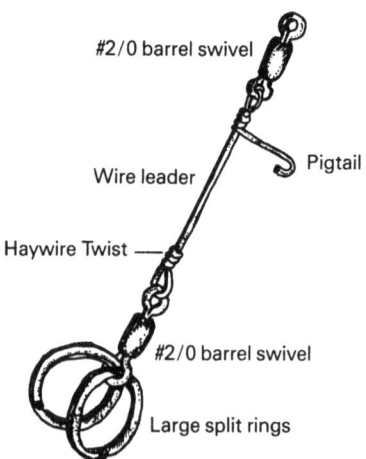

Deadend Rig

Slide-Bait Rig

This rig is the heart of the *ulua* fishing technique. The slide buckle is fastened to the mainline and actually slid down to another portion of the leader. The slide buckle carries the bait, which is usually too big to cast, all the way down to the area where the bait can be displayed for all to see and with luck eat.

All the slide buckle is required to do is slide. Below the buckle is a section of stainless steel wire leader that varies in length. Some anglers make two lengths: one for the first slide, which is short, about four to five inches long; and another for the second slide, around a foot long. The reason for having two lengths is that two baits of the same length dangling on the line causes tangles and an overall mess. When the two slides are different, however, the baits are better exposed and you have fewer tangles.

Normally, the Slide-Bait Rig uses solid stainless steel wire. Some anglers will use heavy-duty, braided wire to connect the hook to the slide buckle. They feel that this way they have a better swing with the bait and, for that matter, more strikes. Again, it all boils down to what the individual angler trusts and feels comfortable with.

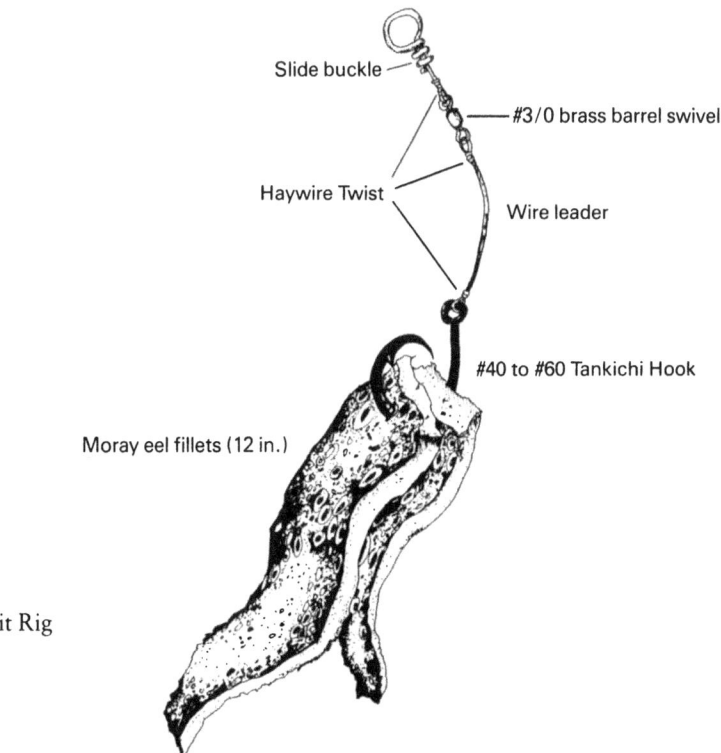

Slide-Bait Rig

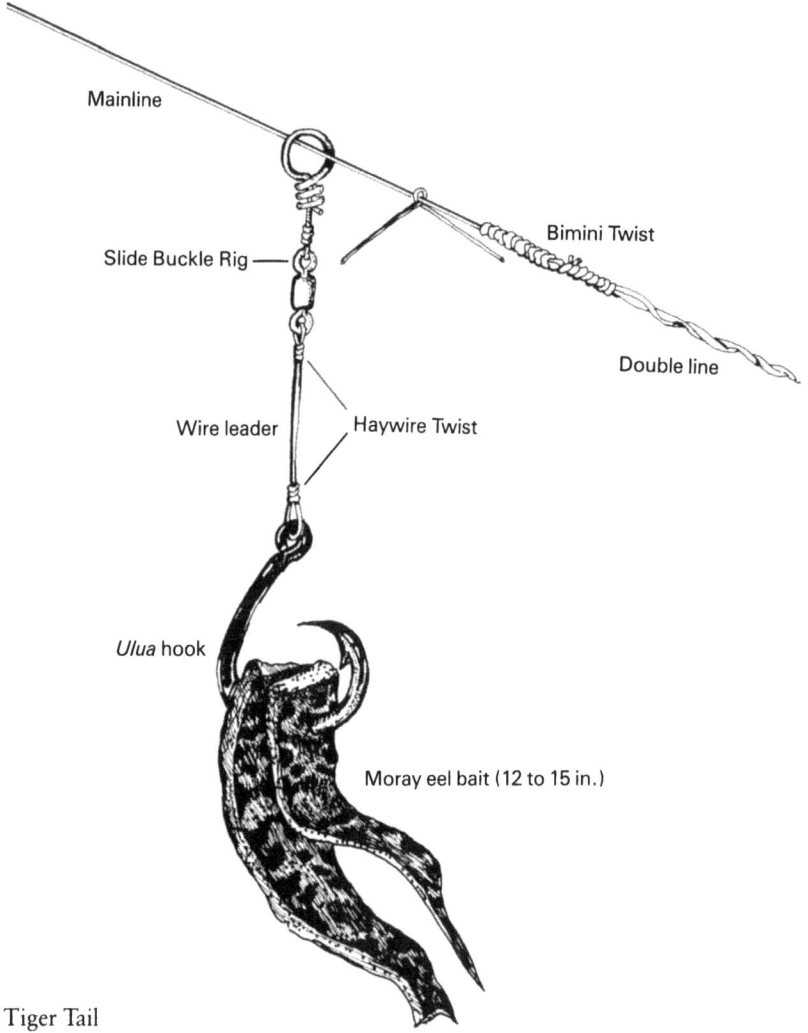

Tiger Tail

Tiger Tail

One of the problems one encounters when slide-bait fishing is the moray eel, which loves to take baits into its hole. The only way to keep it from eating your dangling bait is to keep the bait out of its reach. So, the idea is to stop the bait as high as possible.

To solve this problem, someone came up with an ingenious invention called the tiger tail. All it consists of is a small, three- to four-inch section of wire leader bent into a curl. The curl should be smaller than the diameter of the knot at which you wish to stop the bait.

The way to use this rig is to first slide the tiger tail down the line *before* you send down the bait. The tiger tail will stop at the intended spot, which can be a knotted section of dental floss or a Bimini Twist at the head of the leader. Since the hole of the tiger tail is small, the wire will stop abruptly. Because of its weight, it will not hinder the line or the leader in any way. Slide the rig down as usual and it will stop at the tiger tail. If the bait should be grabbed by an *ulua,* the tiger tail will bend backwards and permit the slide buckle to proceed down the length of the leader and stop at the ring. Except for the fact that the bait is stopped a little bit higher than usual and the morays have a little harder time at getting to the bait, everything else in the leader is identical with and functions the same way as the standard leader rig. The best thing about the Tiger Tail Rig is that it works very well, is inexpensive and easy to make, and you can carry a whole bunch of tiger tails in your tackle box. All it takes is a little time in front of the TV on a quiet night and you'll have a bunch of tiger tails in no time flat.

Sandy Beach Slide-Bait Rig

This slide-bait rig is one of the most basic of all leaders. It is easy to make and works great if the area you're fishing in is sandy and does not have a lot of coral outcroppings. Due to the length of the anchorline, if this style of leader were to be used, the stop ring would have a good chance of getting tangled in the coral heads. If this happens, you will have to break off the line and retie another leader. Since the leader is about three to five feet long, the anchorline has to be short (about a foot). If you make the anchorline long, maybe five feet, you won't be able to cast it. So, the anchorline in a leader like this has to remain relatively short.

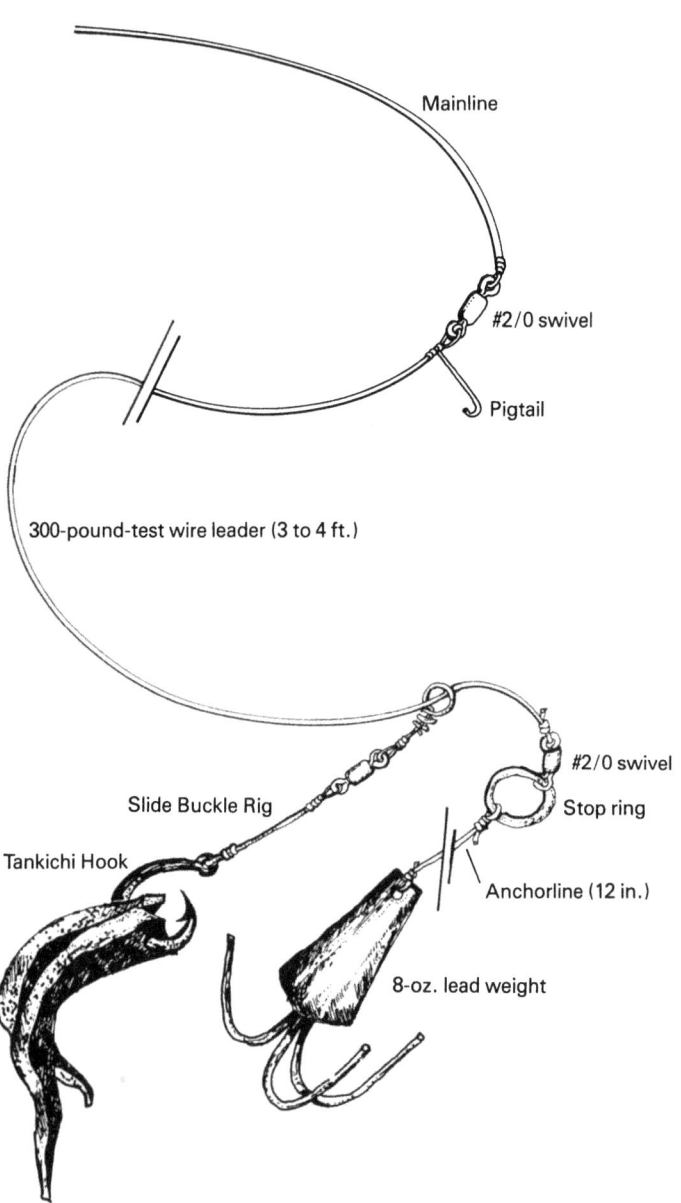

Sandy Beach Slide-Bait Rig

Toilet Paper Rig

The Toilet Paper Rig is a slightly modified version of the Big Island Leader. The leader is basically the same only the anchorline is wound around a section of toilet paper rolled up to about the thickness of your thumb. Each tag end of the anchorline is half-hitched off and tied to either the lead or stop ring. What you have, then, is a rolled up section of toilet paper with twenty feet of anchorline wrapped around it. The entire rig is cast out into the ocean and the lead allowed to sit on the bottom. The toilet paper will dissolve in the water and the tag ends of the anchorline will be released. This will then release the wound up coils. Now you have an anchorline that is super long, and, with luck, when you slide your bait down, it will help you get more strikes and fewer bites from moray eels.

One of the drawbacks with using the Toilet Paper Rig is you have to make every cast count. Once the toilet paper gets wet, the trick is over. The angler that uses this technique, therefore, should be a pretty proficient caster. If he isn't he'll get very frustrated very quickly. Another drawback is having to carry a whole bunch of toilet paper rolls. They have to be kept very dry, and when you're fishing down at the beach, that can become quite a chore.

Ted Tokunaga MD-TP Slide-Bait Rig

As I've said, fishermen are some of the most ingenious people when it comes to thinking up and designing techniques that will help them catch more fish, or that will just make fishing more fun. Some techniques are several ideas melded into one very simple idea; others are totally original and show that much thought and effort went into their design. Whoever designed the original slide-bait technique either had an extremely imaginative mind or the inventor tried different ideas until he stumbled onto the right one. The idea seems almost too simple to have required any thought.

When it comes to *ulua* fishing, I have found that the people of Hawaii have shown much creativity. This is not to say that the slide-bait technique was not developed in other places on this planet. Fishermen on the mainland have devised the "trolley style" of fishing, which is basically the same as our Hawaiian style. However, Big Islanders seem to have perfected the slide-bait technique.

On the Big Island, the extremely rough terrain of the fishing spots must have made it necessary to develop this technique to its fullest. As

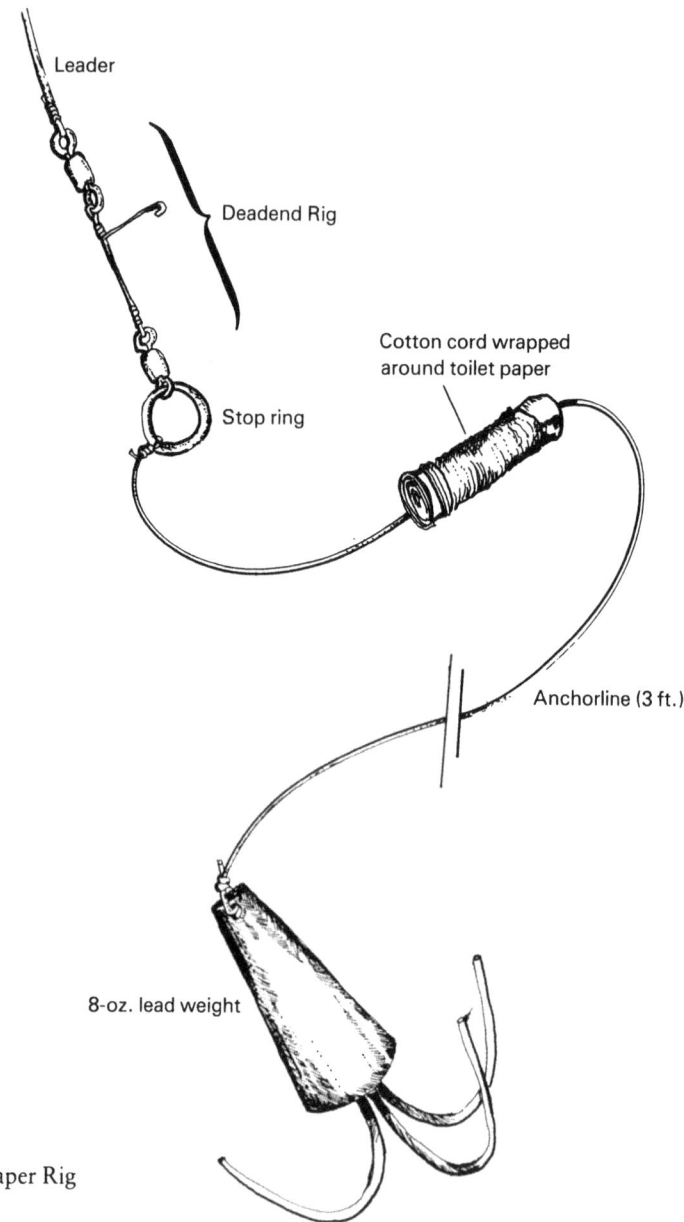

Toilet Paper Rig

a result, the Big Islanders developed a leader style that is totally different from styles found on the other islands. The rig takes more time and effort to make, and it dictates the types of rods and reels that are to be used. But, quite simply, the leader is what enables Big Islanders to hook and land more fish than other fishermen.

Because *ulua* fishing is so popular, more ideas are constantly being thought of and more facts about the quarry are being made available. But to make a style change and move forward takes time and effort. A new idea has to be simple and cheap, not time consuming and too foreign to the individual that would like to try it. If the idea is too offbeat, most anglers will shun the idea as ridiculous and not even pay

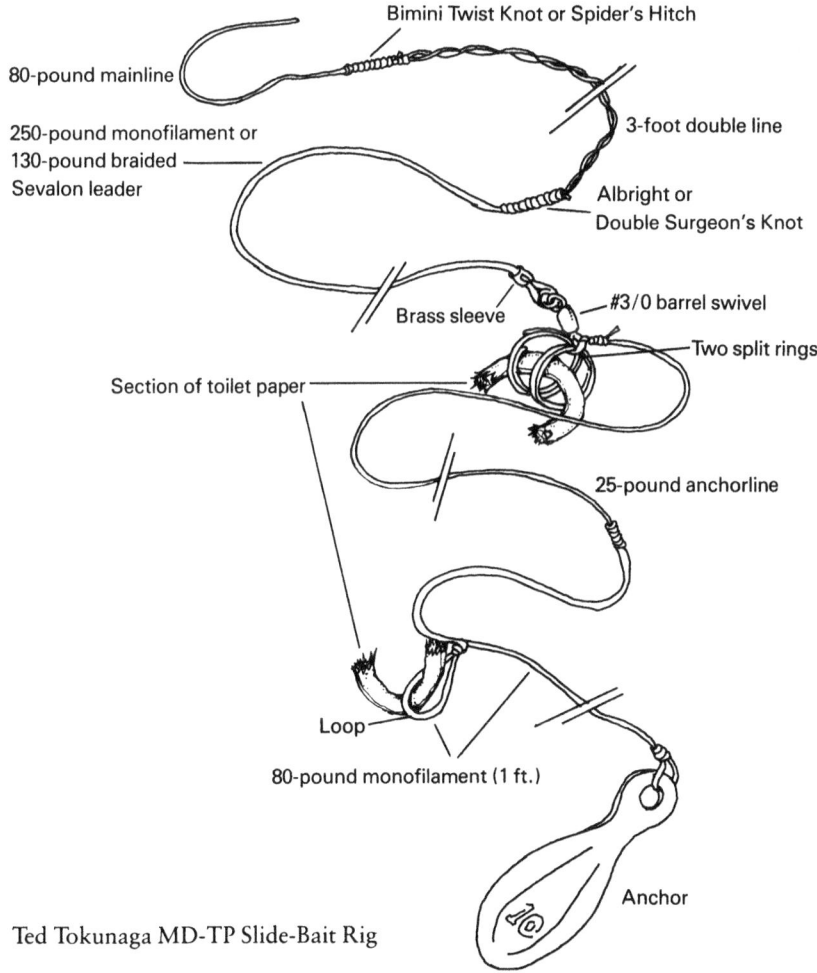

Ted Tokunaga MD-TP Slide-Bait Rig

attention to it. Still, it often is only a matter of time before a fisherman will come up with a fully clever idea.

One such fisherman is Ted Tokunaga of Hilo. His *ulua* fishing ideas have come after a lot of trial and error. With his knowledge of the Big Island style of leader construction with the Bimini Twist and Albright Knot, and of the use of monofilament and Sevalon leader material as a basic starting point, he slowly devised an *ulua* slide-bait technique that makes a lot of sense.

First, he took the problem of making a long anchorline and devised a method based on the toilet paper anchorline idea (see preceding section). The idea is good but obviously not quite good enough for Ted. He thought the idea involved too much preparation time, so he changed the method but kept the basic idea of using toilet paper.

All he uses is a three-foot section of 80-pound test and connects one section to the lead. At the section where he connects the anchorline (25-pound test) he makes a loop and keeps the anchorline as long as he feels is necessary; he can make an anchorline up to fifty feet long or more if he chooses.

He then connects the other end of the anchorline to the basic stop ring section. Next, he rolls three squares of toilet paper—he prefers the MD brand—very, very tightly and puts them through the 80-pound loop and then into the stop ring loop. He loops the anchorline around his fingers in a figure 8 pattern and snugs it down with toilet paper and some spare monofilament. This small, bundled section of anchorline is held together with just the small cord of toilet paper. The section of MD-TP is so small that it will dissolve right away; but, at the same time, it is wound so tightly that it would take some tremendous force to break it on the cast.

This method's only drawback is the fact that you have only one chance to make the anchor set in the right place. Because of this problem, Ted uses none but the straight overhand cast.

"Since the anchorline is now only three feet long, it is very easy to cast this way and pretty easy to put your cast right where you want it. I don't think that the longer the cast the bigger or more fish will take the bait. I feel that as long as the bait is visible and a fish is hungry, you will get a strike."

And with this long anchorline, Ted accomplishes just that. The bait is always visible because the anchorline is extremely long. Fishermen who use a shorter anchorline normally have their baits quickly eaten by prowling morays.

"With this rig, if I get a *puhi* strike, I normally will bring it up. The reason is that if the *puhi* wants my bait, he has to swim up a great deal and leave his hole to grab the bait. If he does, he'll get hooked and can't get back to his hole to drag my bait into the rocks. So my quantity of *puhi* strikes are minimal, but if I get them I usually bring them up. I hardly ever lose my whole leader section and have to remake it.

"The length of the anchorline is governed by the type of bottom that you're fishing. I normally make it very long—twenty to thirty feet —if the area has a lot of big boulders and the bait has a chance of getting lost between rocks and other big boulders. In areas that are flat and pretty much without obstruction, I use a leader that is about twenty feet long. I don't want the bait too high off the bottom. I think that the *ulua* is a basic bottom feeder and likes to look along the bottom areas of the ocean."

The other thing that Ted does is slide his *palu* (chum) along the line with his bait. This is very unusual, as most fishermen choose to simply pour or toss the chum into the water and let it distribute itself in

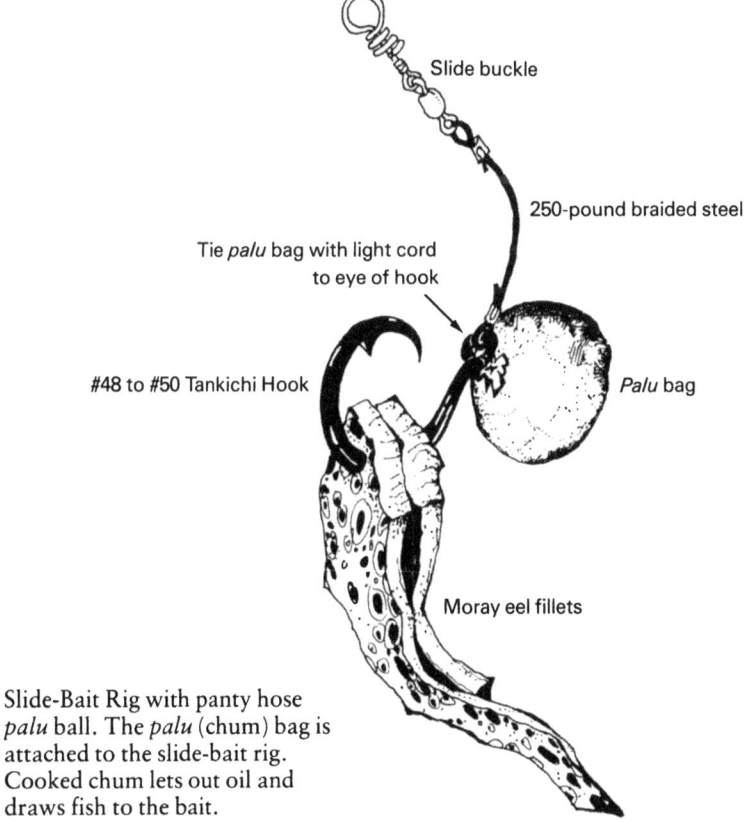

Slide-Bait Rig with panty hose *palu* ball. The *palu* (chum) bag is attached to the slide-bait rig. Cooked chum lets out oil and draws fish to the bait.

the area. Ted feels the closer the *palu* is to the bait, the easier the fish will find his bait. "It makes a lot of sense, but how do you do it?" I asked him.

"Well, the first thing you do is get hold of a pair of panty hose," he said with a straight face.

"Hey, come on Ted. Stick to business!" I said to him with a bashful grin.

"No, no. You stuff the *puhi palu* into the panty hose and slide it down the line."

"Now that has to be the most ridiculous technique of all," I said. "Can you imagine a full-size panty hose full of fifty pounds of *puhi palu* following my bait down my line? If I tried that, I'd be wearing a white jacket with long, long sleeves that tie in the back and would be living in a rubber room."

"No, no, no. You take a small square patch like this," he said as he held up a small 8-inch square that he had cut out from the hose, "and place the *palu* like this and then tie it onto the eye of the hook." What he had was a small tangerine-sized ball of *palu* tied to the eye of the #50 *tankichi* hook.

"The ball will distribute all the *palu* slowly and draw the fish to the area. If you pound the *puhi* bait at the fishing site, you'll have a better grade of *palu*. The more oil you get from the *palu*, the better the drawing power." But before Ted slid his bait down, he had another rig which he also uses for *palu*ing to show me.

"Boy, Ted, you sure *palu* a lot," I said.

"Well, I've been *palu*ing like this for a long time and I've had fourteen out of sixteen trips come back with fish. It seems to help with my percentage so I keep at it."

The other rig was simply a slide-bait rig with a handkerchief tied to the end of the slide buckle at one of the four corners. The slide-bait rig is connected to a spinner. Ted places a hefty handful of *palu* in the handkerchief and ties it with a cord of bound toilet paper. Next, he hooks the slide-bait buckle onto his line and slides the *palu* down it by allowing the line to feed from the spinning reel. Once the *palu* is almost all the way down, he gives the rod a solid tug and then just waits for awhile. After a few minutes, he cranks up the rig. The handkerchief is opened and the *palu* is dispersed.

"I'll do this several times before I slide my bait down the line. I believe in priming the ground before my bait goes down. Once the ground is ready I slide the bait and the small *palu* bag down the line," he said as he reached for a hook and some bait.

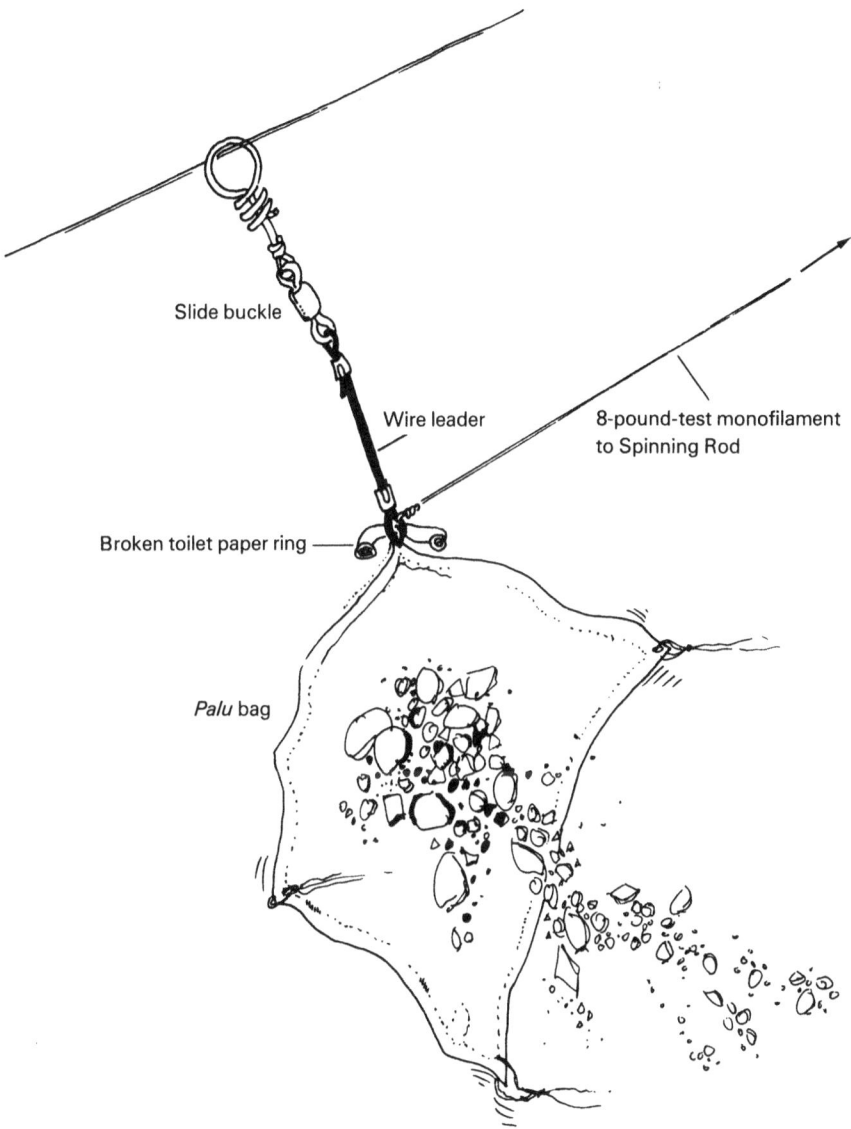

Ted's trolley version of a *palu* bag

"What happens to the small *palu* bag? Does it get in the way?" I asked.

"No, the bag doesn't get in the way. The *ulua* will take the whole thing into its mouth and tear everything up. The hook will set solidly and all I have to do is fight the fish up to gaff. It's simple and it works."

Pat Crozier Slip Pin

Pat is a tall, lanky sort of fellow who likes fishing as much as I do. What's more, he is very inventive. Since fishing is one of his favorite pastimes, he spends a lot of time thinking of ways to greatly increase both his catch and strike ratios. One day while I was in Kahului, Maui, I had a nice chat with Pat about anchorlines and I learned that some anglers had come up with some really fascinating ideas. Some of these ideas fell flatter than a pancake, but each did have some potential and they all fascinated me to no end.

Anyway, after he very politely listened to me ramble on and on, he was finally able to say that he had an idea for an anchorline rig that would be both easy to cast and short. He pulled out a section of surgical tubing and some cotton cord he had tucked away in his tackle box. He already had a rig set up, and I looked at it with great interest. It looked incredibly simple. It took me a while to break down and ask, "How does it work?"

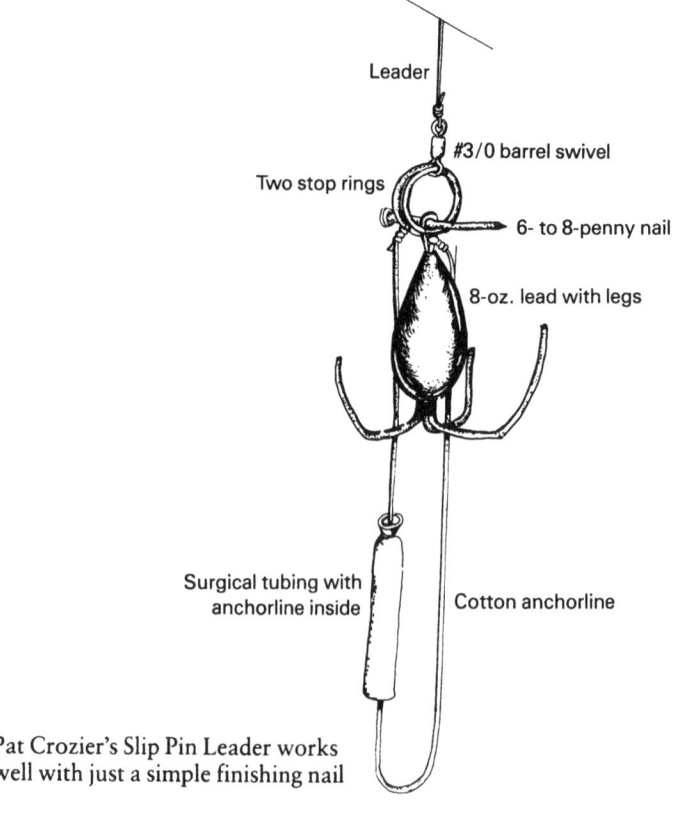

Pat Crozier's Slip Pin Leader works well with just a simple finishing nail

Pat took it from my hand and started to explain. After ten minutes of great gesturing and a million words, I found it was really as simple as it looked. And it worked.

Pat simply cinched close one end of the surgical tubing and tied it to the stop ring. He then tied the anchorline to the stop ring. The line can be made as long as the angler wants and in Pat's case it was about eight feet. He wound a length of cotton cord around a chopstick and forced the coils of line into the core of the surgical tubing. Now the line was out of the way, neatly tucked inside a tube. He tied the other end to the lead. He placed the lead's eye between the two stop rings that he had on the #3/0 swivel, and then pushed a common finishing nail into one stop ring, the eye of the lead, and on through to the other eye of the stop ring. The finishing nail was caught between stop rings and the lead. The weight of the lead kept the nail from falling out and pulling the anchorline out of the surgical tubing.

He cranked up his line and walked to the edge of the beach and made his cast. I followed and watched as he went through all the motions of casting and setting the lead on the bottom. I wondered if the finishing nail had fallen off when the lead hit the water as he said it would. I was amazed at the amount of strain he could put on the rig as he made his cast. The finishing nail was tough and the cast went beautifully.

To prove that the rig worked, Pat pulled the line back up and showed me that the finishing nail had indeed slipped out and the anchorline had fed out from the surgical tubing without a hitch. It worked like a gem. He had his long anchorline and the technique was simple and effective.

Pat told me that the system had been working for him for quite awhile. He was still working at making it more streamlined and more efficient. I told him that the system seemed to work just fine. To this he said with a big smile, "No, not quite yet. But I'm working on it."

Lifesaver–Balloon Rig

Fishermen really come up with some of the cutest ideas for rigs that you can imagine. Some ideas are really original and boast of unusual combinations of techniques; still, all must take into consideration specific fishing environments. The Lifesaver–Balloon Rig is one such idea.

Using this rig is very similar to the South Point style of fishing: A long tag line to which many hooks are tied is connected to a small sail-

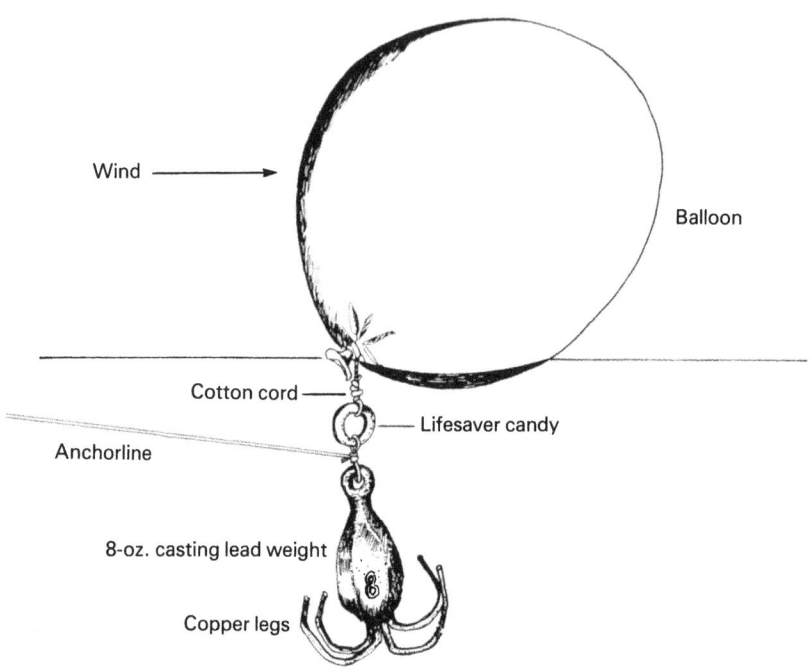

Lifesaver–Balloon Rig. A "sweet" way to drop off a leader.

boat. The sailboat is set adrift without passengers, and the wind is allowed to take it out with all the hooks trailing behind. The next day, the sailboat and the lines are pulled in and the fish are taken off the hooks.

The LB Rig involves the same principle, only in this case a big balloon is connected to one side of a Lifesaver, the other side of which is connected to the anchorline and the lead. The Lifesaver holds the anchorline to the balloon. Once the Lifesaver melts, the anchor is dropped off in deep water. However, sometimes because the Lifesaver will take too long to melt, the line won't be released soon enough. When this happens, the ends of the candy are chewed so that it will melt faster. Once the candy has melted and the lead is dropped, the balloon is left to be blown out to sea. A variation of this method involves shooting the balloon out with a small caliber weapon once the balloon reaches the designated point.

The only problem with this rig is that you really have no control over which way the balloon will drift. Some days you'll get lucky and the balloon will go out just right and you'll have a perfect drop. And some days the currents will be bad and the wind uncooperative. But this still is a good way to get a line out far when the conditions are favorable. And besides, balloons are cheap and easy enough to carry in a tackle box.

Minibuckle Rig

This rig is very similar to the Tiger Tail Rig. Again the objective is to stop the bait from going all the way down the line. The farther down the line the bait is, the worse your chances of getting a strike. Also, your chances of losing bait to reef predators such as the morays and conger eels are greater. Ways to stop the slide buckle rig at a designated spot have been devised; using the Bimini Twist (double-line knot) or a section of dental floss tied onto the mainline, for example.

The minibuckle is exactly what its name suggests it is: a buckle that looks like the slide buckle, only much, much smaller in size. The slide buckle is slid down the line in much the same way the standard slide buckle is, except that it is joined to a smaller buckle with a section of soft telephone wire or a rubberband. Together, the slide buckle and smaller buckle are slid down the mainline. The slide buckle will pass the Bimini Twist, but the minibuckle won't. The slide buckle is now stopped at the designated spot.

Once a fish comes along and takes the high-hanging bait, the rubberband or soft wire will trip or break and the slide buckle will slide

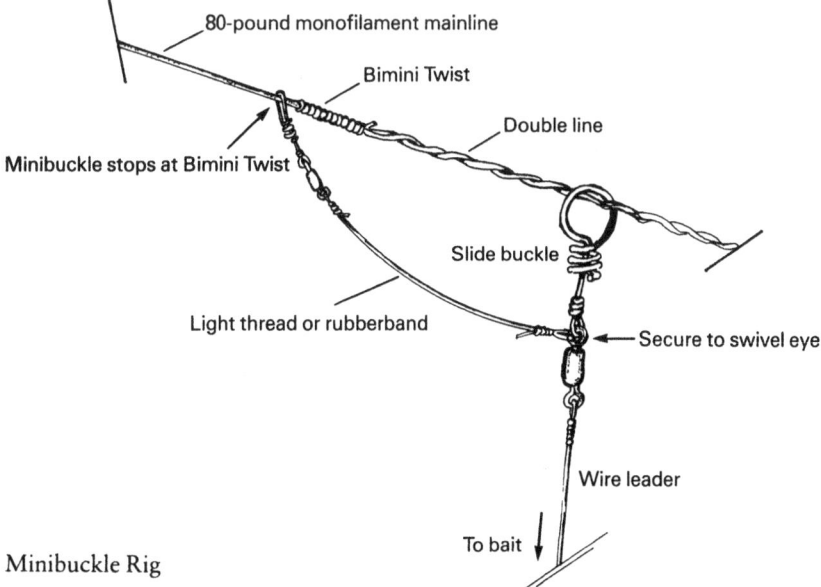

Minibuckle Rig

down to the deadend rig or stop rings. The minibuckle is so small that it won't hinder the fighting of the fish.

The best thing to use with the minibuckle is a paperclip. Standard-size metal paperclips are perfect for this type of buckle because they are cheap and soft enough to bend without much effort. If you know the fundamentals of making slide buckles, this kind of bending is really simple stuff. With the right kind of tools and some dexterity, you can or should be able to make a whole bunch of them while watching TV one quiet night.

Astonishingly enough, the system works very, very well and the cost is minimal. If you combine this idea with other ideas, like the Ted Tokunaga style of using *palu* and long anchorline, you could have a style of fishing that could possibly be phenomenal and just out of this world.

Balloon Stopper

Much like all the other means of stopping baits on lines, this one is very, very simple. The Balloon Stopper functions much like the Minibuckle Rig and the Tiger Tail. In the case of the Minibuckle, the rubberband or soft wire breaks and allows the fish to take the bait down the line and to the stop ring. The tiger tail acts merely as a tripping device and also permits the bait to slide down the line.

In the case of this balloon rig, the fish pulls the bait down and breaks the balloon in the process. This sends the bait and hook down the line. One problem arises: if the stop ring is very far beneath the surface, the fish has a long way to pull the bait before it reaches the stop rings. Therefore, this rig is best utilized in areas where the water is fairly shallow and where the fish won't have very far to go with the bait. If the stop ring is too far away, usually the fish will break the balloon and then break the mainline by pulling laterally. If the anchorline fails to break at that instant, the mainline will break and you will lose a whole day's work, all of your leader, and much of your mainline. So use this system in shallow waters, that is, water ten to fifteen feet deep. It's a great way to keep the bait from the morays and other reef-dwelling critters.

Ultralight Whipping Leader

This is the simplest and most effective of whipping leaders. It's inexpensive and easy to tie, and the only knot you have to know is the

MONOFILAMENT AND MONOFILAMENT KNOTS 113

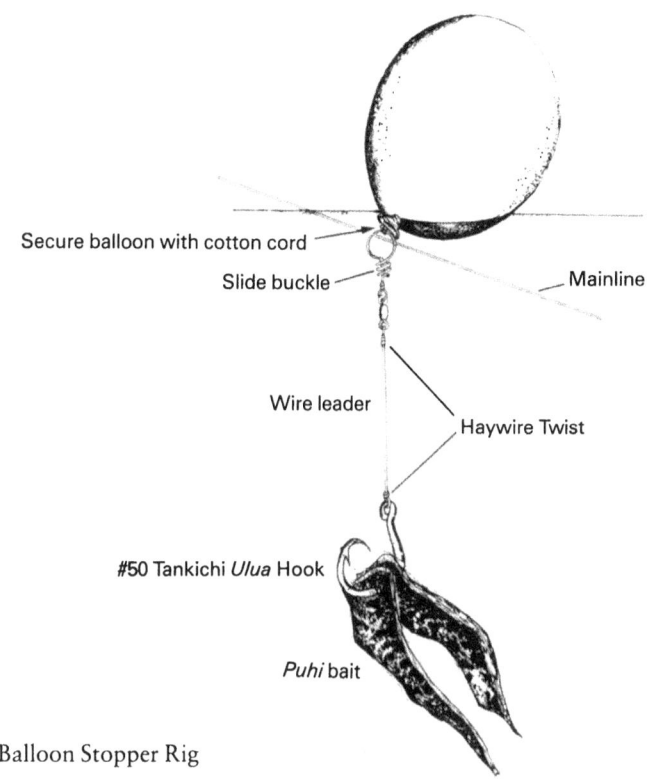

Balloon Stopper Rig

Improved Clinch Knot. What sinker to use is really all up to the individual. Some anglers like to use a small egg sinker with this leader; some like a very large sinker. Other anglers have found that they get many more strikes if they paint their sinkers white. It also seems that the longer the leader, the greater the percentage of strikes. Some anglers use leaders that are as long as eight feet, even ten feet; others stick with three-foot leaders.

What plastic lure body to use is also a matter of individual preference. The basic plastic body lure is a strip of glitter shrimp, which is sold just about everywhere. This one item will catch just about any fish you could possibly imagine. It's the champion when you're fishing for small *pāpio* and other fishes like barracuda and *moi* (threadfin). If you like to catch goatfishes like *moano, kūmū,* and *weke,* you should try using colored shrimp strips or lures with curly tailed bodies, such as the Mister Twister bodies (in red and orange). The *moano* and other types of goatfish seem to like the color enough to attack the lures with great gusto. If you're in an area that has a lot of barracuda,

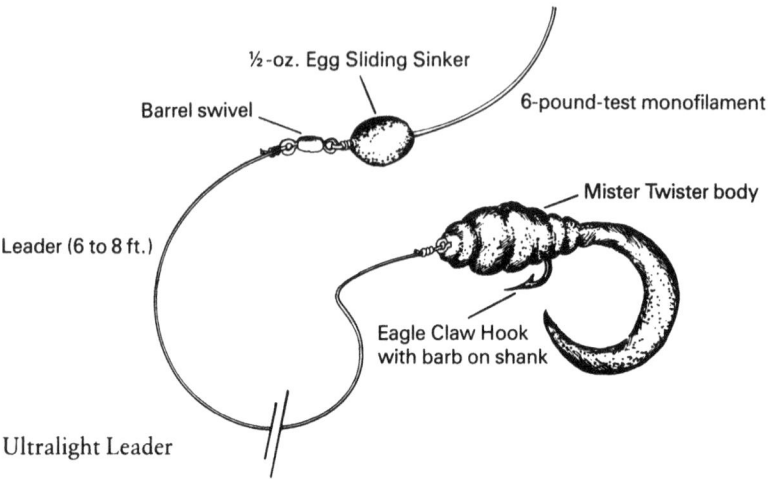

Ultralight Leader

change tactics a little and add a short length of wire leader to the rig. A length of about a foot or less is fine.

Although the whipping leader is great for casting and retrieving, it is also very good for dunking baits or bait casting. Since the line is merely fed through the egg sinker, the bait or the fish that takes the bait will be fighting almost directly with the angler. Also, any tugs and taps on the dunked bait will be instantly detected. Good baits to try with this type of leader are live shrimp or cut baits such as 'ōpelu or ika (see Chapter 5).

This leader is best utilized in areas that are mostly sand. The bait can sit right on the bottom and will move with the currents and tides. If you're after *weke* or big *kūmū*, move the bait, that is, drag it on the bottom. *Weke* are really curious fish and they are attracted to noises made on the bottom. If you drag the bait on the bottom with this rig and stop periodically, you will have a good chance of hooking a *weke*. The routine is drag . . . stop . . . drag . . . stop . . . drag . . . stop. It's very simple yet very effective.

Hanging Spreader Rig

Some fishermen fish off high cliffs, and sometimes it is most productive to drop a bait in the deep water right down below them. Naturally, there are many leader styles for this type of drop-bait method, from the most complicated to the most simple. But the best type of drop-bait rig utilizes a simple spreader to keep the bait swinging freely. This type of leader spreader is easy to make at home and is quick to tie when down at the beach. Just hook on the lead, tie on the mainline and hookline, tie on the hook and bait, and you're ready to roll. With so many swivels, the leader is unlikely to get tangled.

When the rig is scaled down a little, it is easily converted into a whipping rig for *menpachi* and *'āweoweo*. The metal arm again keeps the leader (normally very long in *menpachi* fishing) from getting tangled. The length of the leader varies for bait fishing and whipping. If you're whipping for *menpachi* or *āholehole,* make the leader 4- to 6-pound test and six to eight feet long.

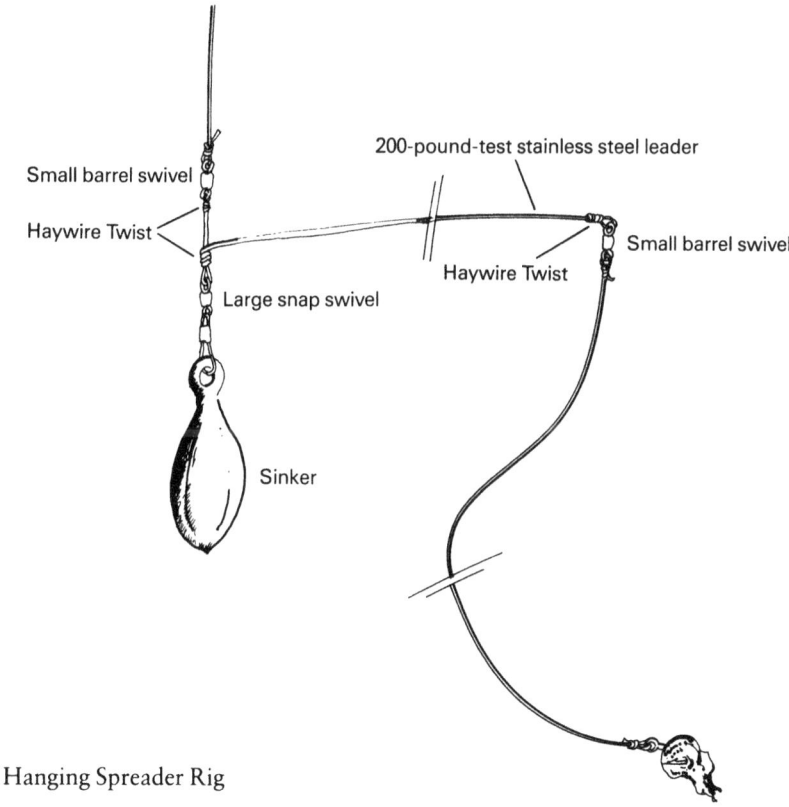

Hanging Spreader Rig

5
The Art of Bait Fishing

Dead Bait Whipping

Fishing with bait is one of the oldest styles of fishing since the worm was first put on a hook. Just about everyone has fished for tilapia or for *'o'opu* with a handpole and a hook neatly adorned with shrimp bait. This is how most beginners start bait fishing, and then they graduate to a little more sophisticated style.

Baits for the shore fisherman range from tender sections of filleted *'ōpelu* to strong smelling fillets of a shark's belly. Both baits catch fish. Although some baits are more effective than others, each has its place and is especially effective in certain types of terrain.

Most of the time the best bait to use is the real live thing, but live baits don't take to being whipped or constantly cast along the rough shoreline. Some baits will last a little longer than others, but most will eventually fall apart and become useless. If you use a dead bait that is already tough, however, you'll have a whipping bait that is better than anything artificial. The moray *(puhi),* for instance, will draw as many strikes as a soft plastic worm will draw largemouth bass. Soft and expensive baits such as *'ōpelu* don't stand much of a chance in coral areas, because before an *ulua* can get at the bait, the bait will either be devoured by small reef fish or dragged into a coral head and neatly dissected by every moray within a quarter-mile radius.

Moray Eel (Puhi)

The best thing about morays is that they are great bait for catching *ulua*. Their meat is tough and fleshy, and when fresh it has a very strong odor. It will last literally for hours and hours. The skin of the moray is such that penetrating it with even a very sharp hook is difficult, therefore a very sharp knife with a sharp point is required for cutting *puhi* fillets.

The normal size of the shore caster's bait ranges anywhere from a six-inch section of a moray to a whole fillet. The amount of available bait for a trip normally dictates how the bait will be cut. With luck a moray will gobble the first bait and quickly hook himself, leaving the angler with more bait to slide.

One slide-bait enthusiast managed to land a moray eel by using "seven-strand" or Sevalon leaders on his slide-bait rigs instead of stainless steel wire leaders. The reason for this switch was that somehow the Sevalon would get tangled up with the hungry eel and the eel would wrap itself up into a neat little ball for the angler to haul to the surface. Of course, the Sevalon was then cut and the moray untangled to be cut up later as bait.

Some nights an angler will come home with as many as ten to a dozen *puhi* but not one *ulua* strike. This means that on his next trip an extra-long or super-large bait can be slid down without hesitation.

This bait can also be thrown on the fire before you slide it. Burning the bait simply cooks the outer section of the flesh and makes the bait look like chunks of tunaflake. Once the bait is slid down, the flakes will slowly break off and spread the smell of the moray for miles around. This practice is intended, in other words, to create some *palu* (chum) and to draw the *ulua* into the reefline and eventually to the bait.

You can also do this trick with old and stale baits. You'll find that a moray that has been in the water for about two hours will look pale and mushy. Because the smell is gone, the bait will seem useless. The inside of the bait, however, will still be good. Burning the outer layer will leave the inside exposed and the bait ready for a final effort. Therefore, burning the bait is a way to get an extra slide, and is an alternative for those who have very little bait for the weekend.

The best way to cut *puhi* is to halve the bait into two fillets. If the bait is very big, one fillet is sufficient. Cut the fillet up the center. With the tip of a knife make two holes about two inches below the top of the fillet. Force the hook into the holes and make sure that the fleshy side of the fillet is facing outward. Now you should have two sections of *puhi* fillet about sixteen to twenty-four inches with all the meat showing. Ninety-nine percent of the hook should be showing. Some anglers will rubberband the bait to the hook to keep it from flipping up and hooking itself and thus preventing the hook's point from finding its mark. It's a good idea, it's very inexpensive, and it works. Also, one of the *ulua* fisherman's primary concerns when it comes to bait is movement. The split in the fillet will allow the *puhi* just the movement that will spread its smell out over the reef.

For bait, the all-time best part of the moray is the head because it has the most blood. The head will draw many, many strikes. For some reason the *ulua* doesn't seem to fear the toothy snake and will take an entire head with one bite. Many big *ulua* have been hooked and landed with a whole five-pound section of a moray eel's head.

The ancient Hawaiians used to favor the tail section of the common brown moray, usually about sixteen inches long. After it was cut off, the moray's tail was slowly pulverized with a small round stone

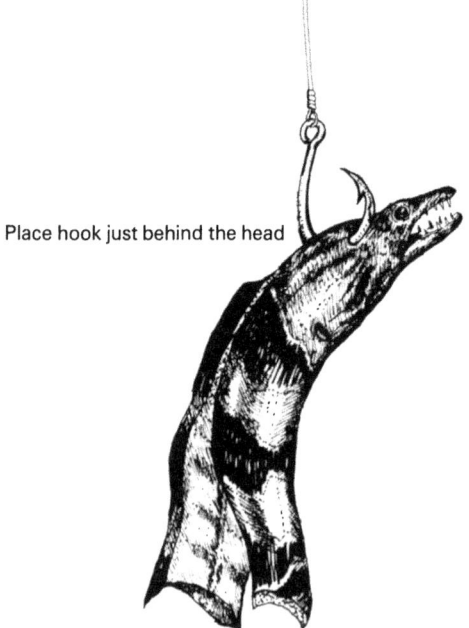

Place hook just behind the head

Split eel to allow smell to escape. Debone for freer movement

Moray eel bait

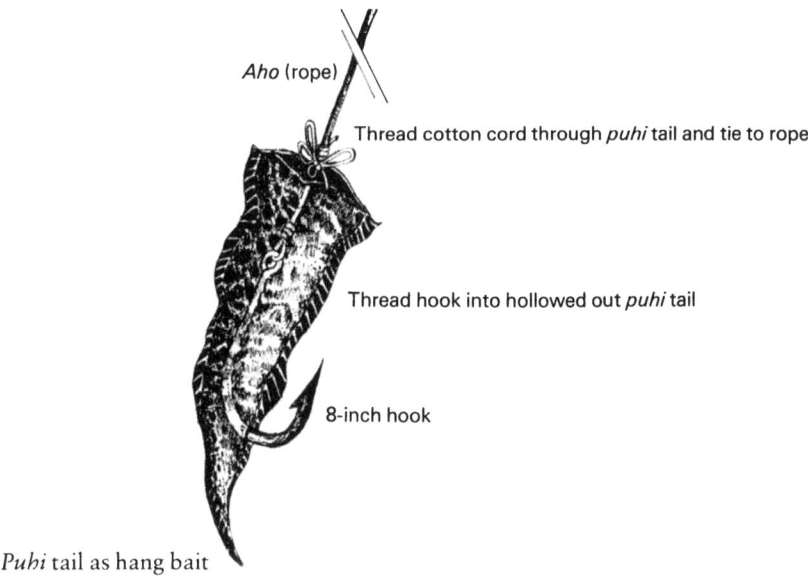

Puhi tail as hang bait

until all the bones and the meat were forced from the flattened tail. Then the tail was turned inside out and the white inner skin was used to attract the *ulua*. A hook was forced into the tail and hooked through the section of hollowed out skin so that the eye of the hook was just about where the top of the tail was. This was quickly cinched closed with cotton cord, and then it was lowered over the cliff's edge with rope, or *aho*. The "hang bait" was left to dangle just at the top of the water until an *ulua* came along and took it. Once the fish was

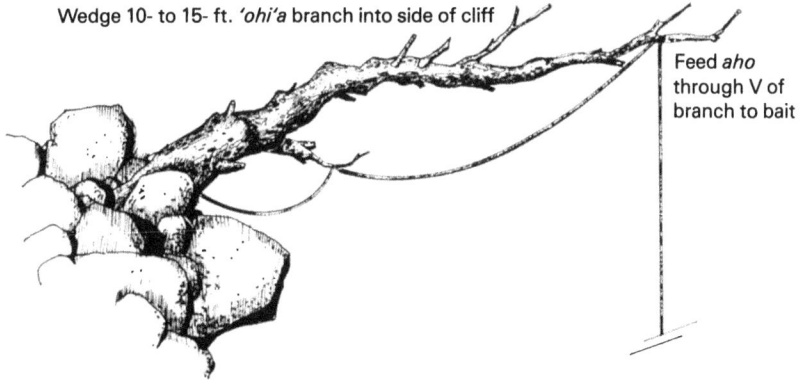

Hang bait

hooked, it was quickly hauled up the cliff's edge by a group of men and quickly dispatched with clubs. Today most *ulua* fishermen won't go to that much trouble with a bait, but they, too, have found the moray to be a choice bait.

Aware of their tried-and-tested methods, we did almost the same thing as the ancient Hawaiians. Instead of using a section of tail, turning it inside out, and hiding a monster hook in it, however, we used a whole baby *puhi* and rigged it like a trolled bait. The following will describe how this rig works.

First, select a moray that is about the diameter of your thumb and about a foot long. This is probably the most effective and easiest size to cast; anything longer and heavier would be hard on the spine, rod, and reel. Next, purchase a #4/0 Mustad to #5/0 Galvanized trolling hook, 250-pound-test monofilament, and a small box of sleeves to fit the monofilament. It would also be a good idea to purchase a selection of ball-bearing swivels or maybe the less expensive "barrel" swivels.

Take the small moray and smash all of its bones with a three-pound sledge hammer. Be careful not to break the skin. As much as possible smash the whole length of its body down to the tail and up the length again. Don't smash the head section. Sharpen a small brass tube (you can purchase one at any local hobby shop) to a bevel. Run the tube from the anus of the eel up through the body and out through its mouth. Next, run the 250-pound-test monofilament up through the brass tube. Withdraw the tube. This will leave the 250-pound monofilament secured in the body cavity.

Connect the Mustad hook to the monofilament and pull it up into the anal opening. Hide the hook carefully as you pull the head of the moray, and stretch the body until it won't stretch anymore. At the point where the leader comes out of the mouth, carefully tie a square knot.

With a five-foot length of dental floss sew the jaws of the *puhi* closed. Tie the dental floss to the square knot and go back again and stitch the head. Every so often tie off on the knot and go back to the head and the eye. Several stitches through the eyes and back to the leader or square knot will make it very secure.

It is important to tie at the square knot so that the head of the eel is held at the knot and not on the hook. If no stitching is done, the eel will slide back on the bend of the hook and invariably form a mess. With the stitching, the weight is off the hook and only on the knot

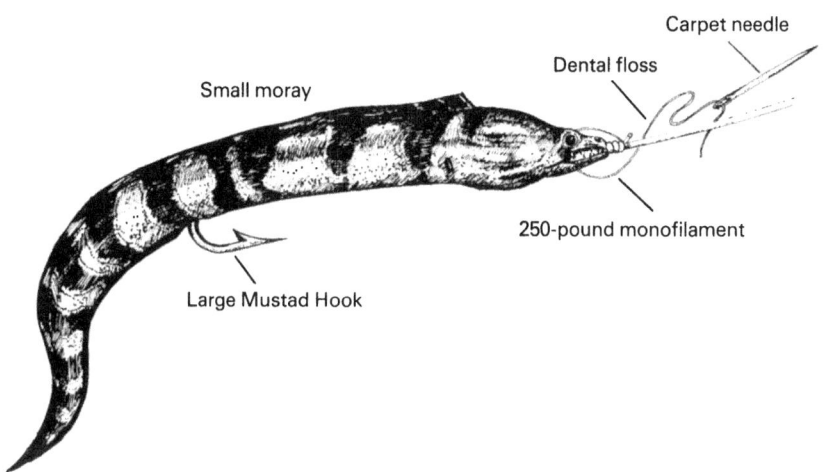

Moray eel for whipping. All but the head section of the moray is smashed with a small hammer. Monofilament is threaded through the eel's body with the help of a brass tube. The Mustad Hook is connected to the monofilament and pulled up into the anal opening. At the point where the leader comes out of the eel's mouth, a square knot is tied. The jaws of the moray are sewn closed with dental floss.

and the head. This leaves the body totally free to impart tremendous action on the retrieve. The best leader for this type of rig is usually up to the angler. Some anglers prefer their leaders as long as possible, and others find a simple three- to four-foot leader sufficient.

Casting baits such as this is a far cry from throwing a streamlined, eight-ounce lead. The bait will fly, flutter, and wobble its way out and land with an ungraceful ker-SPLAT! But this is what you want. The noise of this splash will draw the *ulua* to you and with luck the *ulua* will take the rigged bait.

The retrieve is different with each individual, but a slow, ponderous retrieve seems to draw the most strikes. Working white water and a rough shoreline is fine, and many times the strike will be right in the white water and a few feet from shore.

The first technique I use involves working the moray slow and sloppy. If I draw in a spunky *ulua* that zips back and forth but won't take, I immediately start twitching the rod tip to make it seem like the eel is trying to get away. Once the *ulua* takes the *puhi,* I immediately drop the rod tip and give him some slack. This will give him some time to take the bait further down. If you have nerves of tungsten steel, you can open the bail of the spinner or throw the reel into free spool. This will give the *ulua* more time to run with the bait. Count to ten s-l-o-w-l-y. When you lock the reel into gear, you'll feel the weight of the running fish. Haul back and set the hook as many times as you possibly can.

Some fishermen prefer working the *puhi* down deep and jigging it up and letting it fall back down. Others will work the *puhi* at the coral level and only bring it up when it reaches the white water. Techniques like this draw jolting strikes that make your arms feel as if they're being torn from their sockets. Another breed of fisherman will stick to the old traditional method of cranking the *puhi* bait in quickly and letting the *puhi* skip and splash its way in.

I think that all of these methods work well and should all be tried each and every day. Some days you have to search until you find the right combination for the day; when you do, stick to it.

White Eel (Tohei)

This bait, also called Conger eel or *puhi-ūhā,* is easy to catch. All you have to do is go diving at night and you'll find it swimming over the reefline, looking for crabs and shrimp. *Tohei* love areas that have a lot of sand and shallow reefs. They feed almost exclusively at night and prowl the reefy areas, poking their heads into small cracks and crevices. They don't spook when hit with a diving light, and they are easy to handle once you have them speared. They are not like morays, which will bite anything that gets in their way, but they definitely don't take to being grabbed.

Tohei also come in sizes that will astonish anyone who hates snakes. If you hate snakes with a passion, I'd advise against diving for the white eel. Some of them grow to huge proportions—fifteen to twenty pounds or more—and when seen at night, they look three times as big as any boa constrictor you'll ever see and much more menacing. But to a hardcore *ulua* fisherman, the huge *tohei* is a lot of bait and he'll fight the monster tooth and nail before he'll let it go free.

Like the moray, the best part of this bait is its head. It has a lot of blood, and its smell is very strong. Although some anglers feel that the glowing eyes of the white eel draws strikes, the smell is the most important thing when it comes to prompting an *ulua* to strike.

Hook the *tohei* the way you would a moray. The *tohei* can also be burned and slid after it has been used. Its meat is soft, tender, and almost boneless. The flakes of the cooked flesh will draw a fantastic

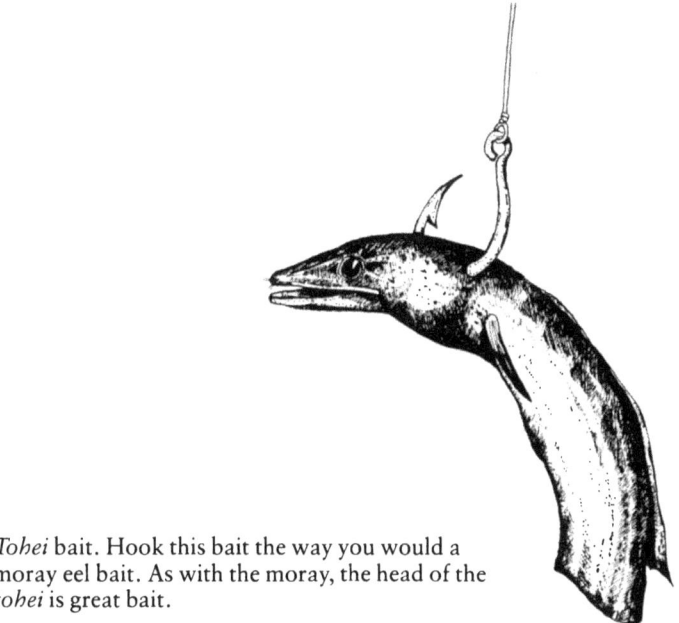

Tohei bait. Hook this bait the way you would a moray eel bait. As with the moray, the head of the *tohei* is great bait.

number of fish into the area. It is also great eating if you decide that you're having your share of hard luck at fishing.

If you decide to try your luck with hooking a white eel, the best rig to use is composed of cut *'ōpelu* as bait and a stout rod with very, very big line. If the area has small *tohei,* then use smaller line; but lines that test anywhere from 80 to 100 pounds are not uncommon in these cases. The hooked *tohei* is a great fighter and many an angler will use an *ulua* pole to hook and land one.

Octopus (Tako)

Every island has its own favorite baits, and for Maui and Oahu it is octopus that has just been speared. Anything less fresh is not even considered, because when fresh the octopus' colors are still vibrant and changing.

Getting fresh octopus means setting up camp, driving to the right hunting grounds, and jumping into the water to look for the bait. But if spotting them were as simple as it sounds, most of the *tako* would have been gone from the reefs a long time ago. Catching octopus is an art that requires special teaching and constant practice. I will discuss this art later in this section.

Octopus bait. Place the hook so that much of it is exposed.

Once the octopus is seen and teased (not speared!) out of its hole, it is put in a holding bag, where it is allowed to die. At the fishing site the dead but still fresh octopus is covered with layers of newspaper to absorb moisture and to keep it from getting too soft and mushy. This bait will still be considered fresh after six to eight hours, but once it is brought to the beach it should quickly be hooked through its bulbous head and slid down the mainline.

In theory, the octopus will continue to change color and will give off a light, iridescent glow. Fresh moray eel and fresh *tohei* will do the same thing. The glow is believed to be one of the factors that draw *ulua* to strike.

Tako is usually slid in very sandy areas. Unfortunately, the white eel is a predator in such areas and, like the *ulua* and *puhi* (moray eel), its favorite food is *tako* and it will devour it at the blink of an eye. Besides the white eel, you'll also run into many kinds of crabs, shrimp, and small reef fish, all of which will take a quick nibble at the tasty morsel on your hook. The angler's hope is that an *ulua*, a *kāhala,* or even an *'ahi* will come by and take the bait before every other ocean animal eats the bait to the bare hook.

Other offshore species have been known to come into shallow sandy areas and pick up octopus baits. My father witnessed this once off a point on Oahu named Bamboo Ridge, a favorite *ulua* spot where many fishermen slide copious amounts of this bait.

"One night I had a good strike on the point," my father explained, gesturing as he talked. "The reel screamed and the bell rang to beat the band and by the time I got to the point the reel was almost empty.

"We all thought it was an *ulua* strike, but then we started to hear something out in the darkness beginning to jump and splash all over the place. I thought it was a *mako* shark [known for wild acrobatics] at first. Everyone was telling me to cut the line before everyone else got tangled up with the shark. But one of my friends said to really rough up the shark and bring it in quick. So I worked in the shark—or what we thought was a shark—as quickly as possible. The fish kept jumping all over the ocean and all I did was crank for all I was worth.

"Within minutes I had the fish close to the side of the rocky point. We all shined our lights and all we saw was a beautiful iridescent yellow *mahimahi* [dolphin fish] floating in the water. Suddenly I held the rod very gingerly and with tender loving care. My friends quickly gaffed the fish and we hauled it up. The *tako* bait was still in its mouth and the *tankichi* hook neatly set in the corner of the jaw.

"Not many *mahimahi* have been landed from shore—this is probably the first in history." The fish weighed in at twenty-four pounds.

In some places the octopus is cut into sections and slid down in small pieces. On the Big Island, for instance, octopus is hard to get and a resourceful angler will make as many as four to five baits from a single *tako.* Some Bamboo Ridge anglers will use one *tako* for the entire evening because nothing will touch the bait during the night except crabs and other small fish. For this reason, the number of slides are very, very few. But the Big Island has more than its share of morays and so changing baits every hour and a half is not unusual.

The octopus is also a very good bait for fish other than *ulua.* When cut into small, bite-size pieces it can land a host of reef fish. *'Ō'io* is one favorite gamefish in Hawaii that will quickly take a section of octopus. But if you can't decide what to do with a fresh octopus, I suggest you drop it in an ice chest right away and take it home for some good eating.

Some anglers take the remaining bait or the bait they have cranked back up and quickly cut it up into small bits to use as *palu.* Each day they fish, they will take the leftover octopus and *palu* the fishing area. This is much better than keeping it, only to have it stink up the ice chest later.

As I mentioned earlier, catching octopus is an art. The only way to catch this bait as fresh as is required is to dive for it in the morning when the tide is low or just on the rise. The octopus doesn't feed extensively when the tide is high because it knows the *ulua* and other predators are around feeding at this time. When the tide is just coming up, the octopus knows that it should be close to its hole or at least on its way back.

What do you look for when you're swimming around and all you see are rocks? What tips you off that you've found a *tako* hole? Well, you look for a slight difference in the coloration of the ocean bottom. Sometimes rocks will look as if they have been overturned and scattered, and have a whitish look to them. This is your first tip-off. Another key point: know where *not* to look for octopus. Its arch enemy is the moray eel, which lives where there are lots of boulders and coral reefs. You'll never find a *tako* within a country mile of these places.

The octopus prefers to live in semihard and gravelly areas. It will build its hole in an area that has hills and dales, choosing as its favorite spot the top of a mound or sloping hill from which it can see a great distance at a single glance. The ground around the area the octopus chooses has to be hard enough to keep eels and other enemies from getting to it, yet soft enough so that it can dig a neat hole in the bottom efficiently.

The holes that octopuses dig vary in size, from Ping-Pong ball size to the size of a saucer. Usually the bigger the octopus, the bigger the hole. At times large octopuses will be found in the smaller holes because they find them more comfortable; but in general the bigger the hole, the bigger the octopus.

The octopus' hole isn't as complex as a prairie dog's hole with its numerous tunnels and back doors. It's an ordinary hole in which the octopus can sit and pull a blanket of rocks over itself. That's its secret. The octopus will literally pull the back door over itself. As was noted earlier, during the evening the octopus will hide in its rock home and not come out until the sun comes up, mainly because the moray eel or white eel are out in the coral reefs looking and hunting for anything to eat. The eels will stick their noses into every conceivable hole, hoping to discover a *tako,* but the octopus will hide itself too well to be found. Amazingly the moray will not even suspect that an octopus may be hiding under a blanket of rocks, and will not even smell it.

An *ulua* fisherman looking for *tako* as bait rarely spears it. He merely sticks the spear into the octopus' home and irritates it until it grabs the spear. He thens pulls it out, and with quick hands grabs the octopus and stuffs it into a small mesh bag. The only time this bait is speared is when it lets go of the spear and speeds off to find itself another hole. The octopus will move too fast on the bottom to be grabbed.

Catching an octopus is really much like catching shiners (minnows) for live-baiting largemouth bass in lily ponds, the only difference being the octopus is caught live but used dead. It is believed that bait should give off a slight iridescent glow to really be a deadly calling card to most shoreline fish. The white flesh of moray eels and white eels that have just been caught and filleted, for example, will give off this glow. Octopus is unusual because if speared and quickly killed, it will turn just a shade of white. So, an octopus that has been allowed to die slowly through suffocation is best because it will still be changing colors when you use it.

Depending on its size, the bait can be cut up and divided into smaller baits. For instance, if the *tako* is two to three pounds, it can be cut up by first taking the head off and then two to three of its legs. The head is the most prized portion of the entire *tako* and also the first portion to be hooked on. The legs are hooked on next and allowed to dangle freely. The hook that is used is normally anywhere from a #42 to #52 *tankichi* hook and has a fine cutting edge. When the bait is hooked, much of the hook is left exposed, but this doesn't seem to affect the quality of the hook-ups.

Shark Fillets

Surprisingly, shark fillets make wonderful bait. Some anglers go down to the local pier during the weekdays and actually fish for small hammerhead sharks so that they can get fillets for the weekend. They quickly fillet the sharks, and to preserve the smell of the meat, they store it in small plastic bags. Most people think that the smell of a shark in the water would cause most fish to quickly vacate the premises. But the smell of the shark meat draws *ulua,* and they will actually hit the bait just as if it were a fillet of *puhi* or *tohei.*

If the shark is big, say, ten feet long, it will still make good bait. Most *ulua* fishermen will land a shark of good size at least once in their lifetime. These sharks put up quite a good tussle. So if you hook one, instead of cutting the line and letting the shark go, land the brute and quickly dispatch it with a sledge hammer or anything heavy. Once it's dead, take a sharp knife and start cutting yourself a good slice of shark meat.

I once cut a huge slab for a guy named Gary Ranne. The piece was about five inches square and about two feet long. It was huge. I quickly poked a hole through the bait with the tip of a knife and hooked the bait. I then held down the slide buckle with my foot and cut the bait from the end up to the hook. This gave the section a split tail and more smell. The shark meat was really fresh and the blood was still flowing.

Gary was skeptical as he slid the bait, but about twenty minutes later he had a strike that was a real gate-crasher. His reel screamed and his rod looked like it was going to break in the rodstand. Gary managed to get the rod out of the rodstand but couldn't stop the rampaging fish. The fish simply tore line from his reel with absolutely no effort. Within three minutes from the time of strike, he was almost out of line. The fish emptied his spool, cut the line, and was gone. But Gary has since been definitely sold on using shark for *ulua* bait.

The best thing about shark bait is that you can use as much of it as you want and not worry about wasting it. Most big sharks can't be taken back home and put in the refrigerator anyway, so use large and fleshy pieces. Although I stated in Chapter 1 that big baits on handpole hooks are not advisable, it is an entirely different matter when it comes to fishing for *ulua* on conventional shore-casting gear. It has been my experience with *ulua* that big baits draw big fish. The smaller *ulua* find the big baits delectable but difficult to handle. The large, ravenous *ulua* will grab a large bait, entire moray eel, for instance, with one gulp. Since the hook is left almost entirely exposed, it isn't difficult to hook large *ulua*. Remember, bigger bait means bigger *ulua*.

The best section of the shark is its belly. Much like an *aku*'s belly, it is thin and bright white. If fresh, the meat you slide probably will glow like fresh *tako* or *puhi*. The shark's belly is a little more tender than most parts of the shark. Hook the fillet cut from the shark belly the same way you would a *puhi* or *tohei*. Simply cut a long strip and hook the very end of it. Leave a large portion of the hook exposed because it is very important to set the hook solidly in the jaws of the *ulua*. If the hook is completely hidden by the shark's tough skin or meat, you'll have a lot of missed strikes or dropped bait.

Skipjack (Aku) *Belly*

Aku belly used to cost about 10 cents a piece. Those were the days when I used to take a bike down to the piers and on the way stop at Oahu Market to buy a section of *aku* belly. It was a section that they were glad to get rid of. Nowadays you have to really pay through the nose for a section of *'ahi* or *aku* belly. The sections that used to be sold to young, aspiring anglers are now sold to people who've found out that *aku* belly is really great eating.

Besides being fantastic eating, it is great bait. We used to cut up the *aku* belly section into neat two-inch squares and bait cast with it. The bait was taken by all kinds of great reef fish. We landed everything from balloonfish to *weke* (goatfish), to good-sized *pāpio*. Whatever we didn't use, we salted and saved for the next trip down to the piers. If we needed *'o'opu* bait, we took out sections of the *aku* belly and had a blast down at the river. The *'o'opu* really loved the smell of the *aku* and gobbled the small morsels down without hesitation. *Aku* is very smelly and will draw just about anything within range. Its skin will retain this smell even if the meaty sections have been eaten away. The skin is very tough and you must have a pretty sharp knife to cut it cleanly; but it is the part of the bait that makes for a secure hook-up.

In the days when we could get a lot of *aku* belly for just about nothing, we used to use whatever we had for *palu*. We tied sections of *aku* belly with some stout string and bashed them against the side of the caissons at the pier. *Aku,* being very oily, was great for that kind of work. The constant pounding created a great oil slick and bits and pieces of meat would drift down and draw in all kinds of fish. If we wanted bottom fish to come around, we would coat lots of sand with the oil from the ground-up *aku* and throw it over the side. The smell of the *aku* stuck to the sand and drew fish to the area. *Weke,* in particular, came around quickly and stayed around, eating the sand and spitting it out.

If we chummed enough, we drew other large fish into the area. Since the waters at the pier were relatively flat and calm, when the *ulua* finally came up to investigate, we would have the show of our young lives. The big fish would come up and eat all the *aku* belly *palu* and eventually eat the smashed up piece too. It was a real show that we all waited for. We hooked a few, but never could hold them when they went under the pier or between the pier pilings.

'Ōpelu *and* Akule

Of all the cut baits at your disposal, the *'ōpelu* (mackerel scad) and *akule* (bigeye scad) are without a doubt the best. *'Ōpelu,* especially, makes a fine cut bait. It's basically a staple for everything under the water.

The one problem with *'ōpelu,* especially if it isn't quite as fresh as you'd like it, is that it crumbles easily. And if you're the type who carries a knife that won't cut butter on a hot day, then you're really in for some trouble. The meat will literally ooze out of the fish if you try to cut it, and all you'll have is smashed *'ōpelu.* So keep your knife sharp. The best kind of knife, according to my dad, was the old military butter knife. It could be sharpened to a fine edge and would last for years. Plus that, in those days, the price was right—it was free.

The best way to cut scad is perpendicular to the center bone. Start from the tail and work your way toward the head. I used to cut about an inch-thick section straight down and then slide the knife along the backbone and lift the section off. I'd cut about three sections at a time and then leave the rest for when I needed it. When I'd cut it all up and not use it, I'd end up throwing the cut sections away and feeling that it was a terrible waste. Later I found out that the best thing to do with *'ōpelu* and *akule* is to precut all the bait at home. A friend told me to cut all the sections that I could get from the fish, salt it, put it in a small container (like a margarine cup), and refrigerate it. Although this drew the moisture out from it and made it very, very hard, it preserved the strong smell fish seem to like so much. So far this has worked great. I also try to drain any water that collects in the container periodically, and check the bait to see if it is getting old. But old or fresh, scad is still one of the greatest baits there are.

The *'ōpelu* and *akule* also make great chum. If you have a whole mess of old and discarded *'ōpelu,* quickly smash it up or run it through a meat grinder. Mix the chum with sand or old bread crumbs. The whole concoction may stink to high heaven, but it will do the trick when you want to draw in some fish. When I was young, it seemed to me that the smellier the bait, the bigger the draw, but then, there's only so much one can stand.

Other Reef Fish as Cut Bait

Most anglers prefer the conventional baits. They don't try using any of the common reef fish, such as the *mamo* (damselfish), *manini* (convict tang surgeonfish), or *hīnālea* (wrasse) for cut bait; however, these fish are great baits and will catch their share of good-sized fish.

They can be salted and filleted much like *'ōpelu*. They also become very hard and make strong baits. Fish that people normally feel are troublesome, such as the yellow lemon butterfly, can be scaled and used as good cut baits. Other fish, like the *ta'ape* (striped snapper or blue-lined snapper), are used by bottom fishermen. Instead of taking a whole mess of expensive *ika* (cuttlefish), fishermen will take only a small handful and after they catch the first of many reef fish, they will simply use for bait whatever they feel they can't market. The fish never stop biting and the baits are always fresh, so don't discard reef fish. If you use them for bait, you'll be surprised at the number of fish you'll catch and the amount of money you'll save not having to buy shrimp or squid.

Crab

Crab is a universal food. Every fish will take a peck at a swimming crab. Unless a crab is fast at getting under a rock or hiding under sand, he'll quickly become someone's meal. In Hawaii there are a multitude of crab species and they all work as good bait. If you have a large supply of dead crabs, grind them up and you'll find they make great *palu* for catching *'oama*. Salting the chum will make the flesh firm so that you can hook it.

When getting meat from a whole crab, pull off its legs, break off one end of each joint, and suck out the meat. It'll come out in small, sausagelike sections, perfect for putting on the hook. The skin of the crab meat is relatively tough and will sit on the hook for many an *'oama*. Once you have accumulated several layers of crab skin, then you'll hardly ever have to add more bait to your hook; just keep on using the crab skin and you'll catch fish after fish until your arms get tired.

Whole crab as dunking bait has landed many an *'ō'io* that wouldn't grab a section of *ika* (cuttlefish). There's something about a crab which draws the savageness out of many reef fish. It's probably a delicacy to many of them.

Some anglers whip a whole crab over the reefline and let the bait drift with a floater. The *uhu* (parrotfish) loves to eat crab and will take a crab as soon as it sees one. The problem is the parrotfish has very parrotlike teeth, making a wire leader necessary. Also, parrotfish love to dive beneath rocks as soon as they are hooked. For this reason, the line that is used is usually about 30-pound test. Once the parrotfish is hooked, you will have to muscle the fish out of or away from the hole.

The *mū* (grandeyed porgy fish) is another fish that loves to eat crab. It is an extra strong fish and lives in reefs. Usually an angler after *mū* will look for an area that is very deep, drop a crab there to about midwater, and wait for a *mū* to come by. Being mostly a night feeder, the *mū* will slowly come up to the bait and then very confidently eat the crab right off the hook. The angler must have sharp eyes and be very patient. Once he sees the rod bend down ever so slowly, he must set the hook with a vigorous tug on the rod. If the fish is hooked, the angler will be in for a fight that he will never forget. The *mū* is one of the toughest fishes that grace the reefline. Most *mū* fishermen use nothing less than 30-pound test and a good length of wire leader to discourage the molarlike teeth of the *mū*.

Live Bait Fishing from Shore

Some anglers have made live bait fishing more than an art—it is a science. They can tell you which baits will catch which gamefish. And to some extent they are right when they say some reef fish are better than others as bait. But the primary reason any reef fish will make good bait is not because the *ulua* or other predatory fish seek them out; it is because all reef fish keep well on the hook and are active swimmers. Predatory fish all have highly sensitive lateral nerves that pick up distress signals and home in on vibrations much the same way that a shark's lateral nerves help it to find its meals for the day. The stronger the baitfish, the farther his vibrations will travel and the quicker the predator will find the bait and, one hopes, the hook.

Thus one of the angler's main considerations when live bait casting is keeping the bait fresh and frisky. This takes quick handling and well-aerated buckets or live-bait baskets. Anglers that deal with this type of fishing come well prepared and know how to handle bait. The secret is to handle the fish as little as possible, even while hooking or unhooking it.

The hook should always be extra sharp when you're working with live baits. Less fish will die if the hook can penetrate the skin and be pushed through quickly. When the hook is dull, people have a tendency to force the hook through and inadvertently kill the fish by squeezing it to death. The place to hook most live baits is just above the head. The predatory fish will hit the head section of the fish 99 percent of the time so it can dispatch the fish and swallow it as quickly as possible. If it took the tail first, it would have a terrible time eating it.

I tried hooking the back section of a fresh *mamo* and stayed away from the head. I thought that if I hooked it through the tail section, I would have a stronger bait and it would last longer. I did get a fantastic strike on the rod with the *mamo,* but the fish was off before I could get to the screaming reel and bending rod. I cranked up the bait and found the *mamo* still kicking, but it was missing its head. The *ulua* had come and hit the mamo, but had missed the hook that I had in the tail. If I had hooked the head, I would at least have had a solid hookup and maybe a fish to take home. I learned from that experience and now I hook all my bait above the head.

Live Bait Size

How big should the live bait be? Should it be smaller than a *mamo* or bigger? The answer to this question is, as big as you can manage. Some *ulua* fishermen have gone to the extreme of sliding five-pound *pāpio* and have landed *ulua* that tipped the scales at over forty pounds. Sounds crazy but it has happened. So, bait size is not that crucial. I have slid down *enenue* (rudderfish) that were easily three pounds, and I've even used huge *palani* (surgeonfish) that would normally be kept for the *hibachi*. Some anglers have even slid down live *kūmū* (goatfish) as bait. Whatever size fish you catch can be slid down. If the predatory fish is hungry, he'll take the bait with no hesitation. Some of the best live baits are *menpachi, mamo, ʻāweoweo, kupipi* (grey damselfish), *taʻape, toʻau* (black-tailed snapper), *palani, kala* (unicornfish), *enenue,* and *weke*. These are all frisky fish and they stay alive on a hook for a long time.

Once again, some anglers wrap rubberbands around the hook and the hooked baitfish. The reason they do this is the hook will begin to keyhole after the baitfish has been swimming several hours, and eventually the baitfish will get away and die in some small hole. The rubberband keeps the fish on the hook but doesn't hinder its swimming.

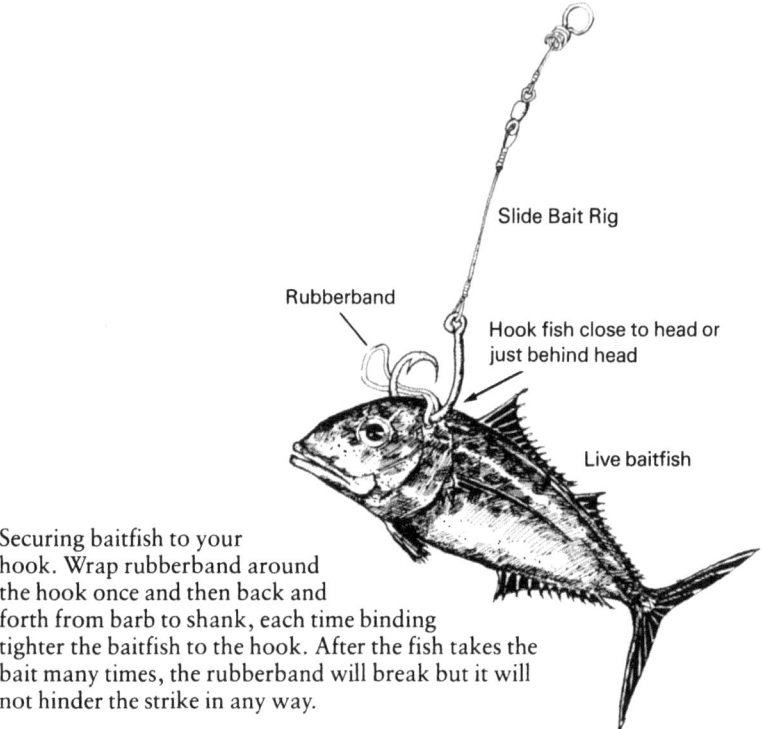

Securing baitfish to your hook. Wrap rubberband around the hook once and then back and forth from barb to shank, each time binding tighter the baitfish to the hook. After the fish takes the bait many times, the rubberband will break but it will not hinder the strike in any way.

Usually when the fish strikes, the rubberband is cut away and the fish hooked.

Some anglers have used common live-bait or carpet needles to poke a hole through the back of the bait. A cord is run through the fish, secured to it, and then tied to the bend in the hook. In this way the fish isn't hooked and the danger of keyholing is gone. The fish lives longer and the hook is completely exposed. It only takes a few minutes to do. Common household or kite string is normally used because it's cheap and easy to handle when wet, and it also makes strong and durable knots.

The best leader rig to use with live baits is the Egg Sinker Leader Rig (see "Ultralight Whipping Leader," Chapter 4). When using live shrimp use the smallest hook possible; numbers 6 through 4 are good choices. The hook should be put through the tip of the tail section because shrimp normally swim backward. When hooked this way, the bait will stay fresh, will not fly off the hook, and have enough freedom to do all the kicking it would like. Many anglers work the hook from the tail section of the shrimp directly through the body and out the mouth or back. This kills the shrimp right away, which is not the intent behind live bait casting. Having most of the hook exposed will in no way discourage the *pāpio* from hitting the bait. The bait will be moving through the water so fast that the *pāpio* will only see the shrimp zipping through the water. If you decide to use the live shrimp on a floater rig, then you should use the same hooking principle. With a floater, the shrimp will swim with the legs located under its thorax. This swimming motion and the floating action will draw a great many vicious strikes.

This style of floater fishing is especially good for *āholehole* (Hawaiian flag fish) and other nighttime feeders that look for free-swimming baits in midwater. Some anglers use the inexpensive lighted floaters to help them see the floaters at night. The cast is not made very far, and the line is normally kept relatively taut to aid in setting the hook when the floater goes under. (See "Floaters," Chapter 1.)

When whipping live bait, you have to check it quite often. Sometimes the bait may fly off the hook, or you may find that only the head section of it will have been bitten off. When the latter happens, quickly change baits and continue whipping. You'll find that the longer the leader and the lighter the line, the more strikes you'll get. If you can handle a leader that is eight to ten feet long, use it and the fishing will be better for you. A lighter line is harder for the predatory fish to see, and it gives the bait a more natural motion than does a hard, stiff line. So use the lightest line that you can manage and add some sport to the whipping of live baits.

Live baits can also be used by hooking one and then just lowering it down to the bottom. Handpoles are good for this type of fishing, but rod and reel combinations are great because you can lower the bait all the way to the bottom if the area is deep. With the rod and reel, you can use the Egg Sinker Leader Rig and let the bait drop straight down to the bottom. Once it hits the bottom, crank it up about three feet and wait for the strike. Once again, the live baits will perform much better with lighter lines and longer leaders. This free-swimming type of action drives the predatory fish wild, and you'll have more action with it than you can imagine.

Whipping Hīnālea

I wasn't loaded for bear like the other anglers were. I had come along just to kind of relax and recharge my batteries after a tough week at work. I fully intended to take complete advantage of the nice warm sunshine and good fishing waters off South Kona.

The rod I selected was my favorite Fenwick GSP1084 and my Penn #550 spinning reel. After I stuffed my pockets full of Boone jigs, I went off to see if I could harass some good-sized *ulua*. I spent several hours casting and dropping my jig in some heart-stopping spots in which I was certain fish were just waiting to pounce. But my efforts were fruitless. "Patience," I told myself after more and more hours went by.

That day brought me but two strikes. Because the hook pulled free, I lost the first fish, which looked to be between ten and fifteen pounds (but they always look big when they get away!). The second was a small one-pounder that committed suicide by grabbing my jumbo Boone jig. On my 12-pound outfit I simply cranked the *pāpio* up the cliff and stuffed him into my pack. I at least had to have something to take home to show my wife that I had really gone fishing.

Although I did not catch anything worth a a story, I did end up following a guy from Hilo by the name of Raymond Okamoto. He was the only guy that was carrying two rods, and for good reason I found out later. After I watched him from afar for several minutes, I finally realized that he wasn't casting a lure like all of us. He was casting a large fish and working it slowly through the rough inshore waters. He had told me that his favorite form of whipping involved using the *hīnālea* as bait, but I thought he was pulling my leg.

As I approached him on the lava shoreline, I realized that he had his short fiberglass rod with him so that he could catch *hīnālea* without changing his leader rig. He simply had to make a standard dunking leader, bait it with some shrimp or cuttlefish, and then wait for the strike. He picked up several *hīnālea* in no time flat, and the ones he selected were between three and five ounces in size.

The *hīnālea* he chose was the common Duperrey wrasse, or saddle wrasse. *Hīnālea* of Hawaiian waters come in a terrific assortment of colors. Although comfortable with looking like aquarium fish, they are the favorite food of roving *ulua*. Ray didn't seem too worried about the color combination of the *hīnālea* that he hooked. If they were the right size, he'd stuff them in his pack, where they were kept cool. But the *hīnālea* that brought the most strikes seemed to be the saddle wrasse *hīnālea,* also called the cowboy *hīnālea*. Basically green in color, the cowboy has an orange brown band just behind its head. It has small, doglike teeth and is hard to clean, mainly because of its slimy feel.

Since the *hīnālea* is such an easy fish to hook, Ray was not in any pain when it came to getting more bait. We, on the other hand, carried tons of lures and other paraphernalia, just so we wouldn't be without or just in case one certain lure worked more than another that day.

It was obvious that Ray had a lot of faith in this technique because he stuck with it through thick and thin. He'd cast out the *hīnālea* as far as he could and then immediately start his retrieve. He never let his fish sink to the bottom or to midwater. He worked the surface completely and with deadly determination.

"I watch for any type of disturbance around or under the bait," Ray told me as he watched his floundering bait. "A lot of times the *ulua* will come straight up from under the *hīnālea* and take the bait with a great swirl on the surface. Sometimes the *ulua* will strike like he wants to kill the *hīnālea* and tear it to pieces."

The main point of his talk was that he had to constantly be on complete guard and ready to set the hook solid. He did not let up on his concentration for a moment, as each cast looked like it would be the one that would draw the strike.

"The best places to fish the *hīnālea* are in the areas that have a lot of white water and reef. The blue water is also deadly, as are the edges of the white water. But you can never be certain where the *ulua* will take the bait, so the best thing is to be as alert as you possibly can.

"I have found that working the *hīnālea* slow and twitching the rod tip to give it just the action that makes the *hīnālea* look like its hurt or dying is the best, all-around action. I'd cast the bait, wait for a bit, then begin my cranking and twitching of the rod tip. I never let the bait sink. I keep it on the surface and keep it working. Sometimes I work an area with one technique and if that doesn't work, I try another pattern of retrieves, which may mean a faster retrieve or more twitches of the rod tip. But basically the variations are small."

Normally Ray would use 20-pound test; now he is considering 80-pound-test and 100-pound-test leader. Naturally, his casting distance will fall off dramatically, as may the quantity of his strikes, but at this point Ray is determined to land some of the monsters that come up for his rigged *hīnālea*.

His rig or leader section is the result of many trials and much frustration. Many fish have been lost to short strikes, to hooks coming loose due to poor hook-ups, or just to the simple fact that the *hīnālea* had too few hooks in it. It was for these reasons that Ray devised an effective three-hook rig that doesn't seem to scare away any interested *ulua*. The first hook is a *tankichi* hook, which is inserted from under the chin of the *hīnālea*, through its jaws, and out through its nostrils.

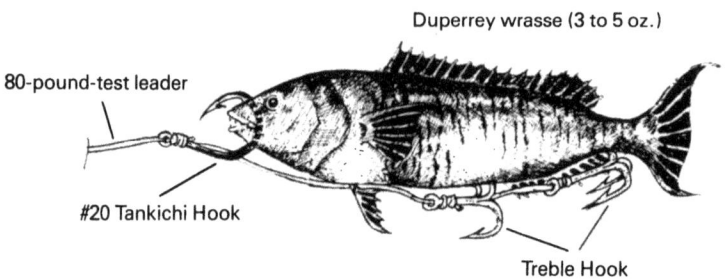

This rig uses three hooks. The first hook is a *tankichi* hook, which is inserted from under the chin of the *hīnālea*, through its jaws, and out through its nostrils. The second hook is a treble hook placed on the lower body of the fish.

The second hook is a treble hook, and it is hooked at only one of the three hooks through the lower body by way of the anal opening. The third hook is placed just past the second and before the fish's tail. Ray does not use weights to help get his bait out further; just the weight of the fish seems sufficient.

The leader's weight is about 40-pound test, and its overall length, six to seven feet. This can vary with the rod he will be using for the day. He does not use a swivel to connect his leader to the mainline but a Surgeon's Knot. This knot allows him to crank some of the leader into his rod tip, and it makes casting the *hīnālea* a little easier. Ray's tackle consists of a fairly good-sized spinning reel that handles about 200 to 250 yards of 20-pound test. The rod he had was a store-bought fiberglass model that stood ten feet or perhaps higher. It had a relatively thick shaft with a hypolon grip.

"When you're casting these *hīnālea,* you need something that can handle the excess weight," he explained. "Also, I like to use a good-sized rod, because when the *ulua* takes the bait, I like to really whale back and set the hooks in deep. On a small rod I can't do that and will lose too many good fish in a day. And when you do as much walking as we do, you'd like to land every fish that you hook too."

That the technique intrigued me is an understatement. I had done a lot of dead *puhi* whipping, but whipping dead *hīnālea* was a new one for me. Although the *hīnālea* has always been considered a fantastic bait by slide-bait fishermen, I never considered the idea of working a rigged dead *hīnālea* the way Ray works one.

While the day wore on I kept pace with him and watched and learned. Every once in awhile I'd flick out a cast and hope for something to happen. Ray kept casting his *hīnālea,* and he'd stop now and then to see how the bait was holding up. The *hīnālea* was surprisingly tough and held up for many, many casts. Then after a time the *hīnālea* disappeared from the center of a huge swirl of white water about thirty feet from the rocky shoreline. Instantly Ray hauled back and gave the rod several good backward jabs. I jumped up and was impressed by the effectiveness of the floundering bait. Ray's rod arched over, and line whispered off of the spinning spool. Two hands above the reel were locked onto the rod's hypolon grips. The battle was on against what looked like a good-sized fish.

Within several minutes the first run was over and Ray had things pretty much under control. The fish was working left and right of the point, but it was on its way in. Ray quickly identified the point's landing areas and selected one in which he could land his fish. After timing the waves, Ray pulled the small *ulua* up on the rocks. The mutilated *hīnālea* was still hanging out of the fish's mouth, and several of the treble hooks were embedded in the jaws of the fish and under its chin. Getting the hooks out was going to be a job, but what mattered was that the fish was landed and not lost, the hooks were a minor concern.

After he put the small *ulua* into his pack, Ray quickly tied on another leader rig, picked out a fresh *hīnālea* from his pack, and went off again. "Still early . . . maybe I'll get lucky and catch another one," he said with a big smile.

"Luck?" I said. Luck had nothing to do with it. It is his confidence, determination, and most of all his innovativeness and dauntless spirit that enables Ray to go out and land many big fish. He succeeds because he believes in his ideas.

Shrimp

One of the most highly prized live baits is the *shirosa* or *'ōpae,* the common saltwater shrimp. Just about anything that swims in the sea will eat this tiny creature, but it is especially the favorite food of the *pāpio*.

Some people catch *'ōpae* by going down to rivers, ponds, or piers. They simply scoop along the canals with a long dip net. Some anglers go into the water and dig for shrimp that are hiding in the weeds along the bank. Others look for this sea creature at night and lay small wire mesh traps with baits that draw the shrimp. Then there are those who look for the shining eyes of the shrimp at night with strong headlamps and tiny scoop nets. They have to scoop them up one at a

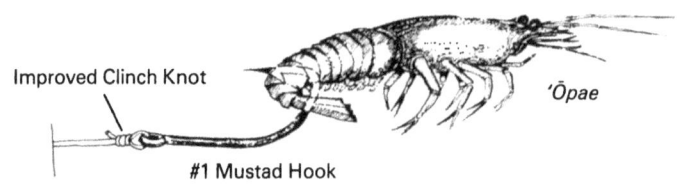

'Ōpae (live shrimp) for spinning. The live shrimp is hooked through the tail.

time, and this makes for tedious work that can end up taking the whole night.

After you've caught your bait, the next most important thing to do is to have some way of keeping it alive. Some resourceful anglers rig up in their homes large 26-gallon aquariums into which they dump the night's catch. Shrimp live quite well in captivity and will quickly get used to the tank. Most anglers will drop in small cut baits for the shrimp to feed on, and they do so readily. When bait is needed the angler simply dips into the aquarium with a net and takes what he thinks he'll need for the day.

Another way to keep shrimp overnight is to store them in an ice chest. A 155-quart cooler is great for this purpose because of its size and portability. Some fishermen will hook an aerator onto the handle, or run a 110-volt aquarium aerator for the shrimp. Most anglers will also simply keep the bait in the same bucket they caught the bait with. If the bucket is full of shrimp, the best thing to do is split the catch with another bucket. If you don't, the next morning you'll find a great many dead because the water will have become stale and polluted overnight. Changing the water just before you go to sleep is a good idea. A great way to keep the shrimp from getting too excited is to place some leaves, driftwood, or grass in the bucket to give them a place to hide. This sort of thing gives them some comfort and settles them down quickly. Adding rocks to the bucket is definitely out. Rocks tend to slide all over the bottom of the bucket and in the process smash many a valuable bait.

Jumping Jack

The jumping jack, also called the blenny or *pao'o,* lives in small tide pools and is one of the best baits for an assortment of predatory fish. They skip quickly over pools and jump headlong into the white water.

At other times they find cover beneath rocks and in small caves. They have long, slender bodies and are hard to hold.

The all-time best way to catch them is by going out at night and scooping them up with a deep scoop net. Some people grab them with their hands; but jumping jacks are slippery and you'll probably lose more than you'll catch that way. The net works best. Once you see a jumping jack sitting on a rock, shine the headlamp away from it and move in slowly. Once you're set, shine the light on it again and slowly put the net over the fish. Shake the net and the blenny will run up into it. Then all you need do is flip the net so that it closes and pull it up.

The water level in your bucket should be kept low and the bucket should have high walls. If not, the jumping jack will jump out of the bucket and back into the pool. Place in the bucket some leaves for the jumping jacks to hide under. The cover will calm them quicker and you'll lose less bait.

The Egg Sinker Leader Rig is the best of the leader rigs to use with jumping jacks. The leader length should be kept short and the line stout, however. If the leader is kept long, the casting of the jumping jack will be very awkward and cumbersome. The total length should be about two to three feet, maximum. The place to hook the jack is in the lips. Hook from under the chin, up through the lower jaw, and into the upper jaw. The hook should be of a reasonable size and a little on the thin side. If the hook is too thick the jumping jack will quickly die.

With this rig, you simply cast the jumping jack out and let the egg sinker take the bait down. Wait a few seconds and then start cranking in slowly. You want to have the jumping jack cruising just above the bottom. The bait should be kept in the water as long as possible. When the bait gets close to the shoreline, keep it there as long as possible. When a wave recedes, let the jumping jack cruise against the backwash. In this area of white water and swift currents, the *pāpio*

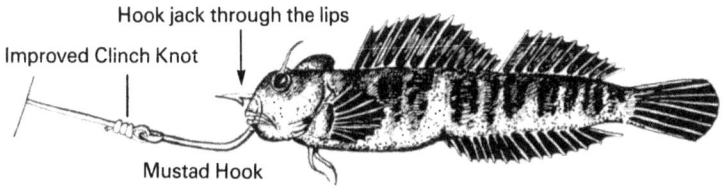

Rigging a Jumping Jack *(paoʻo)*

feels the most at home, so most of your strikes will come right in the shoreline area.

The *pāpio* or whatever reef fish is after the swimming jack will make a quick strike and then run off very swiftly. The predatory fish will take the head first; very few will hit the tail and miss the hook. Some strikes will come as taps on the lines, so be completely alert and ready for this. The lines might also go slack for a second. If this should happen, set the hook with a solid jerk and hope for the best. When the fish takes the bait, it will react very suddenly and panic. Your drag should be fairly loose, and you should hold the rod as high as possible.

Jerk the rod to make sure the fish has taken the hook and that it is set properly. A lot of times the fish will merely hold the bait between its lips and drop it at the slightest resistance.

If by some unforeseen accident the jacks should all die and you're left with only dead but fresh jacks, don't throw them away. One way to use them is to whip them as far out as possible and skip them over the surface of the ocean as fast as you can. Do this about five times. Cast the bait out again and retrieve it with three cranks. Stop and then crank slowly. It is likely a *pāpio* will be following this skipping jack and will hit it with great gusto once the bait stops and its skipping slows down. This technique of skipping and then stopping the bait has proven to be very productive, as those who have landed fish that weighed in the area of thirty to sixty pounds well know.

The meat of the jumping jack also makes great bait. Cut the meat from the dead jack, hook it, and then watch the action start. The skin of the jack is pretty tough and will keep on the hook a long time. Use it on jigs. Bounce it on the bottom and watch the fish climb all over it. I used to fillet jack and scrape all the skin off. I worked the jigs deep with it. *Moano* seem to really like the smell of the jumping jack and will quickly take the bouncing jig.

Another effective way to use jumping jacks is with a floater rig. This technique allows the jumping jack to swim freely in midwater, and it can draw some tremendous strikes. Hook the jumping jack just behind the head with a thin hook. The jack is a very active bait and will draw more than its share of predatory fish. Everything seems to eat the jumping jack, so don't be surprised at what you may catch.

6
Lures for the Shore Fisherman

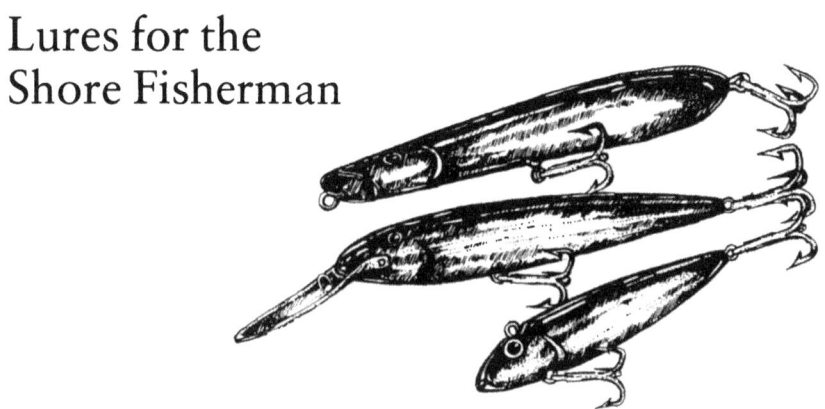

Lures come in such a variety of colors, patterns, and types that it really boggles the mind. Although the number of lures that the angler has at his disposal is overwhelming, in this book only saltwater lures and patterns will be discussed.

Some plugs look so much like the fish they're supposed to imitate that you simply can't resist purchasing one. Some have such pretty color patterns and round goggly eyes that as soon as you look at one, you feel it's a real fish catcher. As you can see some plugs are made merely to catch the fisherman. So which plug or lure do you purchase?

Many lures will produce results, and many, many more will not; therefore the best way to find out what lure really works is to ask the proprietor of a reputable fishing store. If he's sincere and serious about staying in the fishing business, he'll gladly tell you which plug, jig, or spoon will produce fish. The ones that don't produce will not be on his shelves very long. He should know what is selling and what is not. That's his job, and if he's not good at it his store will soon be closed for good.

Another thing about lures is that no two anglers will work a plug the same way. Each person uses a plug quite differently and this affects how productive it will be. A lure may work and catch tons of fish for one guy but not even produce one fish for another. It all has to do with faith and how the angler works the plug. So if you want to work a plug right, go fishing with a guy who swears by the plug and watch how he works it. Also take careful note of the terrain of the area in which he works the lure. That too has to be considered.

Once an angler becomes very proficient at whipping lures and other plugs, he will invariably start to make his own plugs or modify existing lures. The reason behind this is that most individuals will have singled out, more or less, the types of lure that work for them and then will try to make it even more efficient by changing its internal construction and its action.

You'll find that some lures will be quite easy to modify and others will not be at all. Try to make your own lures. You can purchase lure kits through different fishing catalogs. This is a real money-saving venture, and it makes fooling a fish into hitting your lure that much more gratifying. It's much like tying your own dry flies and hooking into a beautiful German brown trout.

Painting lures can be a very effective way to modify them. A simple thing like changing the color pattern on a small lure that has the same general shape as a baitfish of the area can turn a mediocre lure into a hot producer. So experiment as much as possible and test out all your creations. Some will turn out to be real Frankensteins, and others true gems.

If you check an area that has a lot of lure whippers, check to see what kind of concoctions they throw at the fish. You'll find lures made of guava sticks and some made of resin. Some homemade lures will fly a country mile and will draw a great many strikes. Always check the color patterns of specific lures and the manner in which anglers retrieve them. These considerations will make the most difference in terms of hook-ups.

Plugs

Plugs are my favorite lures, especially the surface or subsurface plugs. When working a plug through the water you can manipulate the plug until you get just the right action. You can see the plug working the area, and, even more, you can see the fish come up and follow the plug before it hits it with a frenzy. This kind of action—the sudden rush and uncontrollable attack—is the most exciting thing about using whipping plugs.

There are several different types of plugs and all are made of several different types of materials. Plugs can be made of plastic, wood, or resin. They can have metal lips, plastic lips, or no lips at all. They can be long and thin or short and squat. They can have shoveled-out faces. You can have plugs with jointed bodies that work back and forth during the retrieve. These plugs have a lot of action and don't require much rod tip action to make them work. All of these will catch fish if worked properly and if the hooks are kept sharp.

The most productive plug is the one that moves back and forth in the water. By back and forth I mean in a pattern that causes the plug to dodge and dart from side to side. This action is hard to accomplish, but with a little practice you can achieve some tremendous action with a lipped plug.

The reason this action is the most productive is that when a fish sees the plug dancing on the surface, it'll come up to investigate and follow the plug to shore. Once it comes up behind the plug, it'll chase the plug with determination. The fish will chase the plug as it dashes to the right; and just when it is up to the plug, the plug will dash quickly to the left. The fish will get quite frustrated and become more and more frenzied. After the first, second, and third dodge, it will be so infuriated that it'll hit the plug out of sheer anger. The strike will be furious and solid. At times like this the hooks have to be super sharp and able to set at the slightest touch.

A surface chugger is basically a plug that breaks up the water surface. It normally has a dished-out face that scoops out water, and this makes for a noisy, bubbly retrieve. It is usually worked in flat areas

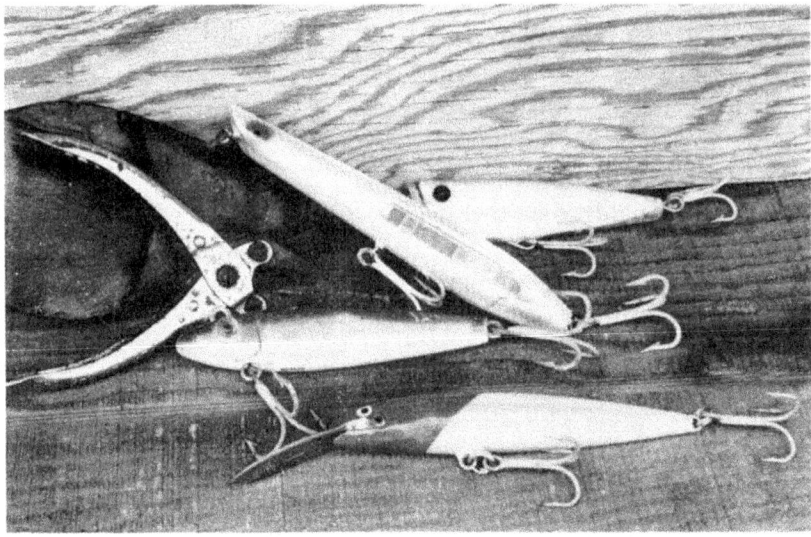

Generally all plugs resemble fish. Types and shapes vary greatly.

along the shoreline, and will not work effectively from a high, forty-foot cliff.

You work these plugs by sweeping the rod to the left or right of your body in determined strokes. This causes the plug to dive and dig into the surface of the water and do a bit of dodging. On the take-up, the lure should pause and then dig down again. If done repeatedly, the lure will work with astonishing results. The noise that it produces will cause a fish from anywhere along the shoreline to come and investigate. To keep the retrieve from getting too monotonous, vary the intensity of the pull and the length of the pause on the line take-up. Some pulls can be slight taps on the line that will cause the plug to dip and dibble on the surface. If a fish is just under the lure, a small simple action like that described will make the fish's nerves tighter than piano wires. As soon as the plug digs down again with force, the fish will come up and with a sudden savage attack either tear some of the paint off the plug or throw it clear of the water. Keep experimenting with a variety of retrieves until you find a pattern that stimulates some fish. Once you do, stick with it and eventually you'll catch some fish.

Lipped plugs also require some rod technique and some experimenting with retrieves. As is the case with surface chuggers, the number of strikes depends on the rod's action. By using a rod that is a little stiffer than the standard rod, you can imitate fish movements by twitching the rod tip upward and back toward you. Crank and twitch, crank and twitch. This will cause the plug to dig down and then pause. The twitch of the rod need not be strong and sweeping; instead, it should be more like a sudden jab on the rod tip. Most lipped plugs sink or are neutrally buoyant and will stay in one place during the line take-up. This makes the plug very attractive to aggressive fish. The pause can be very effective with lipped plugs. So vary your patterns and you'll hook a fish.

The sinking plug is another hot producer mainly because it can sink down to great depths and then be worked up and away. Some anglers weigh the plug down even more to increase the rate of the sink so the plugs can be bounced off the ocean bottom.

Adjustable Plugs: The Mirro-Lure

Although plugs are basically all the same, there are, thank heavens, ones that are different. The Mirro-Lure is one very versatile plug, mainly because it can be reconstructed or renovated. When pur-

LURES FOR THE SHORE FISHERMAN

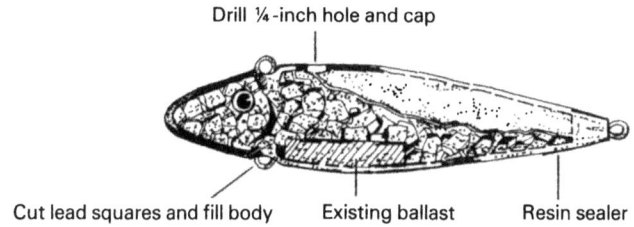

Mirro-Lure for surface splashing and skipping. Approximate weight: 3 to 4 ounces.

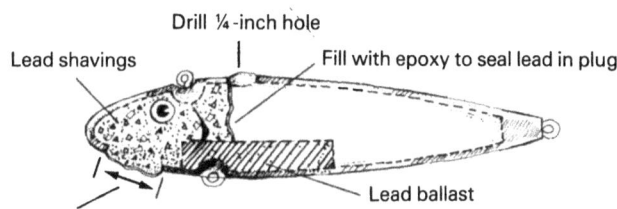

Fully rebuilt plug for whipping from high cliffs

chased, the plug will weigh about 2 ounces; after I'm through with it, it'll weigh about $3\frac{1}{2}$ to 4 ounces and will track well.

You must decide what type of plug you want the Mirro-Lure to be: a surface splasher or a below-surface, fast runner. If you want a surface splasher plug, one that will really kick up a fuss and divide the water like Moses did the Red Sea, then all you'll need is some lead, a hammer, and a junk pair of scissors.

First, drill a quarter-inch hole approximately a half inch behind the screw eye of the two-ounce Mirro-Lure. Pound the lead into thin slabs and cut them with the scissors. Fill the hole up with the tiny squares of lead. Pack it in really tight. Mix a small paper cup of surfboard resin and slowly pour the compound into the tiny hole until it is filled. This will solidify and make the plug totally indestructible and about four to five ounces heavy.

To make a plug that will track well, even when used from high cliffs, first drill the same quarter-inch hole. Take the piece of lead and start shaving it with a large bastard file. Be careful to catch all the flecks of lead on a large sheet of paper, because if these shavings get into your rug, you'll never get them out. If you want finer shavings, use a finer file. Finer shavings make heavier plugs and they make packing easier, but remember, it takes more fine shavings to fill a plug.

Once you've got all the fine shavings you need, slowly pour the dust into the Mirro-Lure. Tap the nose of the plug as you pour to make sure all of the dust is packed in on that end of the plug. This is very important if you want the plug to track down and forward. You'll find that an amazing amount of lead dust will go into the nose of the plug. Once you've filled the plug's nose up to the drilled hole, then once again mix the resin and pour it into the small hole. Make sure you just cover the lead dust; don't fill the plug.

One good way to patch the drilled hole is to pack some wadding in it and seal the hole with epoxy. An even better way would be to fill the plug with a little more resin, tape the hole with masking tape, and tilt the plug until the soft resin flows back onto the hole and covers it. Once the resin is dry, take off the masking tape and sand down until smooth.

After all this is done, I usually take a dremel kit (a tiny drill kit used for model planes) and cut an elongated hole under the lip of the plug. I cut until I gorge out all the plastic and meet the lead shavings I poured in earlier. Then, with the plug upside down, I pour in the lead dust and mix it with resin. This will solidify the dust and bind it to the head of the plug. Finally, I paint the under lip with white paint and the plug is as good as new, except that now it's heavier to cast and will track true and clean. With this modified Mirro-Lure, I have hooked and landed many *ulua*. Also, this lure will work the grounds much more thoroughly and raise many more fish if it is worked with a zig-zag pattern of retrieve.

Tin Squids

This lure, also called a diamond jig, looks like a slab of shiny tin or a chrome-plated lead bar. The lure is extremely simple and can host either one single hook or one treble hook. It comes in a wide assortment of weights but not in a variety of designs. A heavy lure, it is normally cast off of some sudden drop. The lure is brought up with sudden erratic motions, made by cranking the reel and lifting the rod tip vigorously. Because of its diamond-shaped sides, the Tin Squid or diamond jig glitters nicely as its falls and when it is retrieved. The way it falls because of its weight and the way it twinkles are what draws sudden strikes.

Diamond jigs are relatively inexpensive and are easy to maintain. They don't get too badly mangled and don't become worthless after

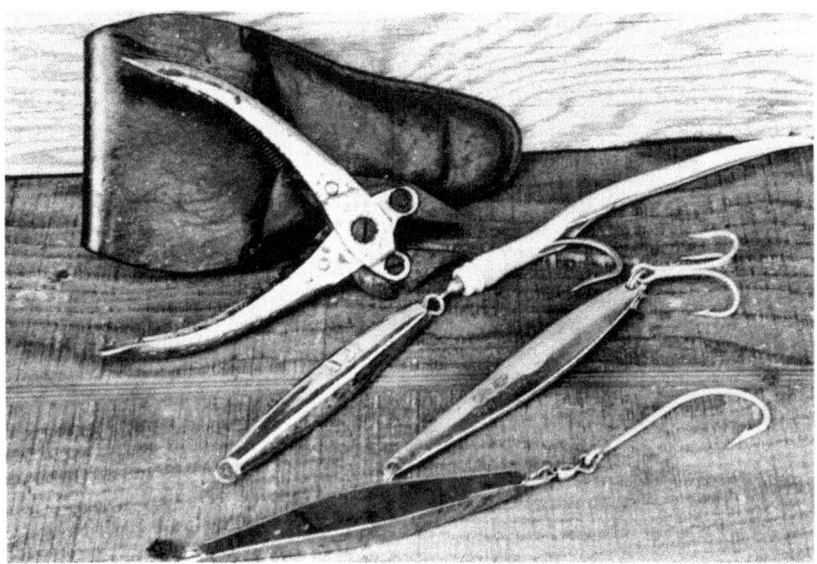

Tin Squids (also called Diamond Jigs)

sudden and vicious strikes. This is especially true of plugs that have finely tuned metal or plastic lips. The only thing that can happen to a diamond jig is the hook may become badly bent and twisted. To fix it, simply bring out the extra hook you should always carry, take off the damaged hook from the split ring, and replace it with a new one. You might even use a new split ring.

Some diamond jigs work a little better with a feather skirt on the shank of the hook. Others can be made more tantalizing with a section of fish belly or a strip of squid. This type of decoration should be used sparingly, mainly because these additions will affect the lure's tumbling action and may even make it ineffective.

Lai Skin Jig

Jigs have been one of the oldest and most reliable fishing lures for almost the entire life of fishing. The reason for their undying popularity is their versatility. A jig can be used for surface action, midwater action, and naturally deep-jigging action. It can be used with a simple bare hook and a slab of fish or cuttlefish as a skirt. If you're a purist when it comes to skirts, you can use anything from bucktail to feathers and rubber skirts.

In this age of innovation, we have seen the advent of the plastic worm, which was eventually converted to saltwater use. Its popularity in fresh water has definitely been undisputed, and now, because of its ability to catch saltwater fish, it has garnered quite a sizeable following. But time marches on and the new generation of jigs have already replaced the standard bucktail and feathers with the dried skin of the *lai* (leatherback).

The *lai* has long been a favorite among trollers, and has more than proven itself a real fish producer. Having this in mind Gary Ranne obtained a few ⅜-ounce lead head jigs and tied to the head of the jigs (not too carefully) some *lai* skin that he had stripped with his wife's scissors (something she wasn't too keen about). This first crude lure looked like it would scare off more fish than it would catch, but Gary was determined and he had faith in his new concoction.

On an eventful trip to South Point with ultralight jig–fanatic Stan Wright (to whom we had given several jigs), we gave the *lai* skin invention the acid test. Within a half hour Stan had hooked into a scrappy, 4½-pound 'ōmilu and proceeded to gaff and land the monster. But before we knew it Stan was thrashing the water again with the proven *lai* skin jig. Several more strikes later only a few *lai* skin strips were left. Eventually Stan lost this special jig to the coral.

After that, Gary hooked into something that he couldn't hold with his ultralight tackle and it was quickly cut off. Something was gobbling up all the jigs that Gary made. By the evening all the jigs were gone. Without a doubt, the *lai* skin jig had proven itself.

Constructing a Lai *Skin Jig*

First, get a set of *lai* skins. This may not be too easy, but if you know of an ultralight-tackle fisherman, contact him because he's your best bet. At times fishing stores have *lai* skins, but not too often. The fun way to get a skin is to go out and catch one. The *lai* is a great fighter on ultralight tackle and will more than keep your pulse racing.

Once you have a fish, simply cut around its outer edges with a sharp knife. Pull the skin off, starting at the tail and ending up at the head. If some belly meat comes off with the skin, take a spoon or dull butter knife and scrape off all the meat until the skin is clean. Lay the flesh side of the skin on a clean white paper and let it dry overnight. Don't use the newspaper for the drying because then you'll be able to read the headlines on the skin after it dries.

Once the skin is dry, you'll find that it's curled quite a bit and is

LURES FOR THE SHORE FISHERMAN

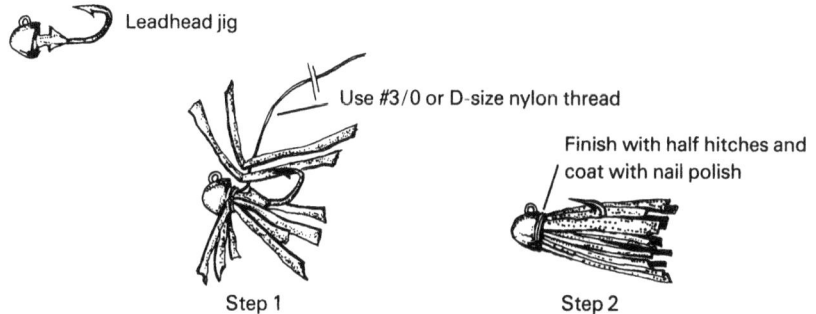

Lai Skin Jig. *Step 1:* Lay each strip of *lai* skin on the jig head shank separately and wrap around the shank. Add strips until all sides of the jig are covered. *Step 2:* Wind nylon thread around the jig and finish with half hitches. Coat the thread with nail polish. Soak jig for five minutes prior to using so that strips become soft and pliable.

very similar to leather. Either force the skin to uncurl and cut it into strips or leave it pressed between two heavy books overnight. The latter method will leave the skin absolutely flat and wrinkle free.

Once you've gotten it flat, get an old pair of scissors and cut the skin into thin strips, ¼ x 2 inches long. At this point, I usually separate the skins into two piles. One pile will consist of dark black to dark grey strips (from the back area of the *lai*), and the other will consist of white to yellowish strips (from the side or belly section of the *lai*). The dark skins will make terrific *lai* skin jigs that resemble jumping jacks *(paoʻo)* and that draw some vicious strikes. The white section is a favorite and will hold its own against any lure around.

The best thing that you can get to hold the jig head while you're tying the *lai* skin on is a "fly-tying vise." If you don't have one, you can use a standard pair of vise grips that will hold the hook very securely. Clamp the vise grips to the edge of the kitchen table with a set of C clamps and you're in business.

Once you've gotten the hook secured, wind nylon thread (size A is good) around the jig several times. After you've put the layer of thread on, cover it with either nail polish (clear) or airplane DOPE (clear). This will secure the thread permanently.

Now select strips that measure approximately three inches. Fold them in half and tie them back. Secure them in that folded position with a layer of nylon thread. Finish the layer with three half hitches and again cement it with a layer of clear nail polish. It would be a good idea to paint the lead head a shade of white with enamel paint.

Paint eyes on the lead head or leave it plain white. It isn't really necessary to paint the lead head but it makes for a nicer lure; also, the white is easier to see and thus correcting your retrieve pattern is much easier. Sometimes white enamel won't stick to the lead so you'll have to use a neutral base paint, which can be purchased through many fishing supply houses or fishing stores. You might want to dip the lead head in vinegar or some lemon juice to make it easier for the paint to adhere to the lead.

When you're down at the beach or before you start fishing, soak the entire jig in a pond or a bucket of water for a time, so the skin can soften up and as a result give the jig more action during the retrieve. It will also be easier to cast. You will find that during the first six casts a jig of stiff *lai* skin will fly like a stiff parachute and your casting distance will be cut in half. Thus you should always soak the jigs before using them.

The lead head jig is basically a very effective lure. With the undulating skin, terrific smell, and durable body, you'll have yourself the ultimate lure. It can be worked effectively in either deep or surface waters.

The very best thing about *lai* skin jigs is they are fun to create. Anyone can tie a bunch of them up. Once when Gary and I ran out of a bunch of them I got a knife, some old monofilament, and some jigs without any dressing that were in my pack. We tied up a batch so we could finish the day's fishing. Gary held the jigs with a pair of pliers while I tied them. I secured them with old monofilament or old rod wrapping thread. Dental floss also works very well and is easy to carry.

The cost of the lures is one other thing to consider about the *lai* skin jig. They are extremely inexpensive and easy to make. They are also very adaptable and can meet any fishing need or want. We make them with long skirts, short, full skirts, or with very few sections of skin. Each can be tailored to the fishing terrain that you choose to fish. So tie up a bunch of them one night and try them out the following day. They work.

Spoons

The spoon is just that, a spoon. It normally consists of a sheet of metal with a dished-out face that makes it either spin or wobble in the water. Because the spoon has a shiny surface and will flash like a neon light, it can draw the attention of fish from a great distance. The

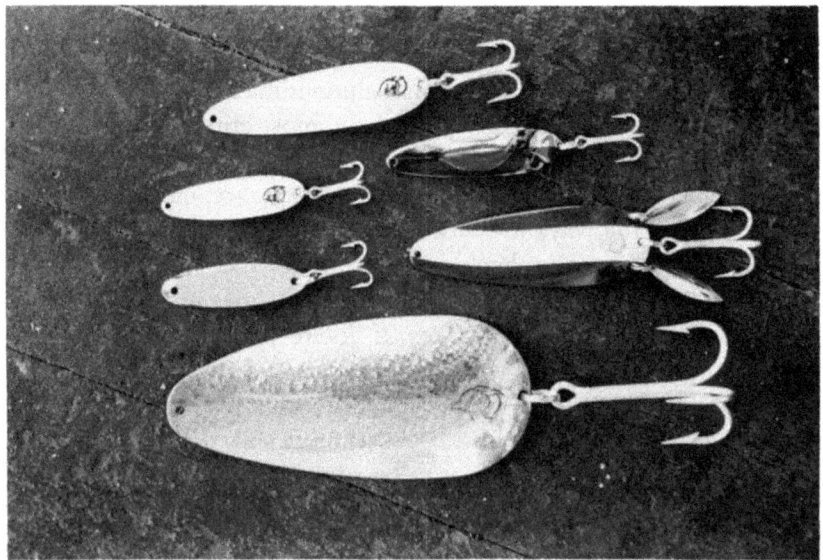

Spoons

spoon can give the appearance of a wounded minnow working its way through the water in search of a place to hide. Its erratic movements, combined with its twinkling action, will lead the predator fish to think that this minnow isn't swimming quite right and therefore will make for easy prey. It is more important, then, to work the rod tip in a pattern that keeps the spoon's movements erratic.

Spoons also come in a wide range of colors and designs. The old spoons that were first introduced to salt water had basic freshwater designs. The common red-and-white-striped spoons of yesterday still land fish if worked right. Why the red and white draws strikes is still beyond me, but it works. So who's to say what colors fish like? Beyond the standard red-and-white-striped lure is the shocking pink spoon. "Shocking" is an understatement, but the lure does draw more than its share of strikes, and it is extremely easy to see in the water. Gold and silver are the standard colors for spoons. The silver spoon, being that it is the easiest to make and that it gives off the most flash, will produce strikes from all types of shoreline gamefish. The gold spoon is another great producer and can be worked very effectively when the silver doesn't seem to draw a nod.

Some people have gone so far as to make their own spoons. It is simple enough to do, and when done correctly the spoon can attract species that don't hit the standard, store-bought spoons. Aluminum and brass are two materials most commonly used by homemade-spoon makers. Stainless steel, another producer, can be used but it tends to be harder to work with than aluminum or brass.

The weight of the spoon is one of the most critical things to consider when selecting a spoon. The angler should be able to cast it without much problem, and it should not create too much wind resistance. One of the ways to work a spoon is to let it sink down to the depths and then work it back up in stripping jerks and twitches. For this method, the spoon that sinks quickly will move much more erratically and thus draw more strikes. If you're working an area that is very shallow and want to work the spoon very slowly and on the surface, then a spoon that is wide and light is your best bet. Even letting the spoon sink a bit won't hurt because it will sink slowly. So, a heavy spoon that sinks very rapidly can be either a great asset or a severe handicap, depending on the depth of the water you're working.

What type of hook you use on the spoon is purely up to you. Most spoons come with a single treble hook joined to the spoon by a split ring. Depending upon one's preference, this hook can be changed to a single hook and then back to a treble hook with no problem at all.

When you work areas that have a lot of rock and coral outcroppings, your hooks may get broken or bent beyond use. Simply release the hook from the split ring and add on another hook. Some strikes will come so quickly that the hooks sometimes get completely torn off the spoon. At times like this just add on a spare split ring and another hook and you're ready to go back to fishing. Needless to say, it's a good idea to carry extra hooks and split rings.

Leadhead Jig

The leadhead jig is one of the most basic types of artificial lures ever created. It is also one of the oldest lures in the world and has never really changed over the course of time. Eskimos still use a jig that is made of bone and fur, and that catches fish as it did many, many generations ago. The key to its effectiveness is that it has a simple construction and it can be used in different types of terrain and under various conditions.

In its simplest form, it is merely a hook with a lead forehead. The lead adds weight to the lure, and the manner in which the lead is molded to the hook makes it ride upright and thus makes it semi-

Feather or Bucktail Leadhead Jigs

weedless, or snag-proof. Because of the single hook, the number of hook-ups is better than average. Also, a single hook is less likely to be worked out during a battle, unlike plugs and treble hooks.

Hooks on leadheads are normally a little bigger than average and much stouter than the treble hooks on plugs. They also require more consideration when it comes to sharpness. Because of the single-hook rig, the hook should have a fine, keen edge. There should be no doubt as to the sharpness of the hook.

But the best thing about leadhead jigs is they cost about a fourth to a fifth as much as some plugs on the market and they stand up to much more abuse. Some well-designed plugs are great until a fish hits them. You may find later that you have a plug that is so well tuned that it is totally worthless. On some plugs, hooks get ripped completely off and metal lips mangled beyond recognition. On the average, these plugs run about $5 to $8. You'll find that losing or demolishing a half dozen in a day can get very, very expensive. This is not to say that some plugs are not cheaper and more durable, but in comparison to leadhead jigs, they are very expensive when you need to maintain a steady supply of them.

Leadhead jigs can be purchased in just about any store you can think of, from the small corner grocery store to the "super" stores and department stores. They are inexpensive to keep on the shelves, as their turn-over rate is fairly high. So, they are easy to find if you need to restock your dwindling supply.

They also come in all the colors of the rainbow, and each color is only as effective as the fisherman who has confidence in it. White and yellow has always been a hot producer under all circumstances, and jigs of these colors will probably be on most shelves. Black jigs have been popular among anglers because of their resemblance to the small reef fish that dominate the shoreline areas. Other colors such as green and red have also been producing and therefore should be saved a section in your tackle box, just in case the fish start hitting jigs of that color more than any other.

Jigs can be purchased from most well-stocked fishing supply stores, or they can be purchased in bulk from a lot of mail order catalogs. If even the latter is too expensive for you, you can purchase a relatively inexpensive aluminum mold and make your own. There's nothing more gratifying than making your own lure and having a fish hit it with gusto.

All you need is a small stove (and your wife's permission to use it), an old peach can, and a ladle to scoop out the molten lead. Paints and bucktail, as well as hooks of all types and sizes, can be purchased in all of the fishing catalogs. Once you've learned the basics of pouring lead, you'll find making a hundred jig heads no problem at all.

Making your own lures will also make your wife and pocketbook much happier. The cost is just pennies, and you'll find that you can always have a good supply for yourself, as well as for your closest friends. Plus that, you can experiment with lure designs to find the one that is extra successful in your area. Streamline your designs and you may have one that is a real killer in your side of the ocean.

Some anglers don't put anything on the leadhead jig except plain old paint; others swear by the addition of well-defined eyes; and some even go as far as to paint on red gill plates. It is purely up to the individual. I personally don't see any harm in painting eyes and gill plates on your jig because I don't think that it'll hurt its effectiveness. So if it doesn't hurt, why not?

Plastic Body Jigs

This is not an invention that just hit the market, but is has more acceptance now in the fishing community than it ever had before. The

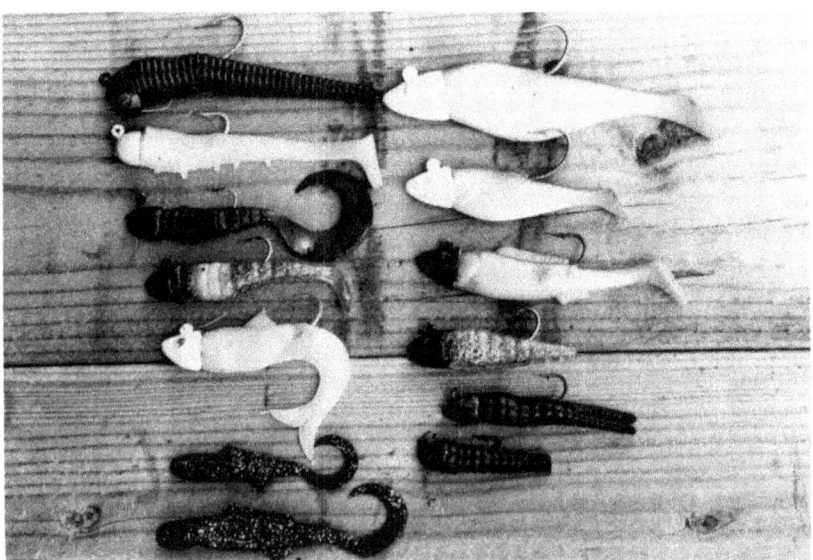

Plastic Body Jigs

plastic body jig has been hooking an increasing number of fish, and its cost is very, very reasonable. The jig is a much more adaptable lure now that the bucktail section of the jig has been replaced by a plastic body that can be molded into a multitude of shapes and patterns.

You can get plastic bodies in any color, from "motor oil" (an olive color) to shocking pink. Each type seems to work in some location or another, and will hook fish with surprising regularity. The most basic colors are white, clear with glitter, and black. Red is right in the running, as is yellow. But it all boils down to the individual and his personal experiences with certain colors. If you have had good results with yellow, you will most likely stick with that color until you find something that works better.

The best thing about the plastic body jig is that the body can be molded into shapes that will wiggle or vibrate in different ways. The typical curly tail undulates, which drives some fish crazy and will provoke strikes that plugs won't. The Beaver Tail vibrates from side to side, and when coupled with a jerky rod tip action, it can stimulate strikes that will pull the rod right out of your hand. Each of these different tails and actions, not to mention the multitude of color patterns they come in, make the plastic body jig the most versatile lure on the market.

But many people forget that the *angler* makes the lure effective. A lure that works on its own is only half effective; the rest of the action is provided by the angler and his rod tip or cranking action. The beauty of the jig is that it can be worked many, many ways. It is relatively inexpensive, which makes it an even more attractive addition to your tackle box. So learn to use the jig under different conditions, in all environments, and for different types of fish. It is only as effective as you make it.

For instance, I normally like to work a solid black Tout or Grub Tail jig. I feel comfortable with its color and get a lot of good results with it. This is the way I like to work it: First, I whip the surface areas in a fan pattern. I start working the areas that look the most productive. If nothing happens, I work the mid-depths. If there's nothing still, I work the bottom. The jig will work under all of these circumstances very efficiently; it only takes some practice and determination on your part. (See "Jigging and Deep Jigging from Shore," Chapter 7.)

Homemade Lures

Many anglers that work the water consistently will eventually start to look into lures that they have heard about or have seen used by someone. Some of the lures, you won't find on market shelves; ones you do

Homemade lures

find, you may not want to use because they don't seem to work. As a recourse, many anglers create their own lures. This is fine and some great lures have been created by anglers.

Plugs are made of anything from broomsticks to guava sticks, and they are painted in all kinds of wild and provocative colors. Some have a chugging action that attracts the surface feeders, and some are so big that it would take a Charles Atlas to cast them. But many of the plugs are tailored to perform a very specific task. They do one job and that's it.

A good friend showed me one such lure. It consisted of one big treble hook, and its body was made of resin. It was molded in a centrifuge test tube. Really a surface chugger, it literally tore up the water surface and left a bubble trail that was about five to six feet long. The average weight for a lure like this is about two to three ounces, and because of its shape it cast like a greased gull. It was a very specialized lure and couldn't be adapted to any other type of action. Although I caught fish with it, if the fish weren't taking on the surface, I was out of luck. Also, the lure required a super-fast retrieve that would steadily make a bubble trail at surface level. Once the lure slowed down it lost its effectiveness. It could only be used in situations where the water was calm and the angler was close to sea level. It couldn't be used from high cliffs or high piers.

Other lures like the long, guava-stick type used on Molokai are also specialized. The areas on Molokai are low and flat and the lures can be worked very close to sea level. They skip on the surface and make a terrific commotion.

All of these lures are very effective yet hardly ever very adaptable. If you are an average angler who fishes a variety of terrains under conditions that change from day to day, these plugs will give you very little flexibility. So if you plan to make one of your own, make a plug that gives you a wide range of lure action, depth-probing abilities, and different retrieve patterns. Learn to use this kind of lure well and you will be able to handle all types of conditions and fish in more than one type of ground.

7
The Art of Whipping the Shoreline

Reading productive shorelines is very similar to looking for good wildlife hunting grounds: after many years of hunting in various types of terrain, you'll eventually find that certain types of game prefer specific types of feeding grounds and resting sights. Gamefish prefer certain depths and bottom contours. Take, for instance, the ʻōʻio (bonefish). It prefers sandy, crushed coral bottoms that harbor succulent crabs and shrimp, the ʻōʻio's main diet. The *ulua* can be found in some of these areas, but it much prefers radical coral drop-offs and boulder-strewn bottoms. The *ulua* is more successful at ambushing his prey off these steep coral drop-offs or in channels and does so with the least amount of effort.

So what features do you look for in productive whipping grounds? First of all, most good whipping grounds are rather shallow (three to eight feet); have a lot of good coral outcroppings, channels, drop-offs, or potholes; and are relatively clean. Therefore, look for a radically changing bottom, not one that is flat and without character. A smooth, tapered bottom that has very few coral outcroppings often proves to have a very small reef fish population. The small reef fish need a rugged bottom for food and shelter, so unless they are sand dwellers, they will seek this kind of environment. The predatory reef fish also prefer just this type of reef structure. There they know where the food fish are, and if they want to survive, they will hunt in these areas.

A lot of times while fishing some productive-looking grounds, you'll find you can't seem to draw a chase or a strike. In this circumstance, the best thing to do is look for a sudden break in the bottom contour, some apparent change in the bottom, and make your cast around what might either be a large coral head or a deep channel. Saltwater gamefish are very much like their freshwater counterparts, such as the large- and smallmouth bass: they seek out a specific type of structure, whether it be a brush pile, roadbed, a pile of rocks, or half sunken tree. Although the type of structure preferred by each fish may be different, its purpose is always the same.

If the water is a very deep blue color, you'll usually find that working the water from the top will yield very poor results because the fish are down too deep (fifteen to thirty feet). They won't want the small bait or plug enough to come up and "equalize." So adapt to the demands of this type of water depth and work the lure or bait close to or right on the bottom.

Small bays and channels that open into the ocean are great spots for roaming *pāpio* and other gamefish. In these areas, the *pāpio* has the advantage a wolf has when it's cornered a single sheep in a box canyon. A lot of times when you're spinning in an area that has no bays, you'll find that the *pāpio* will seem to wait until the plug gets very close to the shoreline before it makes an all-out attack. Again, it seems like they feel they have their prey cornered and at their mercy. Also, because small bays seem to always be slightly sheltered from daily swells and swift moving tides or currents, predatory fish have more freedom to feed there.

Shallow areas with sandy bottoms will produce some fish, but unless you see them after a cast or three, forget the area and move on. This is not to say that all sandy-bottom areas are poor fishing grounds. Some flats may prove to be highly productive, as may some plateau-like shelves. A shelf is a very prominent structure and may be very different from the surrounding general area.

One way of determining bottom structure is to check the shoreline structure. A lot of times the bottom is merely an extension of the shoreline. Points continue into the water and thus a flat monotonous shoreline will indicate a shallow sloping reef with few sudden drop-offs.

Shoreline areas that have a host of large boulders are very good.

Boulders afford fish lots of hiding places, and that's what you're looking for. When the reef is too well developed, hiding places tend to be small and thus few fish will congregate around it. Look for places that have radical drop-offs, channels, and boulder-strewn bottom structures and you'll find fish.

White water is another form of cover for predatory fish. Because fish love the white water and will feed near it very freely, the white water can be a very productive area. You must remember that white water is usually the thickest on the surface and thins or disappears toward the bottom. From the bottom, the surface looks bleach white and anything that moves under it is very easy to see. But from the surface, it is very hard to see the bottom. Predatory fish like to use this to their advantage and will often wait for the plug or lure to run to the shoreline. Once the plug gets to the white water, the fish will rush up and swiftly snatch it. Even if the water is deep, if it has lots of white water, it has some great potential.

Casting with Accuracy

When it comes to working the shoreline, casting with accuracy is of prime importance because a lot of time can be lost when a poor cast is made. You could lose the plug in the rocks or cast into unproductive waters. Also, the angle of retrieve or the path the plug follows is of great importance. If the plug is too far from a target rock and doesn't pass just to the left or right of the rock, you may not get the strike you are looking for. Accurate casting also helps you to work the water in a very methodical way. When casting use a fan pattern, spreading the casts out until you hit a hot spot and a fish. In this way you will find out what kind of bottom structure the fish are favoring that day and can duplicate it at the next point. You can eliminate all the extra steps of fish hunting and get right down to using a system.

Casting accuracy is extremely important when you can see the fish or the direction in which the fish is going. If you make a cast and an 'ōmilu (bluefin trevally) suddenly comes up and makes an attempt at the plug but misses it, quickly take up the plug and make another cast in the same spot. Be sure the plug covers the same coral head in which the 'ōmilu tried to ambush it. If you're cast is off, you may loose the attention of the fish, and before you can get off another cast the fish may be gone. So, casting accuracy is very, very important.

Spinning Presentation and Techniques

Ultralight and medium-light tackle techniques are very similar, only the size of the tackle and size of the fish one would be after are different. It's a good idea to carry both sizes of tackle wherever you go. Sometimes the shoreline is just too rough for the ultralight tackle, mainly because you can't get close to the shore. If you tried, you'd more likely find yourself fishing only the inshore white water. In this case shift to the medium-light tackle and you'll be able to work the area with relative ease. Let the ocean conditions determine the style of fishing you'll be using that day.

Once you have determined the style of fishing and the plug you'll be using, tie your leader on and before you make your first cast check out all the working parts of your reel to see if everything is in working order. After your plug hits the water, start the retrieve with a quick snap of the spinning reel bail, or flip it manually. Retrieve the plug in an erratic, jerky motion by working the rod tip as you crank the spinning reel. It takes some getting used to, but the effort will pay off. The more you get used to working the tip, the better and more varied your retrieves will be. To see if you're working the plug properly, make a short cast and work the plug back to you, keeping constant watch on the action of the plug. If it's not what you want, which is a dodge–dart pattern, then change the pattern of retrieve until you hit on the motion. Then when you make a long cast, simply create the rod action that you want.

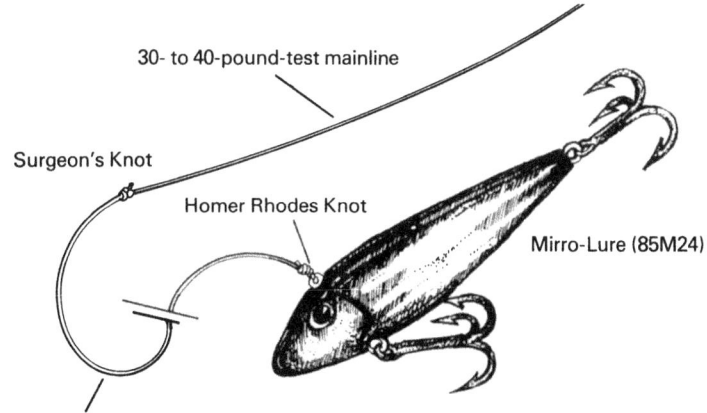

One of the fastest and easiest leaders to tie. It also gives optimum performance on the plug which allows for proper lure manipulation.

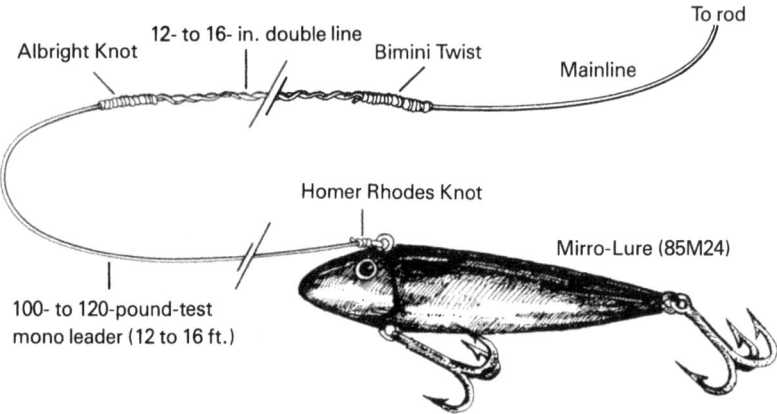

One of the strongest leaders for spinning with plugs or lures. Sometimes the knots seem bulky and make terrible sounds as they go through the guides; nonetheless lures can be manipulated to add much needed action to stimulate a fish to strike.

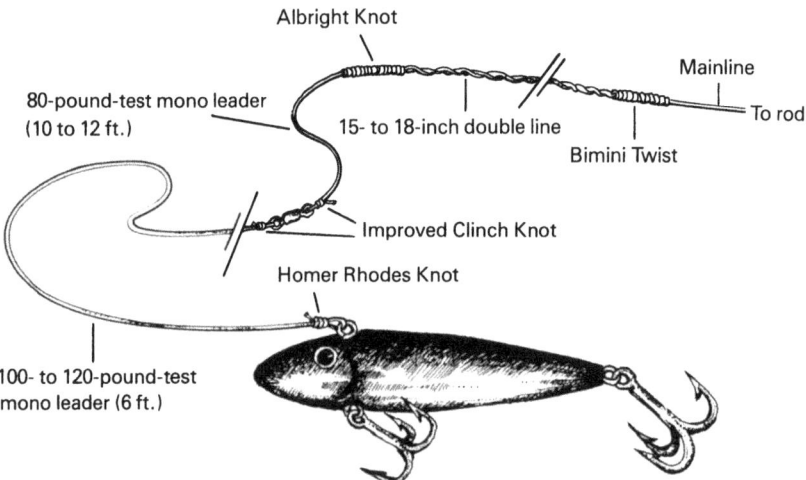

This leader is a good one to use when swivel gaffs are being used because the lure is still allowed a lot of free movement.

Try to visualize the plug in the open ocean as you work it. Work it slowly and methodically. Don't rush the presentation so that you can make another quick cast and retrieve. You'll catch more fish with a few properly presented casts than with several poorly presented ones.

Fish don't always hit plugs because they're hungry; sometimes they hit plugs because you stimulate or tease them into hitting the plug. And tease is just what the plug's motions should do. If you can get a fish to come up to a plug and by dodging and jigging it tease the fish into thinking that it won't get the plug, you'll get it to kill the plug in a mad, frustrated rush. If your retrieve involves a more or less monotonous action, the fish will feel that it's not really worth it, or it'll see that it's an imitation and will quickly swim away. You may raise him for a look, but what you want is to get him to strike savagely. This will ensure a good solid hook-up and prove that your presentation was effective. Fish hit plugs with a lot of power, as is evidenced by badly bent hooks and plugs, or by wooden plugs that have been broken right in half. Sometimes plastic plugs and wood plugs get so badly mangled that deep teeth marks are found all over them. This shows that a fish will take a hard plug with a lot of force and conviction.

A plug that has a plastic or metal lip is worked by twitching the rod tip and causing the plug to dance and jiggle. Although the plug is built to move erratically as the angler simply retrieves it, you still get a better action if you work the plug. So go into the rod action movements again and see what happens. If this doesn't work, try switching from the constant twitching action to some stop–start motions. Sometimes a moment's pause is worth a lot, so stop dead and let the wave action keep the plug moving. Wait two to three seconds and then give the plug a twitch and again let it pause. It will look very much like a wounded minnow—easy pickings to the fish.

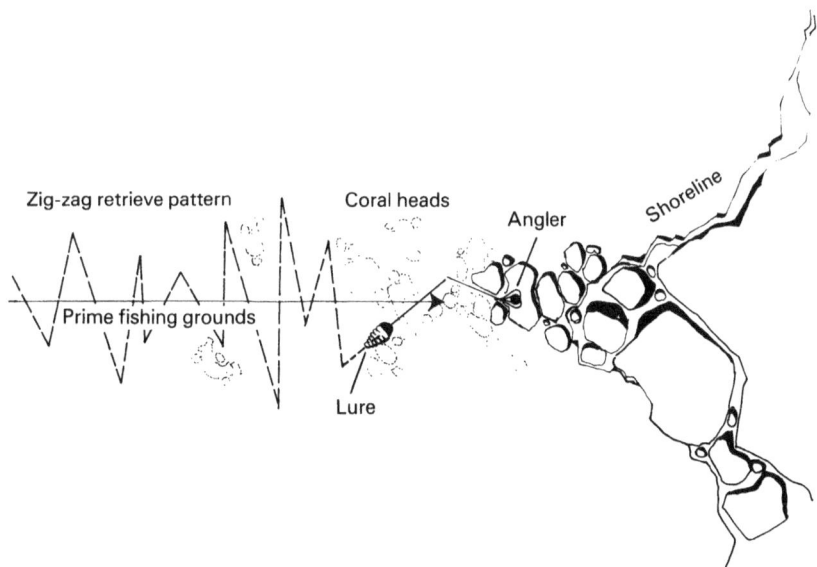

Making the lure perform in a dodge and dart pattern is the key to lure presentation.

Another type of retrieve is the full-on, side-sweeping pull. Vigorously drag the rod sharply to the right or left of your body. Because you must crank up the slack line to do this, the plug will be left sitting motionless for a moment before it dashes off in another panic-stricken run. This kind of action is so stimulating that it literally drives the fish mad and they'll hit the plug with tremendous force. While making the sweeping motion, be constantly on the alert for a sudden, jolting strike. If you're not set, the fish may hit suddenly, and simultaneously cut the line. Again, you have to keep a mental picture of what is happening to the plug. Every once in awhile do a visual check of the plug's action when it comes close to you. Such checks will tell you if the plug is flipping over during the pull. If the lure rises to the surface and flips up and over, you will have to lessen the intensity of the pull. You want the plug to make a mad dash, not jump out of the water and tangle itself in the treble hooks and the line.

Even the least interesting retrieve (the constant monotonous crank) has its place in your retrieve repertoire and can be tried between other more stylized techniques. If all else fails, try cranking the plug in at a very slow and ponderous pace and see what happens. If nothing happens, then move on to another point.

A lot of times the strike will come not when the plug is out working in the reef but just when the plug has reached the shoreline. This is not to say that you shouldn't make long and beautiful casts. The long cast draws the fish out and into the reefline by making them curious about the splashing sounds. It seems that once it chases the plug into shallow water, the fish begins to think that the baitfish has run down a deadend alley and is now left with no place to go. So leave the bait or plug in the water for a moment or two, especially where there is white and foamy water. A plug left in the white water will be silhouetted and from the bottom it will look like a fly on white paper. The baitfish can't see down but the predatory fish can easily see up. As a result, you won't see the fish chase the plug until you reach the white water, at which time it'll come up and suddenly grab the plug as it makes a mad dash and sends white water splashing everywhere.

If the plug you're using is a sinking model, let it sink down to a depth you think is productive. Once you have the plug down, rush the plug back up by cranking furiously for a moment. Stop, and then let the plug sink for four seconds. Then crank again for all you're worth. What you're trying to do is create a sawtooth pattern and work as close to the bottom and midwater as possible. If the water is too deep for just working the top, go down to the bottom and work the baits there. There is always a chance that the plug will get stuck on the bottom, but if you don't go down you won't get any action at all, so it really is worth risking the plug and making the effort. This is really blind fishing and you have to keep close tabs on the line when it enters the water. Sometimes you'll get some hard, vicious strikes, and sometimes the line will just twitch or kick from right to left, so you have to keep alert.

Skipping the Plug

Skipping the plug on the surface of deep water (thirty to forty feet) is usually pretty much a waste of time. Doing it in fairly shallow water (ten to twelve feet), however, is more than worth the effort. Sometimes you'll raise a fish that will look like a big black boulder and the skipping plug will look puny by comparison. Fish this size will make your hair stand on ends and make you think twice about really wanting something that big to hit your plug. Being that the exciting moments in this style of fishing occur above water, it is possibly one of the most popular types of plug fishing.

The technique entails casting a plug as far as is humanly possible and then cranking it in like a wild man. The speed of the retrieval will raise the plug out of the water and cause it to splash violently on the surface. You don't want the plug to go too fast, just fast enough to make some disturbance and attract the fish's attention. If you see a fish coming at your skipping plug, don't stop cranking and working the plug. If you run out of water, then slow down. Once you've reached shallow water, immediately start jigging the rod tip right in front of the water's edge. Whatever you do, don't crank up and take the plug out of the water. Sometimes the sudden jigging will trigger some immediate strikes and you'll be in for some hot action.

Once while I was fishing a spot along the Kau coastline of the Big Island, I found myself in just this situation. I was working a stretch of coastline called Malama Flats, a smooth, *pāhoehoe* lava coastline with a radical cliffline and bottom. I was using a modified Mirro-Lure that weighed in the vicinity of 4 to 4½ ounces. It was loaded with lead shavings, and when it skipped along the surface it tore up the water like a panic-striken mullet. During one of about a hundred or so casts, I thought I saw a black mass come up, take a look at my splashing plug, and then quickly disappear. More than half way back the black mass rose again and followed very closely for a second or two.

It was definitely a big trevally, weighing in the area of sixty to seventy pounds. Not twenty yards from shore, the huge fish rose once more and this time it sped back and forth near the racing plug before it took the plug in one massive charge. I hauled back and tried to set the hook but felt no resistance. I kept cranking and the plug once again started its run back to me. Again the fish rose and charged the plug, and this time its gills and mouth were fully agape. By that time I had run out of water—the plug was at the shoreline. I quickly dropped the rod tip and began some erratic rod action. After I jigged the plug in a very convincing manner, the fish took the bouncing plug with a rush and the battle was on. I hauled back and the fish tore for the security of deep water. In ten seconds he seemed to have taken more then half of my line and was still heading for the horizon. In the next two seconds I felt my line rubbing against some coral far down in the water. The next second, the line cut. It seemed like a long battle, all thirty seconds of it. Although I lost the fish, if I had never tried the jigging technique, I would not even have a fish story to tell. Anyway, it was surely better than pulling the plug out of the water and watching the fish swim away.

For a technique like skipping, the plug has to be fairly heavy so that it can create a good amount of disturbance. The more disturbance, the more attention you'll get. Because of this many plugs that prove to be productive, such as the Mirro-Lure, are modified just for this purpose. Some of these skipping plugs may run two to five ounces in the end and cast like veritable bullets.

Surface Plugging for Big *Ulua*

The lure had a flattish, dug-out face and a huge pair of goggly eyes that made it look like a badly mutated fish. The face of the lure, which was very concaved, was designed for gulping or "blurping" huge gallons of water. It created a bubbling action that seemed to stimulate such predatory fish as the big *ulua, kāhala, 'ōmilu,* and barracuda into striking with absolutely no restraint. Being basically a surface action worker, the lure had a striking action that was just too incredible to believe. And that to me is where the thrill is—in the surface action and the frenzy that comes with working lures in tight little bays, across white water points, and in moderately shallow (twelve to fifteen feet) reef areas.

The *ulua* prowls and hunts in these areas and is constantly on the

An assortment of surface plugs *(top to bottom, left to right):* Bonne pencil popper, Pili, converted Rapala CD18, homemade stick popper, homemade broomstick surface popper, zig-zagger.

alert for a wounded minnow or reef fish, such as the mullet or the goatfish *(weke)*. It will roam in the white water curtains of rough points and cleverly hide in the watery fog so that it can ambush its prey with unyielding authority. Once the prey is found and seems easy enough to snatch, the *ulua* will come up in a frenzy and tear the lure from the surface with a mad ferociousness.

To be able to see the huge, silver-grey back of these Goliaths as they rise out of the white water and smash the lures on the surface is worth all the countless casts surface spinning demands. Both perseverance and determination are the key to surface chugging for big *ulua*.

The big ones are the ones that seem to really go for the surface chuggers. Although this is not to say that the smaller ten- and twelve-pounders don't rush up and take the plug, the majority of the action will come from the bigger thirty- to eighty-pounders. Why this is, I don't know. I can only speculate that the big *ulua* isn't afraid of the chugging and blurping of the lure, but is drawn to the plug's action like a moth to a flame.

The most productive method of working the surface plug is by chugging and pacing the plug on the surface. Lightly "chop" the rod to the left or right of you, all the while keeping a sharp eye on the amount of bubbles the lure is generating. If done right, this rod action should cause the lure to scoop large quantities of water and thereby produce huge blurps. Not too much, mind you; just enough to cause the plug to blurp or displace about a foot of water to the left or right. The next chug should drive the lure through the water again and to the other side of the retrieve path.

If the lure seems to be diving instead of chugging, the lure probably has not had time to come up to the surface. In instances like this, allow the lure to float back up to the surface before you begin working the rod tip. Sometimes these momentary pauses will attract some lightning quick responses from a fish that had doubts about striking the lure.

Unfortunately, a lot of anglers work a surface lure by simply drawing it along the surface and not chopping or working the rod. Make the plug walk along the surface and work the shoreline white waters and the coral-laden points. Sometimes I work a point for several casts and take my sweet time. If no fish shows and the area still looks hot, I try all different types of retrieve patterns. Initially I stick with the stop–go . . . stop–go method, but later I begin to change it a little.

The reason I vary my retrieves is fish never seem to favor one type of retrieve pattern. This is not to say that one pattern won't produce consistently; but some days the fish want something just a little different. So if an area isn't working but you feel that a fish is lurking, why not change patterns and see if the fish wants something with more speed and flash.

Sometimes I change the intensity of the rod action. I will work the chugger for two or three regular pulls and then drive the lure so that it takes a big gulp of water and really makes a big fuss. Once this is done I will drive the lure suddenly and very hard and fast. This causes the lure to really break up the surface and make a lot of commotion. Sometimes the lure will skip out of the water and jump in all different

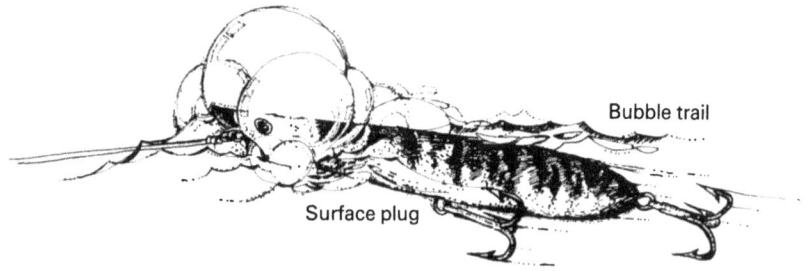

Work the surface plug hard and continuously. The bigger the bubble trail and commotion, the bigger the results.

directions—this is just what you want. Work the lure hard and fast to create a lot of hopping and skipping. This doesn't mean that you should crank fast but that you should work the rod tip faster and harder.

Another method which is radically different requires that the angler take sweeping pulls with the rod. After the cast, crank up until your line is taut, then pull the rod to the left or right in one long sweeping pull. This will drive the lure and leave a long bubble trail like that left by a small runaway torpedo. At the end of the sweep pattern, the lure should pause for a moment. With the next sweeping pull, drive and form another long bubble trail. Depending on the length of the cast, most anglers will get in about three or four good sweeps. Watch for strikes on the lingering pauses or just as a lure is beginning the forward sweep.

Since the strike always seems to come at strange times, constant awareness and a quick eye are mandatory for a fast setting of the hook. Once you have the strike, set the hook with authority. Bang the hook in four or five solid times to make sure the hook is set.

Spinning tackle is normally used for this type of fishing and is tailored for big line and heavy plugs. I use a Fenwick Graphite #GPS 106 spinning rod. It is 10½ feet long and is basically tailored to about 30- to 40-pound test. The reel, the Daiwa BG90, is loaded with 30- to 40-pound-test monofilament. Somehow when the fishing gets hot, the line always seems to develop kinks, weird twists, and a birdnest or two. So, extra spools are mandatory for quick changing and for maintaining your sanity. Have all the spinning leaders pre-tied and secured with rubberbands; that way when you need another spool, you're all ready to fish.

The rod and reel combination just discussed should be able to handle fish of a wide range of sizes. Given good terrain and well-tied knots, lots of fishing luck, and a good strike, you'll have a good chance of landing a fish over the fifty pound range. After they've gained experience and expertise, some anglers will consistently hook and land big fish that weigh in in the double digits.

Basically, all the surface chuggers on the market evolved from the original broomstick plug. One end of a broomstick (or dowel) was tapered and the other end made concave. A hook was attached to the lure, paint was lovingly applied to it, and a popper was born.

There is a wide selection of surface chugging plugs on the market. Of these are Cotton Cordell's Striper Pencil Popper, Cordell's Near Nuthing, the Hawaiian Pili (made in Hawaii), Heddon's Chugger

Spook, and Boone's Chugger. Although they all weigh from about 1 1/2 to 2 ounces and have big concaved faces, each plug is different and will have its own movements. But they all work as long as you have faith and work the rod tip properly. It is the job of the individual angler to find the style of retrieve that will produce the optimal lure action.

The best *ulua* plugs are blue and green, and backed with silver-yellow bellies. Red- and pink-colored plugs seem to produce in the early morning hours, but as the day wears on, the blues and greens dominate in the action.

One of your primary considerations when purchasing a surface lure should be its construction. Since it will be attracting large gamefish, the plug will be in for some heavy assaults and tremendous stress. Many a plug has been literally torn to pieces after a fish has taken a liking to its color and commotion.

The hooks should be secured to the body of the lure with some strong internal wiring system. That way, if one hook tears loose, it will be secured by another hook and on to the forward eye of the plug. Even if the lure is actually torn to pieces the angler will still have the fish. You can always get another lure, and you don't want to loose a fish because of a weak one. This will happen many times until you reinforce lures you now have, or find a solid lure you like.

Besides having an internal wiring system, some lures have "screw eyes," and others have split rings. Both are relatively weak (the latter is the weaker of the two) and tend to get either pulled completely out or ripped apart. Split rings are notorious for opening up. The only way to make sure one will hold is to add a back-up split ring and hope for the best. If enough stress is applied to them, both rings will get torn apart. Some anglers go to the extreme of welding split rings shut with small torches. This takes an enormous amount of time and effort. Another option would be to cut the hook's eye, spread it open, and secure it through the eye of the lure. When the hook is secured, the eye of the hook will be forced shut. Once again one must always hope for the best.

The split ring may not give out and the hook eye may not open, but the hook itself may bend back and lose you another fish. Treble hooks aren't very strong and bend open relatively easily. Some treble hooks have actually been smashed together by the intensity of a strike. Others have been bent inward by a strike, forming a hook that resembles a pretzel.

As you can see, the surface plug has to withstand a great deal of abuse. Big fish seem to eat it without any hesitation. They seem to be drawn to the blurping sounds, the vibrations, and the erratic walking movements of a well-worked plug. So if you are an angler with strong determination, well-maintained tackle, a strong wrist, and a great deal of optimism, the surface plug is for you. The action is there if you want the big *ulua*. And the action you will witness while surface plugging will not be quickly forgotten.

    I recall one trip that I went on with Stan Wright and Jeff Konn of Aloha Airlines. We were after BIG *ulua* and so decided to use surface lures that would make a big ruckus. We ventured into some coves and harbors and started to work our lures along the surface of the choppy water. We concentrated on the white water areas of the coves and rocky points. I made one cast in a shallow area of a bay and worked the lure so that it made loud, bubbly blurps. I worked the lure about five feet before a big *ulua* came up and took it with a smashing pass. Stan stood mesmerized for a moment and then started shouting at me to set the hook. I slammed the hook home with a series of quick pulls of the rod. Within seconds the fish had much of my line and was quickly making for the safety of the deep water. As the battle raged, I kept the skipper on the flying bridge always apprised of where the fish was and of what was happening. This allowed him to make quick steering decisions. We started to chase the fish down. I kept up as much pressure on my end of the rod as I dared, hoping that the hook wouldn't let go. Stan kept close to me and coached me for what seemed like hours. Soon the fish was in deep water and we were right over it. It felt like I had a hook caught on the bottom: I couldn't budge the stubborn fish. I worried about the line, split rings, rod, hooks—a multitude of things. Luckily they all held under all the pressure. The 30-pound line whistled as I strained on the rod. The fish was coming up slowly. Very slowly.

    The battle raged on for over forty minutes and had left a permanent kink in my back. I knew the end of the battle was near when I sighted silver shining back at me. It looked beautiful and turned an iridescent blue as it slowly became larger and larger in the deep blue water. The stand-up battle was getting to me, as the boat kept swaying with the swells that constantly work on the island.

    The Bimini Twist Knot peeked over the water's surface. The double line was close and the fish was almost within clear view. Because I knew my double line and leader line were almost twenty feet long, I also knew the fish was just that distance below the surface. I heaved and hauled the big fish. Soon the double line was completely out of the water and so was most of the leader. I could see very clearly the silvery-white *ulua* as it fought the relentless pull of the monofilament. The fish lay on its left side and swam slowly away from the looming form of the boat. Suddenly the fish took a short but sustained run diagonally downward, taking line with incredible ease. I held the spool of the spinning reel with my left hand and watched as the line melted from the spool. The Bimini Twist was once again out of sight. The battle kept up and my left arm began to ache with a deep stabbing pain. I slowly and steadily worked the fish back up to the double line and eventually got the leader into the rod and into the reel's spool. Once I had the leader, I was determined not to relinquish it, not for all the lures in the store.

The fish was just under the surface of the water, its mouth agape and gills beating as it sloshed water over them. It was totally drained and so was I. I walked the fish to the stern and Timmy gaffed it with a perfect shot under the gills. The fish was mine. It weighed thirty-seven pounds and was a true trophy for me. Later we looked for the lure and found it deep in the fish's gullet.

The afternoon was far from over so we continued to work productive-looking points. We turned up more monster *ulua* with the technique we had settled on. Several came up and took plugs right in the white water, whereas others smashed lures in water less than eight feet deep. The day ended with more smashing strikes and several torn and mangled lures. The adrenalin was definitely flowing and we wanted to tangle with more of these big bruisers, but the day was getting short and so we decided to clip our lines and put away our rods.

On the way back to Maui I kept seeing the big grey back of the *ulua* come up out of the white water to smash the popping lure from the surface of the water. I was already planning what my next trip there would be like. I wanted more big fish but, even more, I wanted to see the incredible surface strikes that come with working surface plugs. For the thrill—that is the only way to go.

Jigging and Deep Jigging from Shore

Jigs are of the oldest but most dependable lures that you could possibly purchase. When the Navy was looking for the ideal lure for their survival fishing kits, they needed one that was easy to use and that brought results. They chose the jig as their standard lure. The jig has

THE ART OF WHIPPING THE SHORELINE

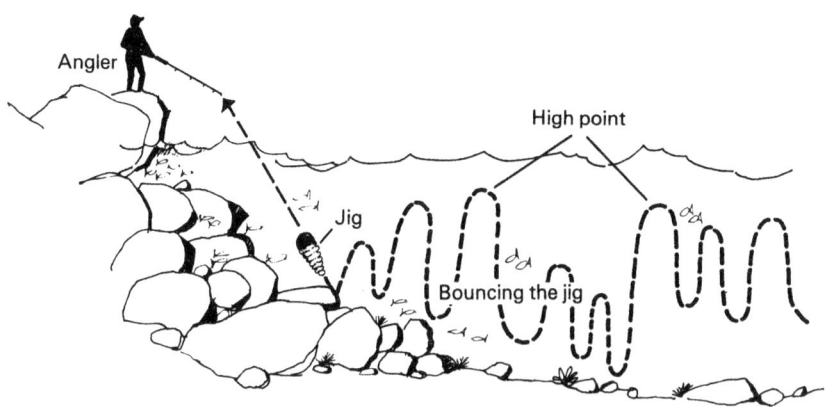

Deep jigging from shore. Try to visualize the jig as you work the bottom. Be patient and constantly on the alert.

a simple construction and is inexpensive in comparison to all other lures. But best of all it produces fish consistently.

Working a jig is much the same as working a plug in that it can be twitched, bounced, and danced until a fish is teased into taking the lure. But one of the attributes of the jig is that the hook rides up and thus is less likely to snag on the ocean bottom when worked in deep waters.

Deep jigging is usually done by offshore fishermen when they feel they have a structure to work, such as a sharp drop-off, a reef, or a sunken wreck, which usually harbors many fish. Basically in deep jigging the jig is allowed to sink straight down and bounce off the bottom. Then it is slowly worked to the surface. In shoreline deep jigging, you cast out and let the jig sink, all the time letting line come off the reel. Once the jig is down deep enough, you engage the reel and begin jerking the rod in a strong upward movement. Drop the rod tip and let the jig sink back down after the jerk. Once the line becomes taut, jerk or twitch the rod tip up again, and at the same time crank in a little line. The procedure is repeated over and over until the jig gets to the shoreline and you can pull it out.

It's a good idea to work the jig in shallow water first. This will help you determine whether you're doing it right or not. Make the jig jump upward suddenly and then let it spiral down a foot or two. Repeat this action. The erratic motion will draw a lot of attention. When a lot of fish begin to congregate around the jig, some competition

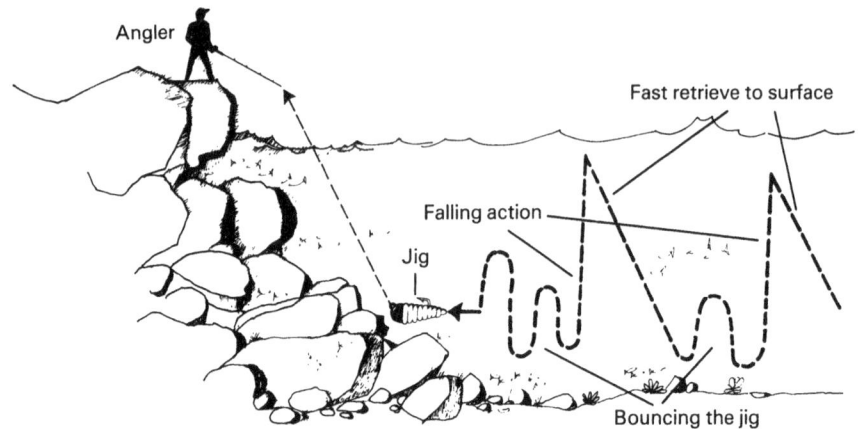

Try to vary the deep jigging action by zipping the lure to the surface and then letting it fall. Be constantly aware of the sinking jig

among the fish will ensue. This competition will be so stimulating that you'll hook some of the weirdest fish you could ever imagine. Some of the fish will be small and not quite qualify as gamefish, but the action will be steady and exciting.

When you're jigging in shallow water, try all different types of jigging patterns and remember the jigging routine after you've made a long cast. Repeat the routine and if it doesn't produce results, change to another and then another until you hit on a routine that draws strikes.

What do you look for in deep-jigging grounds? Well, first of all, the grounds should be deep and the shoreline should allow you to be right up to its edge. If the area is deep outside and very shallow several yards out, chances are you'll hook the ledge when the jig gets close. The only way to avoid hooking the ledge is to jig out in the deep and quickly retrieve the jig when you figure you're getting too close to the drop-off.

Actually any grounds you might feel is poor for surface whipping can still be worked if you use the jig. You can try to work the surface and if nothing happens, go into the deep-jigging routine. In this way you work the area very thoroughly and get the most out of your time. But, all in all, the water in the area should be deep (twenty to forty feet or more). Even if the area is rough and the white water climbs the cliff, you can work the white water—or I should say work under the white water—very effectively. Under the white water is a prime area and shouldn't be ignored at all. A lot of times you get some terrifying strikes that will wrench your arm out of its socket when the jig gets close to you. Keep alert, keep your eyes glued to the line as it enters the water, and all the while keep a mental picture of what the jig is doing on the bottom.

Working the Spoon

A spoon's chief job is to wobble and shine. While trying to wobble the spoon, you'll find that if you retrieve the spoon too fast you'll loose the shine and the spoon will start skipping. Spoons need to be worked a little slower and more carefully than do plugs. You'll also find that spoons have to be worked pretty much from low places. Spoons work poorly in areas that have very high cliffs because they will hydroplane on the surface most of the time and give you very poor results.

Once again, the spoon, like the plug, can be worked in rapid jerks and twitches. When worked with rapid jerks, the spoon will give off some wild flashes and create a disturbance in the water much like that created by a propeller. Its vibrations will easily be picked up by predatory fish quite a distance away. Once they have traced the sound and see the flashing spoon, they usually respond very favorably. The fish will think that the flashing spoon is a wounded minnow slowly dying on the surface. If you watch a dying mullet closely, you'll see that it swims in a very erratic pattern; that is, it seems to twitch and pause as it swims, reacting to spasms of oncoming death. When it occasionally spins in the water, it creates a flash. The spoon is supposed to create the same flash.

With this in mind, when a fish approaches the spoon, I usually keep up the same rapid pattern of twitches and jerks with the rod tip. If it turns away from the spoon, I immediately stop and let the spoon twinkle to the bottom. Sometimes this total stop will trigger some quick responses. Even better would be to give the spoon a wild slashing jerk after the first six to seven seconds of its descent. A lot of times the fish will run up to the flashing spoon and turn away, only to quickly turn back and smash the wildly rising and sinking spoon.

Again, when worked from high cliffs and piers, the spoon doesn't seem to work very favorably. In these areas the best method to use is the "full sinking and jigging" method. As is similarly done in deep jigging, the spoon is permitted to sink almost to the bottom and then brought back up with sweeping pulls of the rod and reel. The sawtooth pattern that results is deadly, but the method requires a lot of

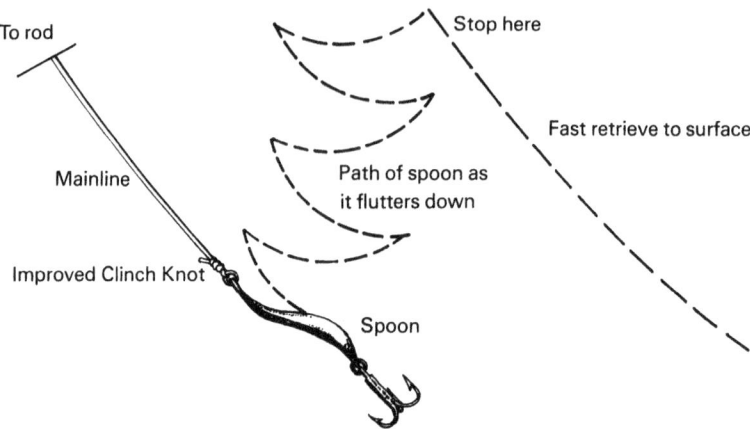

Deep jigging a spoon is a very productive method to fall back on if all other patterns don't work.

concentration on the part of the fisherman. As in deep jigging, the spoon is out of sight and you have to keep a mental picture of what the spoon is doing on the bottom or in midwater.

Being that a spoon twinkles to the bottom like a coin in a wishing well, you'll find that it takes a longer time to get to the bottom than does a jig, which plummets straight to the bottom. The spoon will wobble first to the right and then wobble slowly to the left. Imagine a spoon slowly shine its way to the bottom, make a wild dash for the surface, and then make a twinkling descent to the bottom once again. After it sinks for a five- to six-second count again, it dashes for the surface. The spoon has one very prominent trait: it is constantly working whether you work it or not. When it's sinking, the spoon is shining just as much as when you're retrieving it. If used properly, it is a very hard-working lure. What's more, much like the skipping plug, the spoon can simply be jigged vertically right at your feet.

Once when fishing on the northwest shores of the Big Island, I got some frantic chases from some fair-sized *moano*. I was retrieving my small, gold Kastmaster spoon over a shallow coral reef. Many of the fish followed the spoon until it got close to my feet; then they disappeared down a ledge. After watching a half dozen or so dive down into this shallow pocket without taking my spoon, I decided to drop my spoon directly into the pocket. I merely dropped the spoon from the rod tip and watched as the spoon twinkled down. No sooner had the spoon reached the bottom than two spunky *moano* rushed out and attacked the tiny spoon. I twitched the tip and quickly hooked a small but scrappy *moano*. I managed to take three *moano* from that pocket, and I successfully worked other similar channels and pockets for more fish. I merely dropped or short-cast my tiny $1/_{12}$-ounce gold spoon into small pockets and bounced the lure on the bottom.

A lot of times a tiny piece of shrimp skin or skin of any small reef fish will greatly add to the effectiveness of a bouncing spoon. Skin from jumping jacks *(pao'o)* are especially effective and will stay on a hook for a very long time. You might even use the tip portion (approximately a half inch) of a cuttlefish's tentacle.

Daily Fishing Patterns

The mark of a good fisherman is adaptability. He knows from past experience that down at the beach, each day is a totally new experience. The moon and tides are never entirely the same, even if the calendar says otherwise. Solunar tables, tide charts, and other charts fishermen may rely on really provide only rough estimates; thus you have to adapt yourself to the different requirements of each day and be able to change lures on the spur of the moment. Also, you have to try all different types of retrieve patterns until you hit on the pattern that seems to be bringing up fish. Second, you should experiment with lures of various colors until you hit on a hot color. This constant mental checking and testing of techniques and lures all contribute to the abilities of the angler.

A good fisherman will catch fish even when circumstances change unexpectedly because he knows how to adapt his tackle and technique to different situations. A lot of times an angler will bring two or more types of gear and leave himself open to more styles and techniques. Many bass fishermen keep several types of rod and reel combinations completely rigged and set just for certain circumstances and situations. For instance, one set might consist of spinning reel and rod loaded for ultralight casting and small plugs. The second rod and reel set might be rigged for conventional bait casting and worm presentation. The third set, for spinner baits and surface running. This leaves the angler ready and able to adapt to the requirements of any set of circumstances.

It is much the same with the shoreline whipper. He should be able to change line, lure, and retrieve technique on the spur of the moment. If you watch a good whipper at work, you'll see someone who will change his technique at every new point or drop-off. The computer in his head will call up a past experience in which a point very much like the one he's working produced fish. He'll try the lure-and-retrieve technique at this point, and if it doesn't work again he'll try others until he's satisfied that the fish either just aren't interested or are simply not around.

Confidence and the artifical lure is a curious thing: they go hand in hand, even if the lure looks like nothing that lives in the sea. The key is to have confidence in the plug to make it produce. Someone who has this confidence will always produce fish because he knows how to work and use his plug properly. Once he has learned to work his plug and has caught fish with it, he'll use it more and more. With constant practice, he'll learn a greater variety of techniques; he'll add to his mental arsenal until he's so confident he'll be able to work the plug in just about any situation and under any circumstances.

So learn to use every lure that you can find and learn to use each one properly. This means working each plug in several different ways and using different techniques. Some plugs or lures have multiple uses and some don't. Learn the capabilities and limitations of each.

8
Slide-Bait Fishing

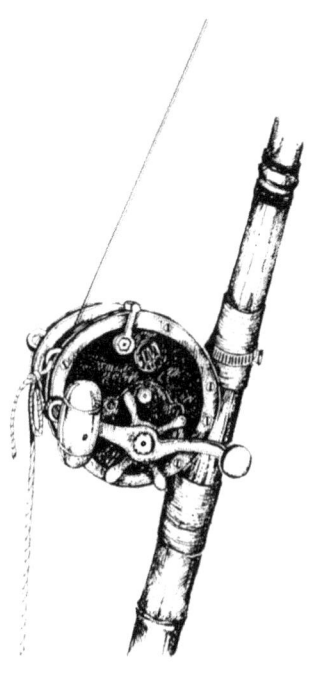

Slide-bait fishing is similar to what mainlanders call trolley line fishing. The technique is simple: all you do is cast out a set type of leader and after the line is secured to the bottom, slide down a rigged line that has a sliding swivel and a baited hook.

In Hawaii, the technique has been refined and is more sophisticated. What's more, a variation of this technique has evolved on each island to accommodate extremes of terrain. Some bottom areas, such as those on Maui and Kauai and around Honolulu, are primarily crushed coral; therefore, less is demanded of slide-bait leaders and techniques. But on the island of Hawaii great demands are made on the angler and his tackle. There the bottom terrain has masses of coral gardens, lava boulders, and lava ledges that sit on the edges of steep drop-offs. The Big Island leader must also be relatively easy to make, reasonably priced, and above all it has to work.

It is also imperative that the leader has a long anchorline, mainly because of the abundance of moray eels that prowl the coral beds. An anchorline ten or twelve feet long is not unusual. The anchorline must be weaker than the mainline. In other words, if you use 80-pound test, your anchorline would have to test around 60 or 50 pounds. If its line test is more than the mainline, when the fish strikes the bait and runs, the mainline will cut first and you'll lose your fish. Some anglers use cheap bulk spools of monofilament, whereas others use cheap box string or cotton cord for their anchorline. It is purely for the individual angler to decide what to use, and this decision is usually determined by his past practices and his pocketbook.

In Hawaii, the leader material is usually heavy monofilament, say, 300- to 400-pound test. Anglers of the past used seven-strand Sevalon or braided steel line. The seven-strand normally tested around 90 pounds and stood up to a lot of abuse, but it still had a tendency to cut under severe stress. It would also eventually rust and become kinky or curly, and hard to cast through the guides. However, because its diameter was small it was easy to crank into the reel.

Primarily because it couldn't be used too long and had to be replaced after several strikes or trips, in the long run the Sevalon also tended to be a little on the expensive side. Then a group of innovative fishermen tried using the monofilament that the deep-sea trollers used. It was much thicker in diameter and was also much less expensive. The monofilament didn't kink as the seven-strand did, and it lasted for many more trips and strikes. Being that the monofilament tested in the area of 350 pounds, the chances of a big fish cutting the line on sharp coral was minimal. After a lot of field testing and after many, many *ulua* were brought up, the line had proved itself. More and more anglers moved away from using the Sevalon and began using the thicker monofilament.

This monofilament's only drawback was that its larger diameter made it a little harder to crank into the reel. To offset this, some anglers went to lines that tested around 200- to 250-pound test. These lines still stood up to the amount of abuse that leaders normally take when used in harsh environments. Other anglers didn't have faith in the smaller test monofilament and stayed with the heavier leader lines, though these lines added a little more bulk to the reel.

The Stop Ring

The stop ring section of the leader rig is very unique in itself. Its purpose is twofold: first, it must bring the slide buckle to a complete stop, and second, it must keep the slide buckle from going back up the line. The idea is to keep the fish in the strongest test area and away from the mainline. To meet this need Hawaii anglers devised the "pigtail," which is connected to the stop ring section. All it is, is a section of the wire leader that is allowed to stick out and that is later bent in toward the wire section of the line. This small, curled back section on the wire leader stops the slide buckle from going back up the line. It is effective and doesn't take that much time to make.

In actuality the stop ring section, which is only about five to six inches long (some anglers make it even shorter), is a smaller version of the Oahu slide-bait rig. The only difference is that the Oahu leader rig is about three feet long, but it still has the stop ring pigtail and stop rings. And being that the rig has one #2/0 barrel swivel on the top and is three feet long, it cannot be cranked into the tip top. So what the Big Island rig is, is a combination deep-sea trolling rig and standard Oahu slide-bait rig. As two ideas in one, it works very well.

The double-line knots (Bimini Twist and Spider's Hitch) are the standard knots used by billfishermen. The Albright Knot is also used mostly by offshore trollers and was invented by offshore fishermen. But these knots have worked wonders on the shore fisherman's rigs and have proven themselves with more than one fish. (See Chapter 4, "Monofilament and Monofilament Knots.")

Working the Baits

Ulua fishing is sometimes called work mainly because one must deal with the ever-present moray eel. Sometimes as soon as you slide down your bait, an eel will be on it trying to pull it into his hole. It can be very frustrating to hear your bell clanging away right after you've made your cast and have slid the bait. But if you wish to land an *ulua* or any big gamefish, you will have to pull up your line and recast the entire rig again.

Recasting takes time and effort. Sometimes rods are situated very close together and recasting can become a real chore. Also, some people have a really hard time recasting at night and tend to cast far to the right or left of where their lines originally were. Lines can quickly become crossed and tangled, and sometimes other anglers have to come out to the point and recast or help untangle the mess. This can get frustrating at times, but with some determination and luck, you can get your line back out and the bait slid down again with no trouble at all. Once you've tried it, you'll find that night casting is entirely different from day casting: the control that you had during the daylight hours completely escapes you at night; the lead will go everywhere but where you want it to; and your thumb will seem to get burned more often. A good idea is to get in a lot of casting practice during the evening hours.

Some anglers will work several rods during a trip. Some will use two rods, and some up to seven rods at a time. This can really become work and by the late evening hours leave you ready for the funny farm. Some anglers insist on using a half dozen rods and work the entire night, hoping beyond hope that one of the rods will go off with a great big bang. Most of the time they'll produce fish; but fishing is supposed to be fun and relaxing and not a part-time marathon. The standard number of rods to use is usually two and sometimes even just one.

What some anglers do is rotate their casts. They will recast a rig after about two to two and a half hours because the bait can become stale and unappetizing to the *ulua*. Once the rod is hauled up and everything is recast, bait is slid down again and at least an hour is allowed to elapse before the second rod is checked or hauled up. By allowing some time to pass between casts, the angler can have fresh bait down all the time. Since the baits are staggered, the angler will always have at least one bait that is either on the way down or that is down, still fresh, and ready for a prowling *ulua*.

You'll find that a serious angler will watch the clock very closely. Every once in awhile he will get up, pull up a rod, slide his bait, and then come back to sit down to a cup of coffee. He'll repeatedly slide fresh baits and repeatedly recast lines throughout the night, but he'll also allow himself time to kick back and relax. If he gets a strike, he'll have enough energy to fight the fish and continue to recast.

To some, this may seem like really hard, and at times unnecessary, work, but if you want to catch fish, this is the price you've got to pay. The fresher the bait, the greater the possibility of a big strike on your rod.

Fishing for *Ulua*

On every island, the terrain determines what style the angler should use with fighting fish. For instance, a Maui angler will let his fish run to its heart's content and actually kill itself outside. The reason for letting the fish run and take line is the fish can then move beyond all the lines, and in this way the angler can avoid entangling his line with others. For Maui, this type of fish fighting is feasible mainly because of the abundance of sand and pebbles there. The fishermen don't have to worry about their lines being cut on sharp coral, or about large boulders their fish may try to hide beneath.

When the Maui angler has a strike his main concern is setting the hook properly. This means getting to the rod right away and banging in the hook as soon as possible. For this reason he'll permit any angler close by to pick up his rod and set the hook for him. This is contrary to the IGFA (International Game Fish Association) angling rules, which specifically state that the angler must hook (and set the hook) by himself. On Maui, it is important not to lose the fish because of a poorly set hook.

If you are fishing in deep water and the area has a lot of boulders and sharp coral, the fish-fighting technique is a little different. The large outcroppings of coral and rocks will leave the fish little free running room. This is not to say that the Big Island angler, for example, doesn't allow his fish to run; he just doesn't let the fish take line without keeping tension on the rod. Once the fish stops and the line is free and unobstructed, the fish is battled up to the gaff as soon as possible.

If your fish should stop his all out run and come to a slow halt, you might feel the mainline rubbing against some kind of obstruction. If this happens, don't put all your efforts into pulling the fish up. Allow the fish more line and hope that the fish clears the obstruction by itself. If you should keep pulling a line that is stuck, it will invariably cut and the fish will be gone. So your best bet is to keep feeding line to the trapped fish. Because in this method fresh line replaces frayed line at the point of contact, the chances of eventually sawing the line off are slim. If the fish is stuck, you'll lose nothing by waiting the fish out.

Usually what is happening on the bottom is the fish is still swimming free and pulling against the still lodged line. It'll swim left and right of the obstruction until it either frees itself, cuts the line, or dies in the effort. But after swimming to the left and right of the obstruction, the fish will usually clear itself and the line will suddenly relax. Once this happens work the fish as hard as you can. Monofilament can withstand a lot of stress. As long as you pull or work the fish in smooth sweeping arcs and don't jerk the rod in erratic motions, you'll be able to bring the fish up to gaff. If the line should once again become entangled, feed the fish more line and repeat this procedure.

There are many things that happen when you fight big fish on heavy tackle and they all require careful and quick thinking. Most of the time you should have someone close by coaching you along throughout the battle. In the heat of a long battle, many anglers cannot think straight and at times don't know their own strength, so the help of the person coaching often proves invaluable.

Sometimes the anchorline will get lodged in the rocks and the already weakened fish will not be able to break the line. The fish will feel like it is stuck and will dive into the rocks in a last ditch effort. Even when you feed it line the fish may not take. You'll have to make a decision. Some anglers will try to cut the anchorline and hope that nothing else breaks. Sometimes this works and sometimes it doesn't.

Other times several lines may get tangled and the fish may come up the line on another pole. If another angler's fish is tangled on your rod, you both should work the tangle out if possible. The other angler may decide to cut his line and hope that you will be able to bring up his fish. If that isn't possible, you might pull up his line and bring up the entangled *ulua* with him. Sometimes, because this is against the club's by-laws, the fish will be subject to forfeit. Still, you will have the fish, and you both can share in the catch; otherwise you both get nothing anyway.

One of the most frustrating things that can happen in *ulua* fishing is the slide gaff will get tangled up with the mainline on its descent. The gaffman may get too anxious and slide the gaff down in such a way that it could only get tangled. The gaff will not be able to go down or come back up. Trying to pull the gaff up the line could easily lead to a cut line, either because of the weight of the fish or because the gaff itself may cut the line. This is one dilemma that has confronted many a fisherman. The only thing to do is to get a second gaff and hook the fish with another rod. Some anglers use a star hook from a fishing plug or spoon and hook the fish with that. Once this is done, they slide down the second gaff and, with luck, hook the entangled fish. When the fish is brought up, they untangle the mess and get ready for the next strike.

Fighting the Ulua

Once the fish is on the line and running, there is hardly anything that can be done. The best thing to do is to simply let the fish run—but with a controlled drag. Monitor the quantity of line being taken and keep the line coming off the spool smoothly.

After the fish has run off quite a bit of line, the drag washers will begin to heat up and the drag will automatically begin to tighten up. The best thing to do then is loosen the drag a little as the amount of line left on the spool diminishes. Too many anglers tighten the drag during a long and powerful run and quickly lose a big fish. It often times seems like the fish is going to run out all your line in nothing flat, but this is hardly the case with most fish. They will run a great deal mostly because they are in a terrible panic and the only thing that they can think of is getting away as quickly as they possibly can. It is at this point that they are strongest, and it is better to feed them line and let them expel most of their energy in that one fatal run. Most *ulua* will stop short of emptying the spool; but then again, some will empty it at the wink of an eye. You'll never see the latter since the run will happen so fast you'll have little time to think anything except "What's happening????"

When the fish is running, let the line out in smooth sweeps. If the reel is feeding out line in quick and sudden jerks, it means the drag washers are worn or glazed and it's time for a new set. More fish are lost due to a poorly maintained drag system than any other reason.

A lot of people say that you should hold the rod high and keep the tension on the running fish. Granted, you should keep the tension on the fish but the rod should be kept low and almost pointed toward the running fish. The rod should be used to lift the fish with smooth sweeping pulls, and the reel should allow the fish to take line before the line breaks. If the fish pulls, let the rod drop down and allow the fish to take line from the reel.

A rod that is held high and back requires more than double the reel's drag tension before the reel will release line. A rod that is pointed or slightly arched toward a running fish will permit the line to come off the reel at a much lower drag tension. Many anglers don't allow the reel to do its job, which is to allow for a controlled drag tension. A pre-set drag will be more than a fish can handle.

A good angler will be very receptive to what is happening at his end of the line. Most fish will get very active before a sudden run. Some fish wag their heads back and forth and then, panic stricken, make a sudden dash. If it's the fish's second run, it'll most likely be short and powerful. Subsequent runs will become shorter and shorter. Each time it decides to make a quick run, let the fish pull the rod tip down and allow the reel to pay out line. The fish will become more and more tired with each run and you'll have it defeated.

Once the leader has reached the rod tip you'll be very close to landing the fish. Work the fish slowly and carefully and keep your wits about you. Many fish are lost at the gaff. Once the leader gets to the rod and eventually into the reel, you've got the fish. Unless the fish is very, very green, you should not let the fish take the leader out of the reel and back into the mainline. The leader is the strongest part of the line and you should never forgo taking advantage of it. Work the fish even harder once the leader is in. The leader should be very heavy, and it will take much more punishment. If the fish pulls out the mainline, you'll have to work the leader back in, and before you do that you may lose the fish; so once you have the leader you'll really be able to work the fish.

Tides: One Key to Ulua *Fishing*

Eventually every serious *ulua* fisherman starts searching for the elusive formula that will help him hook and land the super shoreline gamefish, the *ulua*. The mere fact that the *ulua* is out there isn't enough for the fisherman who has tasted the thrill of battling such a powerful shorefish.

Now, the serious angler will search for the veteran fisherman that has the most impressive record and subtly try to pick his brain for the elusive answer. Some will tell you that the way to land *ulua* consistently is to constantly *palu* the shoreline. The old Hawaiians caught *ulua* this way (see "Moray Eel," Chapter 5), and when done properly *palu*ing yields some huge *ulua*.

Others say that the type of bait is the key. Some fishermen have so-called secret baits and secret ways of preparing the bait that will draw the *ulua* and make him strike. Some fishermen attach the bait by sewing it to the hook or by securing it with rubberbands or even small copper wire. All this to help keep the precious baits alive longer. Other fishermen merely use small hooks on the bait to keep the bait lively. Each fisherman has his own small contrivance that he feels will lead him to the promised land of hooking more and bigger *ulua*.

Other more influential fishermen keep the fishing site their prime secret. They retain access to special private lands and wisely guard their secrets. They too have their own style of bait preparation and special styles of fishing for the crafty *ulua*.

When you look at any *ulua* club record of fish brought in, you'll find that fish have been landed in every conceivable spot in the island chain, from small narrow channels that lead into some of the most traffic-strewn harbors to the most remote private lands imaginable. *Ulua* don't live in just one kind of environment; they seem to live and feed in any place that yields food and that has some easy means of escape. *Ulua* have been seen shimmying across shallow reeflines with their backs just barely covered with water, or even lying on their sides and wiggling themselves over extremely shallow sand flats. It seems that with very little effort they will go to extremes to get to the places that will yield baitfish. They have been known to follow scuba divers and pick off some strung *kole* (surgeonfish) or *mamo*. If the scuba diver plays his cards right, he will have the opportunity to spear a real trophy.

Other fishermen are compulsive about maintaining their fishing tackle, and they purchase nothing but the very best. Rods are imported, custom tailored, carefully wrapped and placed in velvet casings that are like rod sacks, and soaped and scrubbed after every trip. Some *ulua* fishermen try to find the ultimate in fishing reels and even purchase Penn International 50Ws or the costly Fin Nor's. Pflueger-Templar 400s and 500s are prized trophies. If you're lucky enough, you'll find a long lost uncle that has an Atlapac in mint condition and still in an oily sack and in its box. The quality of Atlapacs and Templars are never questioned. Unfortunately, they are no longer in production and consequently parts are impossible to obtain.

You'll also find countless leader systems for *ulua*. Fishermen on each and every island construct leaders in a very concise manner, but often times the designs differ because there are a variety of shoreline environments in the islands. Kauai, for instance, with its sandy and rolling surf requires long rods and lighter and smaller reels. The leaders aren't too critical due to the abundance of sand on the bottom. In sharp contrast to this, the shoreline of the Big Island is so rough and treacherous that leaders of less than 200 pounds are a waste of time. Even the mainline standard is 80 pounds. With this type of shoreline where the cliffs are high and rugged, Big Islanders don't need to have long rods to clear the rolling surf break; they need short powerful rods to stop rampaging *ulua* from streaking off to the Lanai coastline or diving to boulder-strewn bottoms so common there.

Some resourceful individuals will try to "hyperdevelop" their leader systems by adding small innovations to them. For example, some use toilet paper to increase the anchorline length. About thirty to fifty feet of discarded monofilament or cotton cord is wound around a rolled section of toilet paper. Both ends are half hitched and connected to the ends of the lead and split rings. Once the cast is made the toilet paper begins to melt and the anchorline is fed out systematically (see "Toilet Paper Rig," Chapter 4). Theoretically, the bait will be kept high off the bottom and out of harm's way; that is, the *puhi* won't be able to get at the high swinging bait. The roaming *ulua,* however, will have easy access to the delectable bait.

There are countless other ideas, some entail using the small wire twist locks that tie plastic breadbags, and others use paper clips. All of these work to some extent, but they don't really get you fish very consistently.

So what factors in all successful *ulua* fishing ventures? The answer to that question is *tides*. Above all else tides determine whether you hook a fish or not. Some very determined fishermen have been compiling incredible amounts of tide information for years and years. Some records go back to just before the 1950s, and to this day these have been judiciously kept. The information that comes out of this type of research is astonishing, to say the least. These records show the time and place a fish was caught, the tide and the moon phase at that time, the type of bait used, and the size of the fish landed. But the key point that seems to stand out is the tide.

Moon phases have a lot to do with tides, but whether the moon is full or new, the *ulua* will feed. The movement of the water is the determining factor. It seems that the *ulua* feeds most heavily during the slack period of the tide, when there is almost no movement at all. It doesn't matter if the tide is at its highest point or at its lowest, the *ulua* will bite or feed most heavily when the tide is not moving, that is, between tide shifts.

Some *ulua* fishermen, like Melvin Yamanaka, slide bait during the slack low tide. He has had most of his strikes at this time, and for this reason he has the most confidence in this period for *ulua* fishing. This is not to say, however, that he doesn't fish during the coming of the slack. Other fishermen, such as Albert Alejandro, fish only during the prime *ulua* season (approximately six months, from late Spring to early Fall) and will consistently land over five hundred pounds of *ulua* a year. He also fishes almost exclusively during the slack tide. He will rest and prepare while waiting for the coming of the next high or low tide.

According to some record, the strike will come almost precisely when forecasted. It's really odd. The bait will be slid down and the strike will come almost exactly when the slack starts or just minutes after the water becomes still. That is the key. The fish begin feeding when the water isn't moving. The idea is almost too simple to believe and yet the results prove that the *ulua* will feed heaviest when the tide is not moving.

But then again, could it just be coincidence? Could it be that the fish are there at the right time and at the right place? Could it be that more bait is slid at this time and therefore the percentage of strikes are naturally greater? Other facts that came out of the studies show that most of the strikes occurred between five and eleven o'clock in the evening. The main reason for this is that at five most *ulua* fishermen are at their liveliest and are hustling their hardest; by eleven and twelve they are either making their last slide or are already in dreamland.

So what is truly the common factor among *ulua* hook-ups? Some say (and have proven it in fish pounds) that fishing by the tide is the key. Others believe it is the full moon or quarter moon. Still others believe it is the type of bait preparation and even the type of fruits you bring or don't bring. The records suggest one small glimmer of an answer. Now it is up to you to personally put it to the test.

Gaffs

Slide Gaff

One of the important developments to spring from the cliffline style of *ulua* fishing is a method of gaffing and successfully landing a big fish from a very, very high cliff. Since most of the fishing on the Big Island is done from high cliffs, fishermen there have had to devise a way to get a gaff down. What they invented was a sliding gaff that actually slid down the mainline and stopped at the floating fish. For obvious reasons, this gaff was called a "sliding gaff" or "slide gaff." Mainlanders use a similar type of gaff called a "bridge gaff," which also has a line guide system. The bridge gaff is very much like a grapnel and has multiple gaff hooks; but its principle is the same as the slide gaff's.

The slide gaff is normally made of stainless steel and has only one gaff hook. Some anglers, like myself, prefer a slide gaff that has two hooks; some anglers look for three. Two, three, or one, it doesn't matter. The important thing is that the fish is successfully hooked and dragged up the cliff without anyone falling in while making the attempt.

The rope is usually quite long and should handle stress up to at least six hundred pounds. Polypropylene (yellow rope) is a good choice. All of its knots, however, should be made by braiding, not by

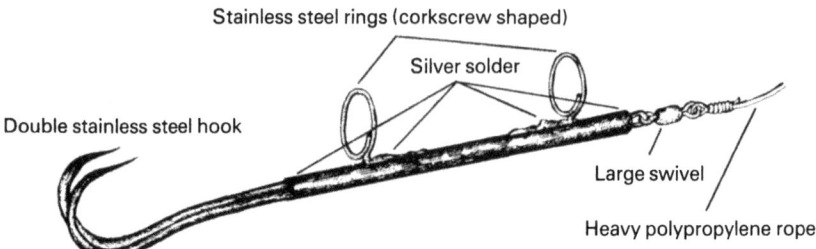

Slide Gaff. This gaff is almost unique to Hawaii. Its construction is very practical and it is also functionally perfect.

tying. Polypropylene is notorious for slipping, and could cause you to quickly lose your gaff and many a fish. However, polypropylene is easy to untie and easy to see in the dark. It is also inexpensive and will not rot like manila rope. Because it does tend to become slippery and hard to hold, especially if you're gaffing fish over seventy pounds, some fishermen tie knots all along the length of the rope to aid in holding the rope and in pulling.

When it is not being used, it is best to keep the slide gaff separate from the rope until you reach the beach and are setting up the rods and lines. Most anglers will purchase a brass snap, which has a built-in swivel that you can just snap on. It's a good idea to wrap some black tape over the snap area, so the gaff's snap doesn't work itself lose and cause you to lose your fish and the gaff at the same time. It takes a little time but will save a lot of grief later on.

All gaffs should have a rubber cap to protect anyone around from the gaff's sharp tips. The cap also keeps a sharp tip not in use from getting dug into a rock or car seat. The only problem is that some anglers forget to take off the rubber cap before they slide the gaff down. This makes for a difficult time in gaffing a fish but a good laugh on the way home. So check your gaff very carefully before you slide it down the line.

The proper way to slide a gaff and hook a fish is to work very carefully and as calmly as possible. In the frenzy of a strike it isn't easy to be calm, but with practice you will find the inner strength to manage it. Once the fish is in and floating, all you do is ask the angler to step back until the line comes to you. You can't go to the line because it is usually at least ten to twelve feet away from the cliffline. So ask the angler to step back and guide the line to you. He doesn't have to see the fish being gaffed. He should stay back and away from the edge. When you have the line, slide it into the gaff rings and be sure that they aren't tangled or put in backwards. Many a fisherman has put a gaff on backwards and lost a lot of time taking out the tangles he made.

After the line is in the gaff rings, gently let the gaff slide down the line. Don't push the gaff down the line to make it go down faster. If the gaff has enough weight, it'll work its way down to the fish in no time flat. The idea is not to let the gaff get tangled around the mainline. If it does as it's going down, you'll lose both the fish and the gaff. SO TAKE YOUR TIME WHEN SLIDING A GAFF.

Once the gaff is down and near the fish, gently lift the gaff until you feel some resistance. Don't jerk the gaff with the intention of stabbing the gaff hook into the fish. If a gaff is sharp enough, the hook will penetrate the fish as soon as it touches it. If a fish is about fifty pounds, that fifty pounds will more than drive the hook right through the body. Some gaffmen will wait for the weight and after they're sure that they have a good hook-up, they'll give the rope a good healthy jerk to send the hook home. But this really isn't necessary.

When the fish is gaffed and coming up the cliffline, the angler should always keep a good amount of slack in the line. This is to ensure that if the fish should drop off the gaff, it will fall down to the water without coming in contact with the angler's tight line. If a big fish drops and the angler has a locked drag and most of the line up with the fish, the sheer weight of the fish will drag him over the side. So keep the line slack and also loosen the drag. Once the fish is all the way up the cliff and safely on the rocks, then and only then should the angler begin to take up line.

Swivel Gaff

The swivel gaff is one of the simplest gadgets to use to land a fish. It does not actually gaff the fish; it gaffs the swivel. So if you're going to use a swivel gaff, use a swivel of the right size and shape. A barrel swivel is your best bet and is stronger than most swivels on the market. Also remember to use a leader (from the swivel to the plug or lure) that is heavy enough to haul up a fairly large fish. The length of the leader is not important, so long as it will not break from the sheer weight of the fish.

Much like a slide gaff, the swivel gaff slides down the mainline. It is worked until it locks the swivel between two bars. Then the line, along with the fish, is hauled up.

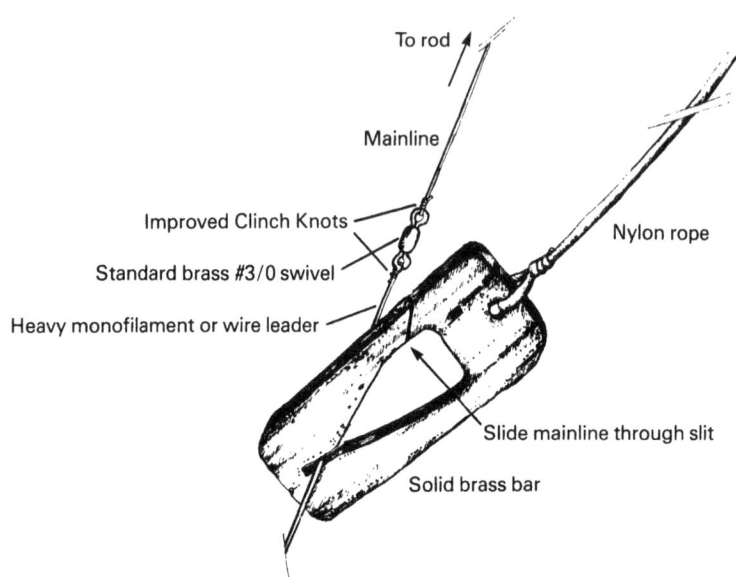

Swivel Gaff. This simple and practical gaff is easy to carry and very compact. The only requirement with this gaff is that the angler must use a swivel on the leader.

The best thing about a swivel gaff is its size and weight. It's small enough to put in a shirt pocket or the side pocket of a daypack, and it's light. It also doesn't have too many complicated gadgets that come loose. The next best thing about it is it doesn't have any dangerous sharp points and therefore doesn't need a cover or cap to keep you from gaffing yourself. Yet, it can land big fish if necessary.

Bamboo Pole Gaff

All a gaff does is hook fish. All that is really required, then, is a shaft of some sort and a good-sized hook. The hook has to be secured to the shaft so that when the fish is gaffed it won't slide off. A friend of mine used to land *ulua* with a bamboo rod blank about fourteen feet long. That was it. No fancy wrappings, no stainless steel wire running the length of the blank, and no fancy stainless steel hook. All he would bring along would be a single rod clamp, a bamboo pole, and a huge shark hook, which he would clamp to one end of the bamboo blank with the help of a pair of pliers. It would take him all of two minutes to make a gaff that you could tow a car with.

I kind of laughed under my breath the time I saw him put his "gaff" together. Now, I have seen many pole gaffs but this was the all-time

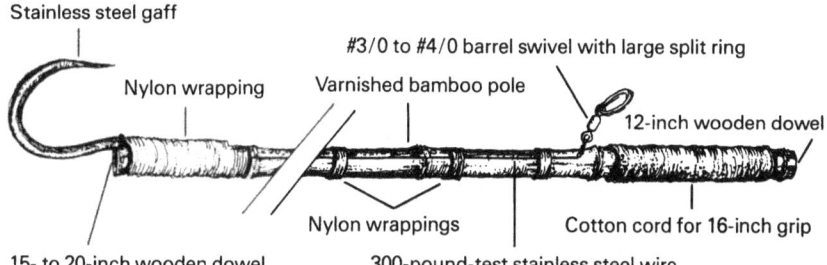

Hawaiian Pole Gaff. The point of the stainless steel gaff head should be triangular to facilitate better penetration and cutting. Wooden dowels should be inserted at both ends to reinforce the stalk. Nylon cord should be used to secure the gaff head to the end of the gaff, to secure the stainless steel wire along the shaft, and to strengthen the gaff pole. The stainless steel wire should be run up the entire length of the pole and secured to the gaff head. Attach rope to the stop ring. Cotton cord is wrapped around the butt section to form a grip. The bamboo stalk should be the finest you can find, and it should be cured at least a full year.

best. It was so basic that it looked almost primitive. But later that night we hooked a beautiful white *ulua,* and my friend gaffed and dragged it up the cliff and onto the rocks. It worked great, and to this day I have not once laughed at it again.

The pole gaff is definitely one of the most important pieces of fishing equipment you could either make or purchase. The most important single part of the pole gaff is the hook. IT MUST BE KEPT EXTRA SHARP! I've seen too many gaffs with terrible points—points that couldn't gaff a limp marshmallow, let alone a tough gill plate. So take a good look at your gaff points and sharpen them thoroughly. Shape them to triangular points with a file and make sure they can cut their way into, as well as pierce, the skin. Unfortunately, after being successfully fought, many fish are lost because of a dull gaff. The gaffer will invariably take a while to penetrate the fish's body with a dull gaff point, and in the meantime, the fishhook will come loose and the fish will escape.

The bamboo pole gaff is a standard among *ulua* fishermen, but each individual makes his look a little bit different. The most ingeniously constructed single pole gaff is one that has a detachable head. The head is unscrewed and can be reattached to a slide gaff. This single head serves double duty and is a very good idea. A lot of times you'll bring along a pole gaff only to find that your favorite spot is taken. You go to your second choice, but you've left the slide gaff at home. The gaff with the detachable head can cover all the bases and allow you to go anywhere you wish.

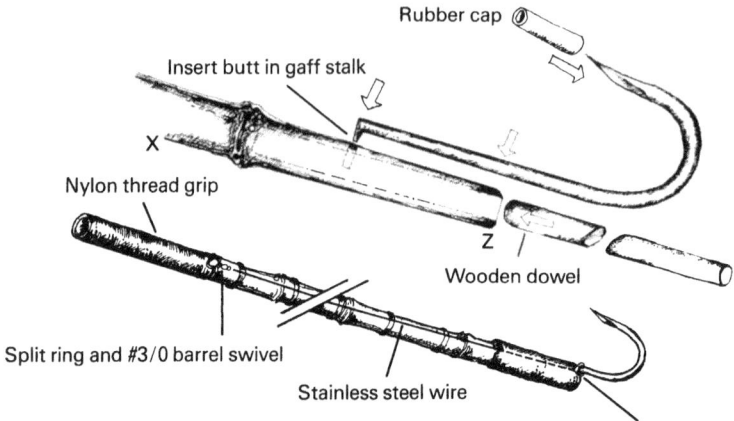

Bamboo Pole Gaff (14 to 16 inches long). As with the Hawaiian Pole Gaff, the stainless steel head of the Bamboo Pole Gaff should have a triangular point. A rubber cap made from a short section of surgical tubing should be used to cover the point. To keep the gaff head from sliding off, drill a hole through the bamboo stalk and into the dowel after the dowel is cemented to the stalk. Once this is done, wrap nylon thread around the gaff shank from point Z to point X. Wrap tightly to ensure that the gaff head will not shift during use. Run 300-pound-test stainless steel wire along the entire bamboo shaft, which should also have a split ring and barrel swivel at the gaff head and at the butt. Secure a rope to the shaft, so that the gaffman doesn't lose the gaff while bringing in the fish. Use cotton cord for a grip. Scattered wraps of nylon cord will also make for easier gripping.

If the gaff head can unscrew, there is a chance that the hook might unscrew itself and lose your fish and the detachable gaff head all in one mighty wave. For this reason, all the detachable heads have a heavy duty wire connected to the head and gaff body. This wire prevents the head from coming off during use.

Most people don't know how to use a gaff. They thrash down at a fish with some vicious strokes and eventually succeed in unhooking the fish. The gaff should be used with great care. Many times the hooked fish is in a very spooky temper and almost always has some reserve energy. It will see you with the light and this great rod in your hand and be ready to try another strong run if need be. So, the gaffers should move as little as possible.

Also, the gaff shouldn't be held high like a sword but low, even put into the water. Let the angler lead the fish to you. Once the fish is close enough, calmly take your best shot. Concentrate on where you want to put the gaff and lightly set the gaff hook at that point. Once you feel the weight, give it a solid jerk and pull it toward you. Don't

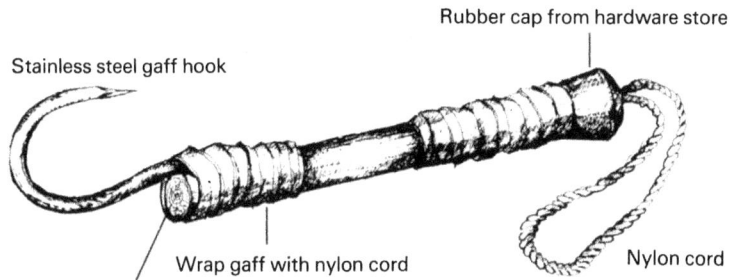

Homemade Short Hand-Gaff. You can buy the gaff head at the store, or bend a stainless steel rod from a welding shop by hand. Secure the head to the shaft by drilling a hole in the shaft, inserting the gaff foot, and then wrapping it with nylon cord. A wooden dowel should be inserted through the entire length of the shaft. The shaft can be a discarded section of fiberglass rod, aluminum tubing, or bamboo stalk. Wrap the butt section to form a grip, allowing space for the butt cap. Drill a hole through the rubber butt cap and insert heavy nylon cord.

thrash the water with the gaff like an old lady trying to kill a snake on the water with an oar. This will almost guarantee a lost fish. The line can get cut or the hook that is hanging on to just the fish's lip can be ripped off. Gaff gently and swiftly, but take the shot neatly and go for the head. Remember the gaff has to be extra sharp to accomplish any of these things.

9
Fishing Accessories and Other Paraphernalia

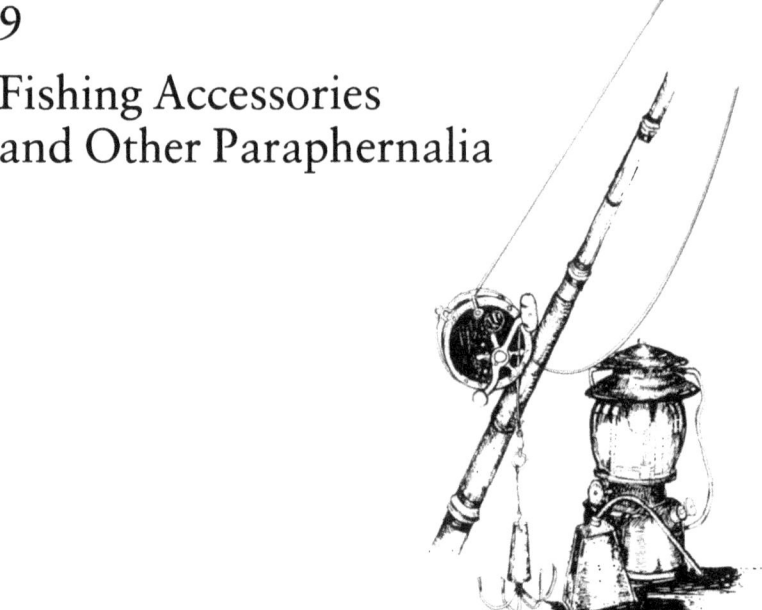

When you first walk into a fishing supply store, you'll be totally amazed at the amount of tackle and accessories the proprietor will have in stock. Usually the tackle supply will start at the ground level and work its way up to the ceiling. If the store has a basement, you'll invariably find that full also.

Besides fishing supplies, the store will most likely have swimming and SCUBA gear, nets, traps, tackle boxes, ditty bags, knives, headlamps, books, magazines, newspapers—anything of interest to the ocean lover. Stores like this tend to have both onshore and offshore tackle. Some stores will specialize in one type of tackle, but a vast majority will handle both. You will be able to find the largest reels that you can carry or reels so small they can literally be slipped into your shirt pocket. Rods will come in every shape and length possible, and in every type of rod-building material known to man.

Besides line, lures, and basic tackle, the fishing store also supplies fishing information. You can get the most current inside scoop on what is biting and where, what type of lure is productive, and what color produces the most strikes. You can also find out where you can acquire baits, where the fishing spots are, and whether you'll need a fishing license or not. Most fishing stores will have an area where anglers can go to just chit-chat, tell their wildest fishing stories, or give valuable information to other serious anglers. The fishing supply store is a world of valuable gossip.

Some stores will also do a little more and repair or overhaul rods and reels. This can help a store's business, as a store that both sells and services what it sells also promotes the sport. And it saves its customers the trouble of having to scurry back to the manufacturer only to find out that it will take ten months to get a single bail spring for a seventy-dollar spinning reel. However, most fishing supply stores will only take in a limited number of fishing reels for repair. More often than not, the fishing supply store will sell you the broken part and show you how to go about repairing the reel by yourself. Reels really aren't very complicated instruments, and it takes only a bit of common sense to dismantle a reel and then make it work the way it's supposed to.

Some specialized stores will also customize rods for select customers. It seems there are rods for all the different types of fish no matter where you go in the fishing world. Some rods can extend to as long as twenty feet; some only four feet. Usually these custom rods are available on a first-come-first-served basis. They may be ordered in advance to come with specific components (e.g., reel seats), or to have specific adjustments made (e.g., having the distance between the butt and the seat increased or decreased). Rods like these normally take anywhere from two weeks to three months to complete. The prices are at times very high; but if the rod matches your body weight, arm length, and reel size, it is truly worth the expense. The true custom rod will fit the angler like a glove and will usually permit him to fish a little longer, as he'll get a little less tired during an average day of fishing. This is not to say that shelf rods don't meet every need that the fisherman has. A lot of them are great for any type of fishing that you would do, and you can normally find a wide assortment on the shelves of most fishing stores. Still, the custom rod has just a little bit more and will do just a little bit more too.

But what about accessories? Do you need all of those different types of lures, swivels, leads, leader materials, knives, and unpronounceable pieces of gear that are in the display window? It really all depends upon the type of fishing that you'll be doing. If you're strictly an ultralight tackle fisherman, you'll only want a fraction of the amount of tackle the store has to offer. If you fish only for *ulua* with slide-bait tackle, then you won't want to have anything to do with lures, ultralight doodads, and swimming gear. All you want are big hooks and grapnel leads.

If you do all different types of fishing—ultralight spinning, slidebait casting, fly fishing—then you'll be needing a storage area much the size of a retail fishing store. But most anglers tend to specialize, and their fishing styles rarely overlap. If the angler has been fishing for a very, very long time, he'll invariably have a warehouse full of tackle that he has tried and found did not work quite the way he'd have liked them to work. Nonetheless he'll have narrowed the possibilities and will buy minimal amounts of tackle—he hopes, anyway.

But as is true with all sports equipment, it is fun just to browse and see what's available. There are always new tackle, new lures, and new techniques that will justify buying a new reel or rod. Much like photography, the assortment is limitless, and the extras stretch far beyond the horizon and the pocketbook. But that's part of the fun of fishing: playing with new tackle and experimenting, and constantly endeavoring to find that one style or technique that is guaranteed to catch you the largest and strongest fish of all your wildest dreams.

Swivels

The basic job of a swivel is to keep the line from twisting, forming massive knots, and making it impossible to fish with. The swivel turns as the line turns and permits kinks and twists to work their way out without any problems. They are invaluable when you have a lot of knots and twists, but they can also become nuisances. They tend to retard the action of a lot of lures, make leader construction a time-consuming affair, and their cost can mount up as you lose more and more of them to the coral reefs and to strong fish. But when used properly, they do the job.

Swivels come in a vast array of sizes and types. The first type is the Barrel Swivel. This is the most common of swivels and is very strong for its size. This swivel can be purchased in black or a stained color if you wish. The reason for using a swivel of either color is that some fish are attracted to shiny swivels and will strike the swivel instead of the trailing lure and cut the line as they make their lunge. Fish like the barracuda and *lai* are famous for this maneuver.

The next type of swivel is the Ball Bearing Swivel. Although it is the most expensive of all swivels, it doesn't have as much strength as the simple Barrel Swivel. Still, it is better in that it turns more freely and thus causes less twist in the line. Because it is so expensive, it isn't used very often in shoreline areas, where it can easily be lost to coral heads or to moray eels that love to tangle leaders in rocks. It is usually used by trollers.

The Snap Swivel is merely a variation of the standard swivel. There are several types of Snaps that are sold on the market and they all work. Some are much stronger than others and tend not to open up as often too. The best type is the McMahon Snap, followed by the Lock Snap, and then the Safety Snap. The other type, called the Coastlock Snap, is usually used by trollers and is simple to use. The McMahon Snap is the strongest and can also be connected to the swivel of your choice in no time flat. Its cost is minimal, and there is no chance of its lock coming loose or being torn open by some fast running fish.

The Slide Swivel is the most specialized of all swivels. Before swivels of this type were made and sold over the counter, shore fishermen used to pry open the elongated trolling corkscrew swivels and make them into round slide swivels. This practice is long gone and most *ulua* fishermen now either buy them over the counter or make their own. Because it is so simple and fast, making your own is really the best way out.

The Three-Way Swivel is another type of swivel that has a special use. It is normally used for bait casting. It provides the dropper section of the leader, and at the same time permits the line to twist as much as it wants. It is a very simple swivel and saves a lot of time in terms of leader construction.

Hooks

Hooks come in so many different styles that many beginning anglers trying to select one don't know where to start. I have to admit that at times even I get totally confused and eventually have to turn to a fishing store clerk for some helpful advice. The clerks pretty much know who buys what kind of hook for what kind of fish. They would have to or they'd be stuck with a lot of hooks no one would want to use.

Naturally, the best kind of hook to use in salt water is a zinc-coated hook. Although it will work and catch fish for you, a hook made for fresh water is far from adequate because it is so sensitive to salt it will rust almost immediately if in contact with it.

The most popular hook used for *ulua* fishing is the circle bait hook, normally used for tunas. This hook has an extensive bend in it and curls almost completely around. (The hook was intended to curve this way.) It is very different from an English hook in that it works very effectively even without the barb. Locally this hook is called a Self-Setting Hook. This means that when a fish takes the bait, the hook will slide to the side of its mouth and work its way in. One such hook is the *tankichi*. It is very strong and very popular with *ulua* fishermen. This type of hook is perfect for the *ulua* fisherman because he is usually far from his rod and must run as fast as he can to finally get to the rod. With a hook such as this, the fish literally hooks itself.

These hooks have a wide price range. The popular name brands are the most expensive and have proven themselves to be more than adequate. They tend to be strong and tapered to a fine and delicate point.

Treble hooks are normally used mostly on plugs and other types of lures. They definitely aren't very strong and tend to get bent back rather severely or even crushed during a terrific strike. Treble hooks are relatively inexpensive and can be purchased in a lot of sizes.

If you prefer whipping plugs and you know that the fish you'll be going after tends to demolish hooks a lot, then I'd advise you to carry spares in your tackle box. Some anglers carry hooks of a size one bigger than what is on the plug. They feel that the plug's hooks are far from adequate, and thus they add their own hooks to it.

All hooks have to be checked for sharpness; this is especially true for treble hooks and *ulua* hooks. I normally carry a small file with me and a small sharpening stone for light touch-up jobs. During a day's fishing I am usually checking the hook constantly. There is never a hook that is sharp enough for me. Too many hooks are bent in after they have come in contact with boulders, coral, and other hard objects.

Lead and Sinkers

As is the case with swivels, the selection of lead types is vast and complicated. With one type of fishing goes one type of lead; that is, not all leads are used for all purposes and so you have leads that have specific tasks. They all do have one thing in common, however, and that is that they make casting easier and more efficient. The style or form of the lead determines the job that it will do or should do. Some lead shapes are variations of other types, and incorporated in each new shape are all the good points of the original form. The result is a lead shape that will serve the specific needs of particular types of terrain.

For the shoreline fisherman who dunks his bait is the Bank Sinker.

It looks very much like a teardrop, and it can be found in most fishing stores. It comes in many different weights, from the small quarter ounce to the sixteenth ounce or twenty-four-ounce monsters. It is used mostly by bait casters and slide-bait fishermen.

The hybrid of the Bank Sinker is the Wire Bank Sinker. It has four wires coming out from its base. The wire is usually a common #4 tie wire, averaging around six to seven inches in length. Sometimes copper wire is used to make legs that are completely rust-free and reusable for many trips. The copper is also softer than the tie wire, and for this reason will bend back and release itself from the coral when pulled up. For an area that has a bottom that is all coral, this type of sinker with the copper wire is the most useful.

When in use, the legs are turned or curled upward toward the eye of the lead. This grapnel-like posture makes the lead grab the bottom very quickly and thus prevents it from sliding constantly along the bottom, a problem with most legless leads. The grapnel legs also work well in sandy or pebbly bottoms. The legs dig down into the sand and hold fast to the bottom, enabling the line to be pulled taut so the bait may be slid down without trouble.

The second lead type that holds the bottom fairly well is the Pyramid Sinker. It doesn't have any legs like the Bank Sinker, but it has a planed face that grips the sand as soon as it is pulled tight. Being that the butt end is pointed, it makes for a very streamlined lead that can be thrown a great distance. It too comes in many different sizes and weights.

The sinker most commonly used by whippers, especially ultralight whippers, is the Egg Sinker. This lead is shaped exactly like a chicken egg, and it has a hole through which the line is passed (see "Ultralight Whipping Leader," Chapter 4). It is used by small-game bait casters and fishermen that hang their baits straight down from cliffs. Some shoreline whippers paint the Egg Sinker white to enable them to see the lead coming through the water. It also tends to attract *pāpio* to the bait, which trails close behind. At times the lead is hit before the fish sees the bait.

Another type of lead is the Torpedo Lead. It looks like a long torpedo because both ends of the lead taper to a point from which a copper or brass ring protrudes. It comes in many different weights and is used by shoreline whippers because of its streamlined features, which prevent drag in the water. It is an alternative to the Egg Sinker. Since it is so streamlined, it also makes for a good dunking lead. It doesn't tend to hang up on the bottom as much as the Bank Sinkers do.

Leader Material

First, what is a leader? It is usually a length of line that is stronger than the mainline, and usually used to eliminate the problems of line being cut by rocks, by fishes' teeth, or from repeated casting. The right size or length leader to use depends upon the type of fish you're after and the terrain of the area you're fishing in.

For instance, let's say I'm whipping for *pāpio* with 12-pound-test mono and I want to construct a good leader. The area is rocky and shallow. Knowing that the fish love to dive down among the rocks when they're hooked and that the section of line likely to be cut off will be the first two to three feet, I make my leader fifteen feet long and such that I can crank it into my reel when whipping.

The best size leader to use would be anything that is about triple the line test. If you're using 12, try about 30- or 40-pound test. If you're an ultralight angler and using a 4-pound-test mainline, then use 10. Try to keep the leader length long, and make sure that the leader is stretched well for casting from a spinning reel or bait-casting reel.

Heavy monofilament leader has a strong memory, so you'll have to take out the curlicues and the twists by running it through some folded rubber or by simply stretching it out with your arms. Pull each section until the leader becomes straight and true. You might also try to put it in warm water and then stretch it tight. The monofilament will straighten out and will remain that way for the entire trip. After the trip, crank the leader back into the reel and leave it for several days. When you use it again, you'll have to restretch the leader to make it straight. The leader will take the shape of the reel's spool and will become twisted again.

The best thing to use when stretching monofilament is a cut section of an innertube folded in half. Run the monofilament through the rubber sections and it will cause some heat to build up. The heat, coupled with the pulling of the leader through the fingers, will make the leader very straight. But be careful when using the inner tube because the heat can build up and cause the monofilament to break down and become weak.

Every so often the leader should be taken out of the spool and rechecked. This is especially important for the whipping leader. The knots should also be rechecked. If the line shows any wear and tear, it should be cut off, as should the abraded sections close to the tip. This is another reason for making the leader so long: you have the option to simply cut sections off, after which you can tie your plug back on quickly and go back to fishing. Check the leader often and make sure that it is working for you and not against you.

Braided Wire or "Sevalon"

The best thing about braided wire is its suppleness. It bends much more freely than other kinds of wire and can be tied when sleeves are not available. Some braided wires have smooth plastic coats which make knot tying much easier. The only drawback with the plastic coat is that salt water tends to stay in the sleeves and corrode the braided wire as time goes by.

One of the braided wire's greatest qualities is that it can be cranked into the reel—wire leaders can't. The braided wire also comes in sizes smaller than monofilament leader material in the same weight, and it is just as strong. It comes in small rolls or by the bulk on spools that can carry several yards of it. It is reasonably priced and has a long shelf life in relation to monofilament, which deteriorates with age.

One of the braided wire's drawbacks is that it tends to get very curly or kinky after several casts. If you have just hooked and landed

Braided wire comes in different spool sizes.

a fish on the leader, you'll almost always find the wire curly as a spring and the plastic coat stripped away. Sometimes small bits of the wire will stick up. This presents a hazard if the leader is to be reused. Those small spurs that stick up can inflict a painful bite on the casting thumb if the angler is not careful. For this reason most braided wire is discarded after one use and a new length is attached to the line.

The bare braided leader is also used by the shore caster, but it tends to be much more expensive than the Sevalon. Some anglers use it for the slide buckle section of the slide rig. They claim that it's a little more supple and thus gives the hanging bait a little more movement. Although the bare braided wire can be tied, it is better if it is crimped solidly with a good pair of crimping pliers.

Twist Weld Wire Leader

This type of wire leader is new on the market. You don't need sleeves and knots to connect this braided wire to your line. All you need is either a match or lighter to make the connection. The wire has a plastic, black coating that when heated will bind the wire together. The bind is just as strong as a knot but much simpler to make. Simply put the wire through the swivel or lure, twist the wire around itself four

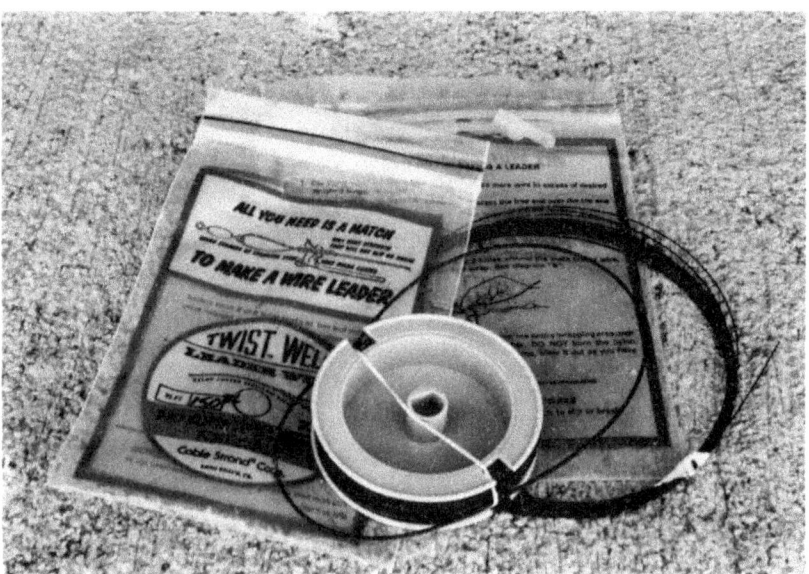

Twist weld—all you need is a match!

or five times, and heat it with a flame. As you wait for the black coating to melt, move the flame along the entire length of the twist. Once the wire is sufficiently heated it will fuse together and all you need do then is trim it off cleanly.

If you don't trust this type of connection, you can still use the standard brass sleeve or the braided wire knots which are available. All in all, this leader is a revolutionary idea and works like a champ.

Pliers and Other Fishing Tools

Every fisherman should carry some sort of fishing pliers. The long nose pliers that have a cutting edge is a good choice. However, this combination cutting tool and pliers usually doesn't last too long and the cutting edge gets dull or dented in several places. Most anglers end up with one set of cutting pliers and one set of long nose pliers.

A second type of long nose pliers that not all anglers carry and that is relatively hard to find is the long nose with a round beak. This type of pliers is used to make perfectly round loops in the wire leader. It can't extract a hook or cut lines very well so it is more or less considered a very specialized tool.

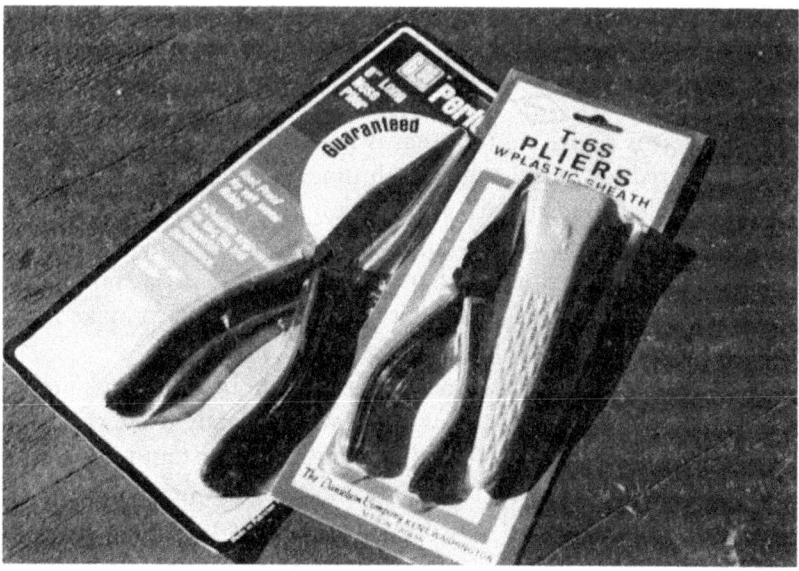

Pliers

If you can't find a set of pliers with a round beak and still need one to make round loops for wire leaders, then the second best thing to do is to get a file and file down one of the two beaks on a standard set of pliers. Spread the jaw open and carefully file away the sides until one beak is round and tapered. Now you'll have the round nose pliers and a set of pliers that will extract stubborn hooks and tighten reel clamps with ease.

One of the best pliers on the market is the Sargent's Fishing Pliers. It is a short, squat set of pliers and is great for tightening knots, pulling hooks, tightening clamps, and a multitude of other odd jobs. The cutting edge is on the top of the head and will remain sharp for a very, very long time. A good one will have a black, anodized head that resists corrosion and that is supposed to stay sharp for a long time. It also has a spring-loaded handle and will always open when not held down. This spring loaded system makes it easy to operate and also helps to keep the pliers snug in its case.

You can purchase a case along with the pliers, or go down to a leather shop and have the owner make one for you. It won't cost you much; maybe only $5. The leather case that is custom-made for the pliers is normally around $10 and will last for a very long time. Because the pliers sits very neatly in the case and the case is very stiff, there is little chance of the pliers slipping out without your knowing it.

Hemostats

A hemostat is a surgical tool that is normally stainless steel. It has a long, tapered jaw with jagged teeth that interlock with a quick snap of the handle. It's terrific for extracting hooks that are stuck far down a fish's gullet. This tool is also good for taking out treble hooks because it has a narrow jaw that won't bend or mash them. Since the point of the hemostat is so fine, it is sometimes used to make a hook hole a little bigger so the hook can be pulled out easily.

Since the hemostat has a locking jaw, it can be quickly clamped to the lapel of your vest or shirt, where it will be handy when you need it again. Made of stainless steel, the hemostat is resistant to salt. It is a useful fishing tool, and you should have several hemostats in your tackle box or the small repair kit you should be toting around. They are great tools for locking things in place when you must make quick and necessary repairs in the field.

Nail Clippers

Last but not least is the household nail clipper. It is the cheapest and handiest tool a fisherman could ever carry. It will cut through just about any size monofilament with relative ease and can be tucked away in the shirt pocket, pants pocket, or tackle box. Cutting monofilament with a nail clipper sure beats cutting it with your teeth, especially if you have dull teeth that you have to secure with Poligrip.

There are nail clippers made specifically for fishermen. You can find them in sporting goods stores or the camping section of department stores. These aren't as small as household nail clippers and tend to have a small groove in the lever of the clipper. This small groove is used to help pull hooks out or push them in to take them out. Some also have a "nail-knot tying tool" slipped in where the nail file normally would be. The tool consists of a tapered section you can use in place of a nail when you need to tie a nail knot (see "Straight Splice Knot," Chapter 4). It works well if you tie the nail knot regularly; but if you don't, it will get rusty and you won't be able to pull it out later.

Some nail clippers come with a lanyard, which is a clip on a cord that goes around your neck like a coach's whistle. It's a great invention and easy to make. Make your own by just getting some old, discarded cord, a large snap swivel, and some dental floss. Put the ends of the cord through the swivel end, tie off with a knot, and secure again with a section of dental floss. Coat the floss and knot with nail polish. Open the snap and connect it to the hole at the end of the nail clipper. There you have it and at a cost of about 2 cents each.

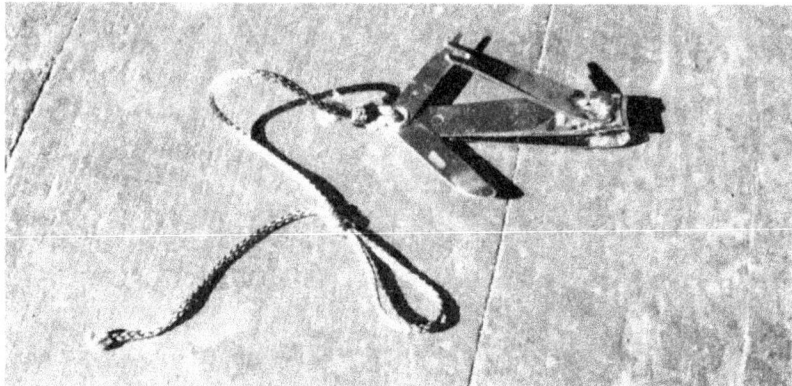

Nail clippers trim lines and knots in a pinch.

Make up a bunch of these lanyards and connect a whole bunch of clippers to them. Tuck them away in your tackle box in a small ziplock bag. You'll find that you'll start losing them or they'll be borrowed and never returned; but they're easy to make and their cost is minimal.

One thing about tools is they always tend to get very rusty when they come in contact with salt. Even if the tool is brand new, as soon as it comes in contact with the salt air, it'll seem to rust right before your very eyes. There is no way of stopping this oxidation, but you can always give the pliers a good coating of high quality lubricating oil regularly. Oils such as LPS and WD-40 now come in small spray containers that can be slipped into your tackle box with lots of room to spare. These oils also make quick work of lubricating dried-out leather bushings on lanterns, tight reel handles, slow moving bails on spinning reels, and the small nut on the top of a Coleman lantern.

Shore Fishing Lights

How much light do you need when shore fishing? Some anglers scorn using any light at all and shudder when they see someone shining lights on the water. To some, lights scare away fish; to others, they attract fish. Which of these two theories holds the most water?

Well, to some degree both theories are true. It's a proven fact that plankton are drawn to light, and predatory fish feed on the small plankton. I've seen *pāpio,* not bothered by the presence of light at all, gather in water lit by lights from piers or boats. They tended to stay just out of reach of the light's rays, then every once in a while they'd zip into the light to pick off some small fish or shrimp. *Akule* are also drawn to light, and with the *akule* come the *menpachi ulua.* Both feed very well under light and don't seem to be bothered by either floating lights or car headlights.

Menpachi fishermen also carry their Coleman lanterns with them in the water to attract feeding *menpachi* to the area. This is especially effective if the night is extra dark and there is a new moon. The *menpachi* fishermen feel that small shrimp are drawn to the light and that with them come the *menpachi.* This method has been proved true time and time again and is still practiced today.

So what about *ulua* fishing? Well, some people say that the *ulua* is afraid of lights. I don't think this is true when a steady light source such as a lantern is used, but it may be true for a strong flickering light from a waving headlight.

I've been down underwater many a night with SCUBA gear and can attest to the fact that light penetrates water quite well. But light doesn't travel through water at an angle too well. At fifty feet I've been able to see clearly the moon shining above. The bottom is clearly lit, and you can see the coral gardens with no effort at all once your eyes get used to the dim light. But once you turn on the light you will become startled and your eyes will have to get used to the sudden infusion of light. I think this is true for the predatory fish that swim in the very deep waters and come up at night to feed in the shallow reefline. They slowly move into the areas lit by a lantern and it doesn't bother them too much. The transition is slow and easy. But shine a headlamp or a strong flashlight in the water and flicker it along the bottom and it'll startle the fish for a moment. If a fish is still hungry and smells something that it wants, it'll come back to investigate. This knowledge is useful for underwater diving. An *ulua* will come to a light and at first, scared, will move away, but later will come back to investigate the blood and smell in the water. Once it gets used to the light, it'll be back.

The lesson behind this story is that light draws the small plankton, which draw the small night feeding reef fish, which in turn draw larger predatory fish such as the *ulua*. For example, the *menpachi* fisherman frequently will hook into a *menpachi* or an *'āweoweo* and have it torn off the hook by an *ulua* that is also feeding in the area. Barracuda, *kāhala,* and sharks will all move into the area when they hear or feel there is a feeding going on. Some *menpachi* fishermen will also hang live baits under their lights when fishing for the small night fish. Frequently, an *ulua* will come in for the struggling *menpachi* and follow it until it finds the hooked and free-swimming bait. The *ulua* will take the small *menpachi* right under the light with a great splash and not show much concern about the lantern at all.

In all situations the light should be steady and should not flicker. A headlamp that is constantly flashing will spook the fish. This is best evidenced by the fact that flashing lights are commonly used to chase a hooked *ulua* away from rocks and shorelines. This practice works well if the water is shallow and the light can penetrate down into the depths.

When fishing around rocky areas you have to have a light, otherwise you'll quickly break either your legs or neck if you don't see where you're going. This is especially true if you're half sleeping when you get a strike in the middle of the night. Some anglers get to their screaming reels to fight the fish and later don't even remember how they got to their rods. This scares the hell out of me, so I always carry a light or lantern when running to the poles.

Lanterns

There are about four different types of lanterns to select from. The first is the white gas lantern, also called a pressure lantern. It is practical, dependable, and relatively simple to operate. What's more, its maintenance cost is ridiculously low. The best lantern to purchase is one that has only one mantle. It gives off just about as much light as

Coleman White Gas Lantern. Carry extra mantles and a lantern case for protection. The case *(in the background)* is a six-inch PVC conduit made into a carrying case with a dog chain handle.

the two-mantle lantern. The main differences are that the single mantle lantern lasts much longer through the night; you don't have to pump it as often as the two-mantle version; and it also is much smaller and lighter than the cumbersome two-mantle version. For these reasons, fishermen that travel a long ways tend to carry this lantern.

The best way to carry an extra mantle is to tie a pack (two mantles per pack) onto the handle of the lantern. Simply tie the handle to the mantle by wrapping with a section of soft telephone copper wire several times, twisting the wire to secure it. In this way you'll always be able to see if you have extra mantles and also keep them out of the way.

The Coleman company also created a cover that caps under the hollowed out section of the lantern's bottom. In this compartment you can keep extra mantles, pliers, nuts, oil, and generator. The cover is very handy but it can make the lantern tipsy when it is set down in rocky areas.

If you're the type that hates to deal with gas cans and the mess that comes along with it, then you will like the newer propane lanterns on the market. All you do to replace a cannister is disconnect it, attach a new full one, and fire up the lantern. Then you're off to the races. The cannisters don't cost very much and they are good for approximately twelve hours of continuous use. It really eliminates all the mess and bother that come with other lanterns.

One drawback with propane lanterns is a lot of them tend to be left at fishing sites. They litter the ground, and when still half or partially full, they are a great fire hazard. The best thing to do, then, is haul back the rubbish you bring with you.

KEROSENE LANTERNS

The old standby, the kerosene lantern, is easier to operate than the white gas lantern. All it consists of is a wick, a tank to store the oil in, and a glass casing to keep out the wind. Unfortunately, it doesn't give off much light, and the smoke that billows out of its top can become very irritating for all. If you don't shorten the wick as soon as the flame starts to burn, the side of the glass casing will become black with soot and this will dim the light. The kerosene lantern also tends to start many more fires than any other type of lantern. If the lantern falls in a tent or in the back seat or trunk of a car, the spilled fuel will quickly catch fire and you'll have a scorched tent or a blazing inferno.

The Coleman company now offers a kerosene lantern that operates in the same way a white gas lantern does. The light is much brighter than the standard kerosene lantern and a little yellowish in comparison to the white gas lamps. But they work great and are very reliable. Places like Christmas Island use kerosene Coleman lanterns extensively. They burn a high-grade kerosene that is really jet fuel and that is brought in by tanker. It burns better than regular kerosene and is much, much cheaper than white gas.

Some anglers, like *menpachi* fishermen, prefer to hang a lantern over the sides of cliffs to draw in fish. Some hang the Coleman white gas lanterns. Most have found the kerosene lantern is much easier to replace after a wave has unexpectedly come up and smashed the lantern against the side of the cliff. The kerosene lantern can take much more beating, and still can be lit and reused as long as the glass casing isn't broken. You simply have to dry off the inside of the glass, resoak the wick, and relight it with a match. You'll be back in action sooner than you think.

Some anglers feel that Coleman lanterns give off too much light for shore fishing, and for this reason they prefer the yellowish light a kerosene lantern gives off. They feel that this yellowish light is softer and more like moonlight, which the fish are used to. Selection, then, involves personal interpretation and trial and error. But, all in all, kerosene is a much cheaper fuel and just as dependable as any other.

FLUORESCENT LANTERNS

If you like white light but hate to mess with white gas lanterns, then your only alternative is to buy a battery-operated fluorescent lamp. They are quick and safe to use. They will also do the job of providing light when you're making your way to the point, when you're tying hooks, or when you're cooking under the stars. The only drawback with fluorescent lanterns is they require two expensive batteries that tend not to last too long. If you're the type that likes to leave a lantern burning the entire evening, then you'll be disappointed. The light will get weaker and weaker as the evening wears on.

Some anglers swear that the fluorescent light of this lantern will draw in small plankton much faster than the standard Coleman lantern. Its light is a different color (bluish white) and seems to filter through the water better. This is all purely speculation and hasn't been proven yet, so take your pick and use what you're most comfortable with.

Headlamp or Miner's Light

For night fishing there is no substitute for a good, reliable headlamp. A cheap one lasts about a dollar a trip. After a half dozen trips either it will rust away, its switches won't work, or the reflective material inside it will begin to deteriorate. So purchase a headlamp that is a good, tested brand.

Nowadays there are available headlamps made of strong, durable plastic. They cost much more than the old aluminum type that you find in drug stores, but they last for a long, long time. They are very dependable; they don't get rusty; their switches always work; and they sometimes come with a small clip on the inside where you can keep an extra bulb if you want.

Some have two operating bulbs, one for scanning an area and another for close work, like tying hooks and making leaders. One switch controls both lights. The light is pretty much watertight. It comes with a small case that holds four type C batteries and that wraps around your waist. It also comes with a small nylon webbing belt for the waist and a wide elastic band that fits snugly around your forehead.

Most anglers customize the headlight for heavier use. Usually they don't use the small plastic battery container and replace the webbing

Headlamps

belt with a military ammo belt and surplus canteen pouch or similar type of canvas pouch. Instead of the usual four small flashlight batteries, they use two heavy-duty dry cells. Some anglers go to the extreme of purchasing a wet cell (normally used for motorcycles), which is sealed in plastic and then placed in the canvas pouch. The batteries are rechargeable and will put out an amazing amount of light. The only drawback is the battery may leak while it's being used. Frequent checking of the battery is necessary to ensure that the angler won't get acid burns.

Another trick some anglers use involves installing a switch at the point where the wire comes to the battery pack. With the switch here the angler doesn't have to reach up to turn off the light but to the side to knock off the power. This is only one of the many conveniences that the shoreline fisherman has thought of.

Some anglers take off the elastic strap that comes with the headlamp and connect the headlamp to a welder's headband (purchased separate from the facemask). This headband is used in place of the headlamp's elastic headband, mainly because the latter tends to squeeze the head, making it rather uncomfortable. With the welder's headband, the headlight can be slipped on or off just like a baseball cap. There is also an adjusting knob in the back of the band to ensure a good fit. The headlamp cable is run either along the plastic band or along the top of the band so the cables don't get in the way.

Personally, I prefer the elastic-band-and-baseball-cap combination. The cap provides some protection against wind and rain and keeps my head warm. On very cold nights I also wear a bandana around my neck, and I'm kept even warmer.

Tackle Boxes—Big or Small?

A tackle box is *never* big enough. A beginning angler usually starts off with a small tackle box, thinking that it will hold more than all the gear he could possibly use. But as the years go by, the box will get smaller and more cluttered with lures, floaters, leader material, and anything else that the angler could possibly use down at the beach. Some *ulua* fishermen have gone so far as to use large wooden boxes that have multiple shelves and trays. These boxes take two good-sized anglers to carry them, as they sometimes contain everything from a TV guide to the largest *ulua* hooks any manufacturer could possibly make.

Tackle box

There are anglers who carry small plastic boxes that have slots in them and that are all labeled for different types of fishing. The small film containers are also used by some to hold hooks, swivels, and other small doodads that seem to litter most tackle boxes. You'll find that some of these small film containers fit just right in the drawers and slots of the right tackle box. If you look around carefully, you'll be able to find the transparent containers made by the Fuji film company. These are better than the solid black ones because you can see what's inside without opening them.

Most tackle boxes nowadays have trays that are wormproof, a vital feature of a tackle box especially if you intend to use a lot of plastic lures. If the tackle box isn't wormproof, then I suggest you store the lures in several small container boxes or in ziplock bags. Arrange the whipping lures in your box so that they are stored in good order. Too many plugs stored in one tray will only make for more problems and a frustrating trip for all.

No matter how big and well stocked the tackle box, there will always be something you'll have forgotten. I've traveled to many islands with my 747 tackle box and more than once saved a trip by either coming up with a repair kit for someone with a serious problem, or by supplying enough lures for everyone so the trip was sure to a memorable one. The tackle box becomes a portable store, and if arranged right it can become a valuable asset to everyone fishing with you.

When selecting a tackle box, look for good construction and simple handling. Naturally, try to buy one from a reputable dealer. Check for cracks and defects before handing over the cash because many tackle boxes are damaged during shipment, and you may not be able to return a damaged tackle box.

If you fish in an area where it rains a lot, select a box that is pretty much weatherproof, in other words one that will keep the rain out once it is closed. This is especially important if you're on a boat that is very wet. The less salt water you get in the box, the better for the tackle and leader material.

If you travel a lot and have to lug a big tackle box around at the airlines, then find a tackle box that is lockable. The money you invested in those valuable reels, lures, and cameras should make it very important to either lock the tackle box during transit or bind it somehow to stop people from getting their fingers inside it. To travel thousands of miles only to find upon reaching your destination that your tackle box is without your reels and other vital components is to ruin a well-planned trip.

The well-made luggage straps that you find in department stores come in very handy when it comes to discouraging sticky fingers. They also help to keep the tackle box from opening suddenly during handling, and from spilling all over the baggage loading area. It can be very frustrating for a luggage handler to chase fifty ½-ounce egg sinkers.

Ice Chests and Insulated Fish Bags

Ice chests come in so many different sizes and shapes that you never seem to have enough of them. They're great for camping trips or fishing trips, and they can serve as cutting boards or tables for moonlight dinners for two. In a pinch an ice chest can become a tackle box in which lures, lanterns, and reels can be stored. It can hold baits and fish, or become a live bait well. In emergencies it can be tossed overboard and serve as a floatation device someone can hang onto if they have to. For this reason I normally select colors that are easy to see from a long distance. Yellow is the easiest to see in the water and is a fairly common color.

As soon as I buy an ice chest, I paint my name squarely on the side. Too many ice chests have neatly walked away because no one knew who's ice chest it was. I also add a note on its top that tells everyone the chest is not for sitting on. I have had to discard too many ice chests because of caved-in lids and ripped hinges.

One of the newest things on the market are insulated fish bags. They can be folded and stored with relative ease in the back of the family car or behind the seat. They are leakproof (except for the zipper section) and can hold a small amount of ice longer than an ice chest can because they don't have as much dead air space. The bag is shut with two sets of heavy-duty plastic zippers. Most of the air is squeezed out, but the cold air is allowed to stay in.

What some of the *ulua* fishermen bring on trips are an insulated fish bag and a smaller ice chest. They not only leave the larger ice chest behind but they tend not to bring as much ice, period. If they catch a big *ulua*, they put the fish into the bag with some ice and leave it on the side. They know that the ice will keep the fish more than cold enough, even if the bag is left out in the sun.

When you are sleeping on rocks or lava, the bag has another purpose. Being that the bag is made of heavy-duty, rip-proof nylon and the foam is sealed foam (not sponge), it makes a very nice sleeping mattress. The bags are also very light in relation to their size. They are not as clumsy as large ice chests, and can take much more punishment than the chests made of brittle plastic.

Much like the ice chest, the insulated fish bag can also serve as an emergency floatation device. It can be tossed over the side quickly, and you can depend on the bag not to absorb water and sink. The bags can be purchased in many different colors, too, including red and yellow.

Tail Carriers and Meat Hooks

Another item that comes in very handy is a contraption called a tail carrier. It makes carrying large fish very easy and less messy. All it is, is a stainless steel T with a length of rope that is formed into a loop. The loop is put around the tail of a large fish and pulled tight. Fish like *ulua* have very sharp and tough scutes on their tails; with a tail carrier you won't have to grab this part of the fish. The meat hook is

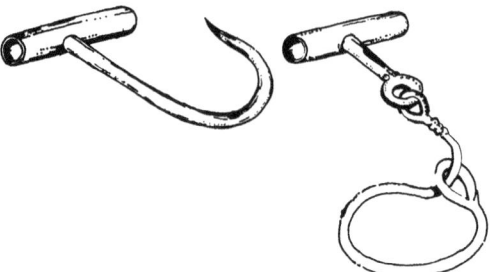

Tail carriers and meathooks are terrific for carrying big fish on the rocks. If a meathook is put into the *ulua*'s mouth and tail carrier on the tail, two anglers can carry a big fish with hardly any problem.

also stainless steel and looks just like the standard meat hook you find in meat-packing plants. It is used to grab the mouth portion of fish, and two anglers can use it, together with the tail carrier, to carry any fish with great ease.

The best part about these two pieces of equipment is that they do not take up too much storage space. They are handy for all kinds of chores, and you can gaff fish with the meat hook if it is absolutely necessary. They are easy to make and don't have to be stainless steel.

10
Shoreline Gamefish

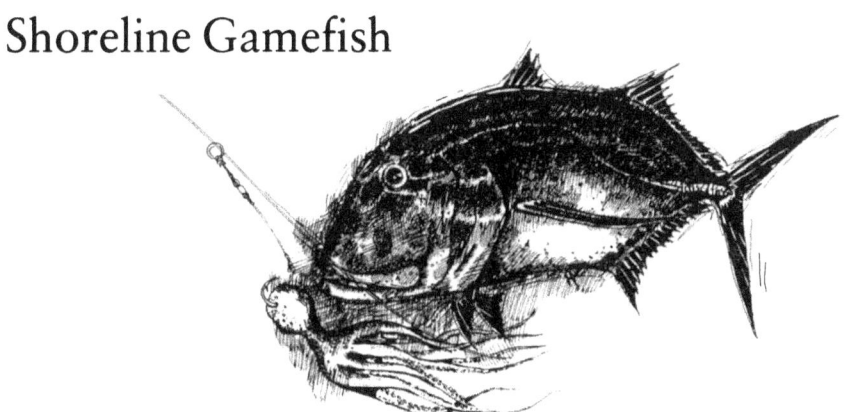

The following is a listing of various gamefish that eventually wind up on the shoreline fisherman's hook. Although it does not include all the species that can be found in the Hawaiian reefs, this section does describe the species most often sought as gamefish or as meals for the dinner table.

Included here, along with general background on these gamefish, are brief descriptions of some angling techniques. Of course this is not to say that these are the only angling methods available to fishermen; anglers from each island have their own methods of catching these fish and each of these methods works. The proper way to find out how to catch these fish is to ask around at local fishing supply stores and learn the techniques that work in that general locale.

ĀHOLEHOLE (Hawaiian Flag Fish)
Kuhlia sandvicensis
This fish is a favorite among handpole enthusiasts. The large adult flag fish is called *āhole,* and the juvenile is called *āholehole.* The banded flagtail is another *āholehole,* only the tail of the flagtail is striped with black lines.

This fish lives in bays, harbors, river mouths, culverts, and rough areas in the open ocean. The *āholehole* that frequent harbors and bays are very small in comparison to the ones hooked and landed in the open ocean. In general, they can grow to between 4 and 8 inches in length, and can be hooked with either bait or artificial lures. The most common way to hook *āholehole* is with a handpole and sections of common California shrimp. In deep shoreline areas, the fish is chummed and then hooked right through the night and into the day. In the open ocean the best bait are live river shrimp.

When artificial lure methods are used, the spinning reel combination is kept pretty light. Ultralight tackle is the best because the *āholehole* is small and bites better when the line is very, very light. The 4-pound test is a good choice; 1- and 2-pound test are also good and probably will produce more strikes. Good choices for tackle include a long leader (approximately six to eight feet), a small hook, and a section of glitter shrimp or strip of plastic. The retrieve should be relatively slow and you must concentrate on the lure. The *āholehole* hits with enthusiasm, so there will be no mistaking a strike or take.

This fish tends to hang out in large schools, and can be caught while you're whipping for *menpachi* and *ʻāweoweo*. They usually stay closer to shore than do *menpachi,* so most of the strikes will come almost at the end of the retrieve.

The *āholehole* is a little on the spiny side and if it is not handled with care can inflict a rather vicious cut. As you unhook the fish, handle the sharp, razorlike gill plates and the sharp-pointed fins carefully.

Āholehole (4 to 8 inches)·

AKULE or AJI (Bigeyed Scad)
Trachurops crumenophthalmus

The small *akule* is called *halalū* or *hahalalū*. *Halalū* schools come into harbors and bays in the summer months of July and August. Once the schools are in, anglers come from all over and congregate at the piers with their fiberglass or bamboo handpoles. If the schools are far out, the spin fishermen will be out in full force and will either snag the fish or whip strips of plastic or *ika* bait.

The best bait to use is the small *nehu*. If you can find a place where you can scoop them up fresh, then you will have the best bet for good bait. If not, catch what you can and salt up the *nehu* as quickly as possible. Once the school is in, the salted *nehu* can be hooked and

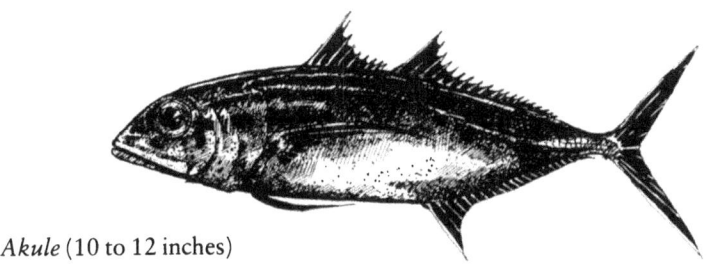

Akule (10 to 12 inches)

lowered over the side with a handpole. Dead or alive, it will make great bait for the *halalū* or the *akule*.

If the *nehu* is nowhere to be found, then the next best bait is live shrimp. If shrimp is hard to get, then hook strips of finely cut squid. Jiggle the strips of squid with your handpole and the *halalū* will take the bait. Each school is different and you should experiment to see what kind of action is required to get them to bite. The fisherman that adapts himself the fastest will catch the most fish and do so the most consistently.

Like the *'ōpelu,* the *akule* should be allowed to swim freely after it is snagged. The *ulua* and *kāhala* also follow schools of *akule* and *halalū,* and they can be hooked using the snagged fish as bait. The *akule*'s meat is firmer than the meat of the *'ōpelu* and is just as good a bait, although it also doesn't last too long on the hook.

The most common way to hook one is by anchoring in deep water and handlining the fish, using small flies as bait. The *akule* feeds very heavily during dark nights. Since it feeds on small white shrimp and other crustaceans that swim in deep midwaters, the small flies you use should look or move much like small brine shrimp.

If a commercial deep-sea fisherman were asked to choose between the *akule* and the *'ōpelu* for handlining, he would very quickly choose the *'ōpelu.* When after *akule,* commercial anglers will use small, single-engine planes and fly over shallow shoreline areas to locate their schools, which from the air look like dark greyish balls. Commercial netters will then head for the spotted areas in small, swift boats, and with huge surround nets they will harvest tons upon tons of *akule* for local markets.

'AMA'AMA (Mullet)
Mugil cephalus
The common striped mullet is both good eating and a fair gamefish. It is normally caught with thin seaweed found in freshwater ponds and

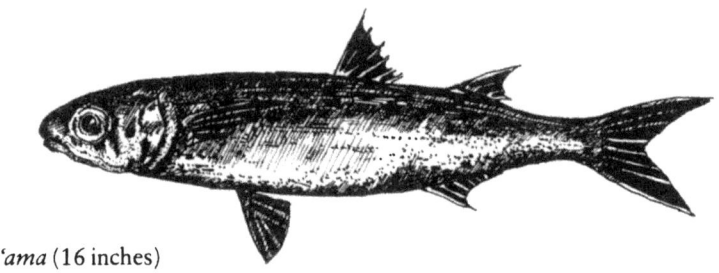

'Ama'ama (16 inches)

streams, although some anglers use pieces of bread. The angling technique requires a very sensitive floater rig, normally painted a bright fluorescent red or orange. The leader requires a double-hook setup, and the entire rig is cast with a long spinning rod and reel combination (see "Floaters," Chapter 1). The angler keeps a sharp eye on the floater and once it twitches or tips up, he snaps the line back with, he hopes, a mullet on the other end.

The mullet is most often caught in small harbors, piers, brackish water ponds, and slow moving rivers. They tend to like these areas because of the abundance of seaweed found there. Mullet are also found near reefs and in the white water areas of the surf. The ancient Hawaiians used to raise mullet in huge ponds. These ponds can still be found along the Molokai and Lanai shorelines. Today the mullet is a commercially raised food fish.

The mullet grows to some astonishing sizes, and it performs very well on light tackle. Although it depends upon the area in which you catch the mullet, generally this fish will have a very sweet flavor and will taste very good. Mullet from very muddy and polluted ponds or rivers will have an unpleasant taste and odor. The ocean-running mullet is the best and naturally the strongest.

The smaller mullet (one and two pounds) make very good whipping baits. Rigged properly, the mullet can be cast repeatedly and will draw some incredible *ulua* strikes. It is also good for slide baiting, and it will stand up to a considerable amount of punishment when slid live. It is a popular baitfish because a variety of deepwater gamefish will take it. So when using the mullet for bait, be prepared for anything and everything.

The most popular way to cook the mullet is to have it steamed with a combination of different sauces and spices. Its meat is white and very moist. In some places on the mainland the mullet is considered a trash fish; this is definitely not so in Hawaii.

AWA (Milkfish)
Chanos chanos

Pound for pound the *awa* is just about the strongest shoreline fish that I know of. It has a powerful tail and a long silvery body that's built like a silver bullet. The mouth is situated a little under the nose, and the eyes are large and keen of sight. On light tackle they are true fighters and you will need to summon all your fishing experience and knowledge to bring one of them to gaff. From the time an *awa* is hooked to the very end, it will fight.

The *awa* is a vegetarian and is known to feed on seaweed quite extensively. The season you'll find *awa* is usually during the summer months, when they come up the rivers to feed on seaweed and on other vegetation that grow abundantly along the riverbeds. Because they feed on seaweed, their mouths tend to be soft, tender, and toothless. For this reason you don't need to use wire leader or braided steel to catch them.

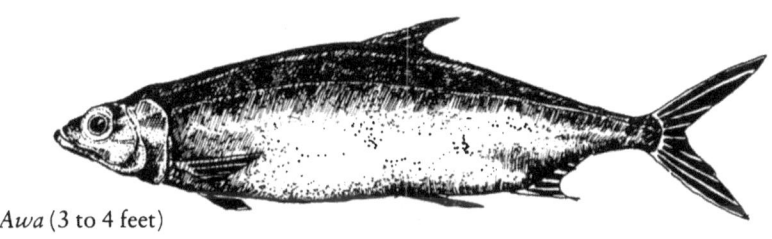

Awa (3 to 4 feet)

The rig that is commonly used by *awa* fishermen is very similar to the floater rig used by mullet fishermen. The only difference between the rigs is the monofilament size and the floater size. The hooks don't have to be very big, but they have to be very, very strong, otherwise the *awa* will bend or break the hook back without any problem at all. Hooking *awa* on light tackle is a battle that has been known to last a long time. If hooked on ultralight tackle, the *awa* will give you something to remember.

Awa have been hooked with artificial hairs such as wool, rug yarn the color of seaweed, goat hair, and other materials. They have never been hooked with store-bought tied flies or hooked on a fly rod, but it is not unlikely that they would take a homemade fly that looked like a ball of seaweed.

Awa grow very quickly in captivity and are raised commercially in many tropical islands and in Asia. The meat of the *awa* is nice and thick and tends to have a slight milky taste, thus its name, milkfish.

AWAAWA or AWA-'AUA (Hawaiian Tarpon)
Elops hawaiensis
This fish is also know as "the poor man's tarpon" because of its size. It resembles the Atlantic tarpon and jumps and feeds very much like one. *Awaawa* don't get very large, averaging around two to three feet in length. However, larger ones have been seen, usually traveling in small schools and feeding on baitfish, which are abundant in small bays and harbors. They tend not to like rough water, like most of the bigger reef species, and are more likely to frequent shallow reefs and calm waters. They will hit a well-trolled plug and are great fighters with light tackle. Normally the plug shouldn't be very big; it should average around two inches or so. Because it feeds mostly on small fish, the *awaawa* will hit small *weke ('oama)* that are whipped or cast out under a well-placed floater. They also hit flies and surface-worked jigs, favoring flies that are white and blue, and jigs that are white. They are great jumpers and will put on a great aerial show if hooked on light (4- to 6-pound) spinning tackle.

The *awaawa* tends to have lots of small bones, making it a little hard to eat. Most people make fishcake from the beautiful white meat, and this does very well on the dinner table.

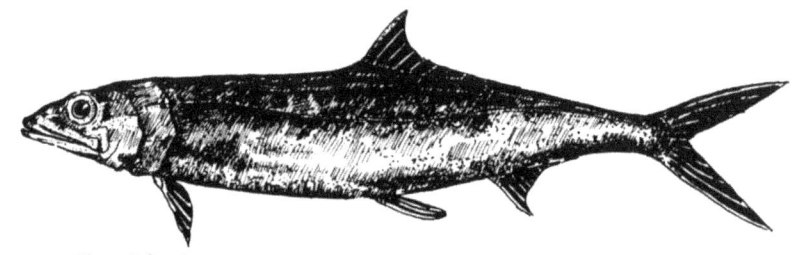

Awaawa (2 to 3 feet)

'ĀWEOWEO (Schneider's Bigeye Fish)
Priacanthus cruentatus
The adult bigeye is called *'āweoweo,* and the juvenile is called *'ala-lauwā.* It is a nightfeeder and can see very, very well with its big owl-like eyes. It feeds mostly on small white or clear shrimp. The average length of this fish is about ten inches; it is well muscled and bright orange or red in color. Its small scales are a real pain to scrape off. Many people fry the fish with the scales left on, and after the fish is fully cooked, the skin, scales and all, is peeled off.

The *'āweoweo* is most often hooked and landed by whipping small white flies or small plastic curly tail lures. The best types to use are the white and the clear with glitter. The angling technique for this fish involves casting as far as possible and then cranking in very slowly. The 'āweoweo can also be hooked with a handpole (twenty to twenty-five feet in length) and cut baits of shrimp, mackerel, or cuttlefish. The 'āweoweo is much like the *menpachi* in that it holds onto the bait as it is being retrieved; it doesn't hit the bait like the *āholehole,* however. So, a sensitive hand is required for hooking this fish when whipping.

The 'āweoweo lives only in the open ocean, loving deep water and the shelter of a lot of boulders, which protect it from the rays of the sun. Rough ocean water doesn't seem to bother it. It feeds mostly on nights when the moon is small or when there is no moon at all. As soon as the sun hits the horizon, it will begin feeding and will feed right on through the night.

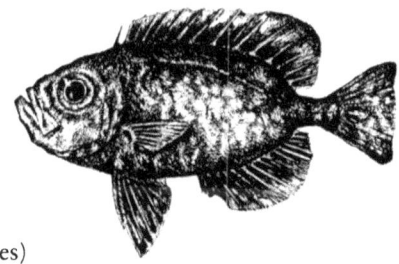

'Āweoweo (10 inches)

ENENUE (Ash-Colored Rudderfish)
Kyphosus cinerescens

The *enenue* is a wonderful fish for *poke* (sliced meat, usually raw fish, cut crosswise). It has a strong flavor that fish eaters like. When marinated with special sauces and spices, it is wonderful to eat. The fish is usually ash-colored, and its belly is a silver grey. Once in awhile someone will hook a golden-yellow *enenue,* or *nenue pala* (*pala* meaning "yellow"). The commonly held belief is that the yellow one is either the queen or king *enenue* and that if caught, should be thrown back to keep the group together. *Enenue* with partial yellow coloring or with a yellow tint only on the head have been seen. It is basically a vegetarian and feeds on seaweed found on the shoreline rocks.

Although the *enenue* normally feeds during the day, it has been caught at night by anglers equipped with handpoles or spinners. The best way to hook one is with a floater and long leader. Don't use a split shot on the leader. The *enenue* will take bread if the area is *palu*ed. Allow the bait to float freely and blend in with the floating chum. A mixture of canned mackerel and common baking flour will stick to the hook well. The mackerel should be made into a fine pulp, and then blended with flour until it becomes a tough, doughy ball. Cover the hook with small pieces of the mixture and toss it over the side with the floater.

When fighting, this fish is very strong for its size. It has a tendency to run under rocks or ledges to get away from the hook. So once the angler has the fish hooked, he should put as much pressure on it as possible. When the fish has tired, it will stay away from the rocks and will come up easily.

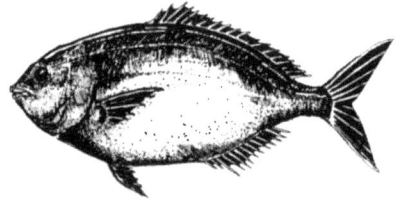

Enenue (12 inches)

KĀHALA (Amberjack or Yellowtail)
Seriola dumerilii

The young are called *kāhala ʻōpio*. The fish is long and slender, and normally has a dark, diagonal streak through its eye. It is a bronze color and has small scales. This fish tends to have a lot of small reddish worms throughout its body and is also known to cause ciguatera poisoning.

The *kāhala* is normally hooked by slide-bait anglers who fish in very deep waters. Much like the *ulua,* the *kāhala* is mostly a bottom feeder and is usually found in waters four hundred to five hundred feet deep. It will take octopus or squid baits, as well as jigs and other

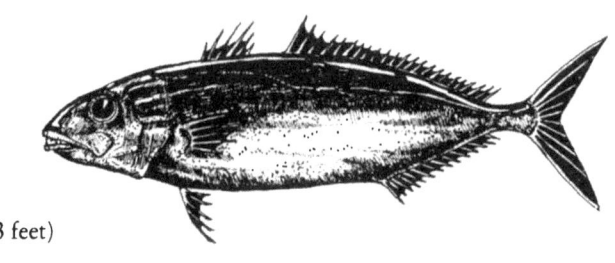

Kāhala (3 feet)

leaded lures. They don't hit surface plugs too often, but they have been hooked and landed on trolling lures. When hooked, the *kāhala* puts up a tremendous battle.

KĀKŪ (Pacific Barracuda)
Sphyraena barracuda

The *kākū* is fairly abundant in Hawaiian waters. They have been known to grow to lengths of over five feet. The largest *kākū*—seventy-six pounds—was landed from shore by Jason Gushiken on 80-pound-test line. They don't normally run that big, and are frequently found in small ponds in harbors and bays. If you look along the Nuuanu River, you'll see quite a few along the bank. They average around two feet in length and are very hard to catch.

The Japanese call it *oni-kamasu, oni* meaning demon or devil. With its massive rows of sharp teeth and mean-looking face, the *kākū*'s resemblance to a demon is quite remarkable. Because it hangs around large schools of *akule* and *'ōpelu* (mackerel), the Hawaiians call the barracuda "*akule* mama" or "*'ōpelu* mama."

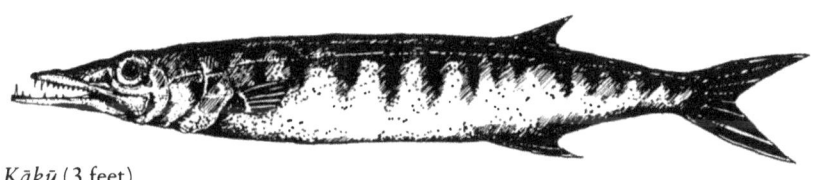

Kākū (3 feet)

The barracuda is a great fighting fish and is known to be a jumper when hooked on light tackle. It hits plugs and spoons, as well as nice yellow feathered jigs or hair jigs that are whipped and retrieved with great speed. Because of its vicious attacks, the barracuda hooks himself very easily; however, if the angler doesn't use a wire leader or braided wire, the barracuda can cut the line and make a quick getaway.

The Pacific barracuda is a great eating fish. It doesn't have many bones and its meat is moist and succulent. It can be prepared in just about any way conceivable, including *sashimi*.

KAMANU (Rainbow Runner or Hawaiian Salmon)
Elagatis bipinnulatus

The rainbow runner is usually hooked by slide-bait fishermen. When the angler fishes in very deep areas and uses squid or octopus as bait, he stands a good chance of hooking and landing a runner. Mostly a deep-water fish, the runner is often hooked from boats by handline fishermen. It is a fish that will live in a variety of ocean environments and depths.

Kamanu (3 feet)

KAWELEʻĀ (Heller's Barracuda)
Sphyraena helleri

The *kaweleʻā* is a little smaller and much more slender than the Pacific barracuda. It also doesn't have the massive rows of teeth the Pacific barracuda has. Small as it may be, as a table fish, it is probably second to none. Its meat is firm, very tasty, and easy to eat because it is almost boneless.

You won't see the *kaweleʻā* as much as you will the Pacific barracuda. It doesn't seem to hang around the shoreline much or go up into rivers and harbors. Large schools of *kaweleʻā* can be found in the deep waters of the outer reefs. They usually follow large schools of baitfish or they feed on shrimp.

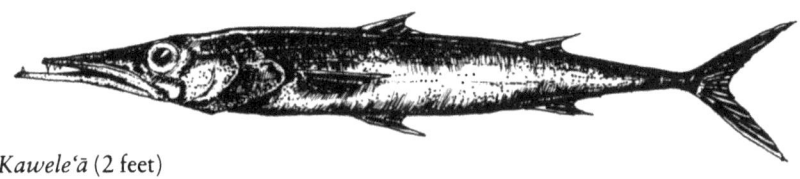

Kaweleʻā (2 feet)

The *kaweleʻā* isn't the jumper the Pacific barracuda is. It also doesn't hit plugs at all, mainly because it feeds in such deep water during only the darkest nights. While spinning, *menpachi* fishermen catch them quite often; but the angler must be on his toes or the *kaweleʻā* will cut his line with only a moment's notice. The fish will make blazing runs that will make many a fisherman's heart pound to beat the band. Once the first run is over, you can be sure there will be more to come. Once the runs have stopped, however, you will find that the fish can be reeled in quite easily. The time it is more likely to get away is during the haul up the cliffline. One shake on the light line and the fish will cut the leader with its weight and sharp teeth.

Some places will be overrun with *kawele'ā*. The best way to hook them is to cast out your slide-bait rig and slide down a half section of *'ōpelu* bait. The only difference between this type of slide and others is that the treble hook and not the *tankichi ulua* hook is used. Some anglers rig together two treble hooks so that the *'ōpelu* fillet covers both hooks. The *kawele'ā* will hit the bait with such force that the trebles will set solid in its jaw and gill plates. Naturally, the leader should be made of stainless steel wire.

Lai (20 inches)

LAI (Leatherback)
Scomberoides sanctipetri

The *lai* is a very slender fish with tough, leatherlike skin. Normally the skin is stripped off, dried, and later tied onto Kona heads or jet heads as an outer skin. This dazzling silver skin makes trolling lures look very realistic. Once wet, the skin becomes supple and smelly, and this adds to the delectableness of the lures.

The *lai* is a great gamefish on ultralight tackle and is one of the few fish in Hawaii that actually jumps. Its aerial acrobatics are delightful to watch, and its powerful runs on ultralight tackle make it a fish well worth hooking. The best bait to whip with is a strip of glitter shrimp. This small strip will catch more than its share of *lai* in no time flat. The leader below the lead should be a length you can handle. Retrieve the strip in short jerks.

The *lai* is one of the best fish to hook on fly tackle. It takes flies very well and will come into fly-casting range if the area is chummed very heavily. The fly should be small and white and rigged with little strips of mylar. The plastic glitter strip also works well as a fly and will stand up to a lot of casting before it is snapped off.

The average length of a *lai* is around twenty to twenty-four inches. The biggest *lai* I have landed weighed in at about five pounds. It travels in small schools and comes into bays and harbors quite freely. It feeds on small schools of mullet and *nehu* (Hawaiian anchovy). As a table fish, the *lai* is average in taste. Once the meat is filleted, it makes for fine *sashimi*. Breaded or floured and deep fried it makes for a great fish sandwich or a good main course.

MENPACHI or 'Ū'Ū (Squirrelfish)
Myripristis murdjan

The *menpachi* is one of the best-eating small fish from the Hawaiian reefs, and it carries a very high price on the market. It is a very prized fish particularly during the New Year season because of its deep orange red to bright red colors.

However, it is not one of the better fighters of the reefs, although it will hold its own on ultralight tackle. The *menpachi* is normally caught only at night and in and around areas that have a lot of rocks and reefs. It hides in caves and under boulders during the daylight hours and feeds almost exclusively on small white shrimp and plankton that live in the reefy areas. For this reason, anglers who fish extensively for *menpachi* use small little white flies or little twister tails about an inch long. The *menpachi* has been known to hit colors other than white—red, orange, as well as blue, for example.

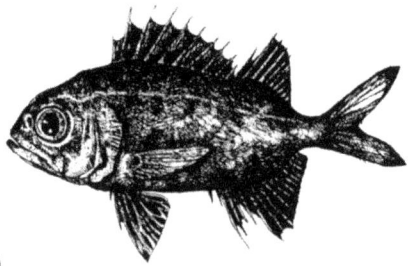

Menpachi (9 inches)

The tackle normally used is light spinning gear and long, long whipping rods. The rods can be as long as sixteen feet and throw a 1½-ounce lead quite a distance. In areas that are shallow (five to ten feet), floaters can be used along with small white flies. Some anglers use cut baits to catch these fish and are quite successful, but being that *menpachi* live in such rough, rocky areas, they usually lose more lead than catch fish.

Fly fishing for *menpachi* is a lot of fun if you can draw the fish close enough to make your cast. The technique used is similar to the nymph fishing techniques used in trout streams. Fast sinking Hi-D fly lines are the best to use, along with small white flies or white wooly worms.

In areas that are easily accessible, some anglers use handpoles to catch this tasty fish. Long handpoles that reach over twenty feet will do the job nicely (see "Leader Material," Chapter 9). Small bits of shrimp and other cut baits will do the trick all evening long. California shrimp work very well, as well as cut sections of *'ōpelu* and cuttlefish. As do all species of squirrelfish, the *menpachi* tends to have a lot of sharp spines, so when handling this fish you should be careful of the gill plates and the fins.

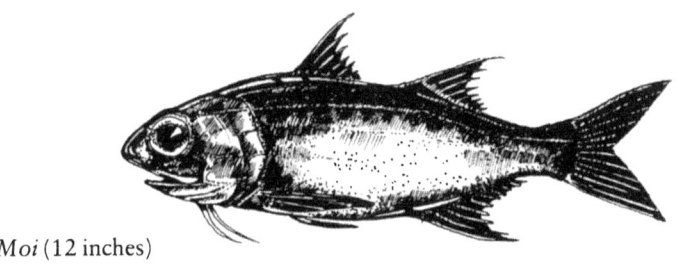

Moi (12 inches)

MOI (Pacific Threadfin)
Polydactylus sexfilis

The *moi* is one of the better-eating fishes of the reef. It is hard to find nowadays and anyone who finds a *moi* hole usually keeps it very, very quiet. The smaller *moi* (two to three inches in length) are called *moi-liʻi,* and the intermediate-sized *moi* are called *pala moi,* or *mana moi,* depending on which island you come from.

The *moi* feeds exclusively along the shoreline and normally travels in fairly large schools. The *moi-liʻi* move up into rivers, brackish water bays, and harbors for cover. They are great baits for the larger reef predators, and if used live they will draw a great many strikes. When the *moi-liʻi* move up into the rivers or bays and shallow reefs, they travel in huge schools and feed very heavily.

The best way to catch *moi-liʻi* is with a handpole and a bit of shrimp bait. They tend to hang around with the *'oama* and small *pāpio,* so you may catch *moi-liʻi* when fishing for these fish. They can also be hooked and landed with artificial lures. The big *moi* will hit a curly tail jig such as the Scrounger Lure. The white or clear glitter is a good choice. The smart fisherman will choose an area that tends to be shallow and a little on the rough side. The Scrounger is cast out and the retrieve is made slowly and steadily. In this way the lure stays close to the bottom where the *moi* likes to hang out. Being that the Scrounger has a built-in wiggle, the rod is not worked the way it is with most lures. The *moi* is a good fighter and has a tender mouth, so the battle should be waged with a light and tender touch. If too much pressure is applied, the fish's mouth will tear and the fish will be lost.

Moi can also be caught by simply dunking some cut bait in inshore areas that have a lot of white water and sand. The *moi* likes baits such as *'ōpelu* and shrimp, and it will pick up these baits with no hesitation.

Places where there are high cliffs and deep water have *moi*. Fish in white water with a spinning rod and some cut baits and you'll have a good chance of picking up some *moi*. Remember they travel in schools, so if you catch one, keep fishing because there should be more around.

The *moi* has firm, moist meat and is best served steamed or fried. Cooking it over a charcoal fire is another way to make the *moi* something to remember.

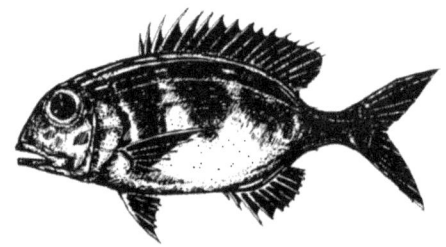

Mū (18 inches)

MŪ (Grandeyed Porgy Fish)
Monotaxis grandoculis
The *mū* is basically grey in color. The young *mū* has vertical bands on its body that seem to disappear as its gets older. The adult will weigh over ten pounds and at times up to twenty pounds or more. This fish has molars and feeds on shrimp, crab, and other crustaceans. It tends to inhabit the midwaters during the daylight hours and move into the shallows during the evening.

Mū meat is hard and firm and very, very moist. It was a favorite of the Hawaiian kings and is still greatly prized by fish eaters. The fish is best prepared steamed and served with onions and salt.

The *mū* angler will tell you that it is a hard fish to catch. It has tremendous strength and will put up a battle that will make your hair stand on end. For this fish, most fishermen use nothing less than 30-pound test; some handpolers use 100-pound test with a very long wire leader. The wire leader must be such that the *mū* can't grind right through the line while he's eating the bait. The hook has to be of stout proportions and will have to endure severe stress. The bait commonly used for catching this fish is crab. Some anglers use shrimp, but crab is best. The best kind of crab to use and the easiest to get is the common *'a'ama*.

When you are fishing for *mū* your rod should hang over the cliff with the bait lowered down to the depths. The bait simply hangs and drifts with the tide. When the *mū* comes along, he will grab the crab and start to eat it right there on the spot. With its powerful molars it will grind up the crab along with the hook and wire leader. If the fish is eating, the rod tip will slowly begin to droop. The experienced angler will wait for several minutes and then quickly set the hook with a strong sweep of the rod. What follows will be a battle second to none.

'Ō'IO (Bonefish)
Albula vulpes

Acclaimed as a great gamefish in both the Atlantic and the Pacific, the *'ō'io* is known for its long powerful runs. It prefers shallow, sandy reef areas, and travels in large schools; it is not surprising, therefore, when one hears that someone has hooked and landed several dozen. Like the *awa*, the *'ō'io* has a lot of bones; thus its name, bonefish. It can be made into good fishcake and other types of fish dishes.

The *'ō'io* feeds almost exclusively on sandworms and bottom crustaceans such as crabs and shrimp. It crushes all of its food with a set of hard, bonelike crushers in the back of its head. Able to hammer its food to a pulp, the *'ō'io* can handle hard crabs and other hard-shelled crustaceans. Although an *'ō'io* weighing over twenty pounds is not

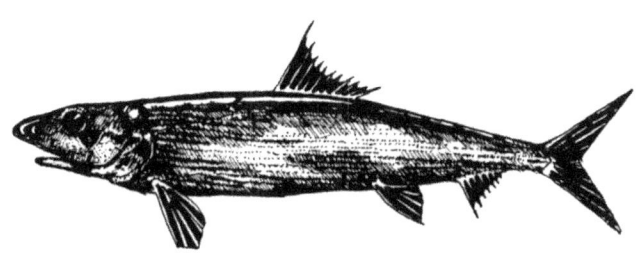

'Ō'io (18 inches)

unheard of, the average ʻōʻio in Hawaii weighs in at between five and ten pounds.

The best way to hook ʻōʻio is to dunk crab (soft shell, if possible) in some sandy-to-pebbly bottom area. It will also take strips of cuttlefish, even sand turtles, which you can find at the waves' edge. In the Bahamas, Florida Keys, and Biscayne Bay, the ʻōʻio has been hooked with flies, but only in shallow, ankle-deep water. In Hawaii, where the waters tend to be much deeper and rougher, fly fishing for ʻōʻio is not always productive, although ʻōʻio could probably be taken with a fly in the shallow shoals common off Molokai and Kauai. Off the sandy reefs of Christmas Island you'll find innumerable ʻōʻio cruising the flats. By bouncing small #6 or #8 flies along the bottom, you can pick up some pretty good size ʻōʻio.

This fish also makes good bait. If it is small, say, one to two pounds, it can be slid down whole. The *ulua* love to eat ʻōʻio for some reason. In the open ocean, I don't know how the *ulua* is able to catch the speedy ʻōʻio. Still, this fish will draw more than its share of strikes.

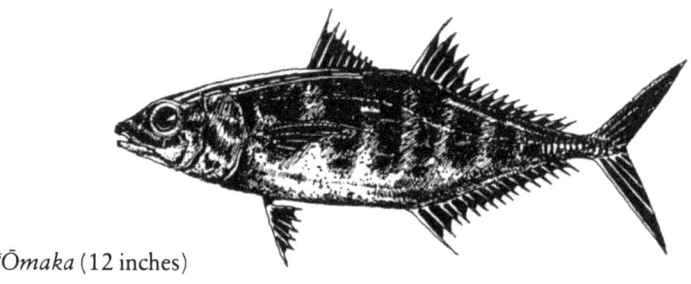

ʻŌmaka (12 inches)

ʻŌMAKA (Yellow-Tailed Scad)
Caranx mate

The ʻōmaka is of the *ulua* family, although it looks very much like an *akule*. The most striking difference between the two fish is their color. Greenish yellow stripes run vertically along the ʻōmaka's body. The fish is a good fighter on light tackle. It is known to frequent harbors and bays quite extensively, and to travel in big schools, which are often followed by *ulua* and *kāhala*.

The best bait to use to catch ʻōmaka is *nehu*, either alive or dead. (It will also take strips of cuttlefish and cut sections of ʻōpelu and *akule*.) Dunk two or three hooks on a single line. The tackle should be quite light; 10- and 12-pound test is used most often. Once the bait is down put a small bell on the rod and wait for the ring.

When traveling in large schools, *'ōmaka* can be hooked by whipping plastic glitter strips through the schools. Small white flies towed behind a whipping leader will also draw a strike. Some anglers cast with small orange floaters to get some action in the water. Sometimes this bit of surface action will add to the effectiveness of the whipping technique. Some anglers will simply drag the line through the water at an easy pace; others will jerk the rod tip to make the floater chug through the water and make big blurping sounds. Each technique can be effective and should be tried until the one that produces is found.

This fish can also be used as bait. Once an *'ōmaka* is caught, it is usually slid down *ulua* lines to prompt vicious strikes. Another way to use the *'ōmaka* is to live bait it and drift it out to sea with a balloon or floater. It will draw strikes from all kinds of gamefish, including *kawakawa, mahimahi,* and other deep-sea dwellers. Use this fabulous bait in very, very deep waters. The *'ōmaka* is frisky on the hook and will last a long time. Its skin is tough and will hold a hook well.

'ŌMILU (Bluefin Trevally)
Caranx melampygus
The *'ōmilu,* also called *hoshi ulua* in Japanese, is a favorite among shoreline whippers. It inhabits the inshore areas and feeds on reef fishes, moray eels, jumping jacks, damselfishes, octopi, and various crustaceans. The *'ōmilu* is often caught with whipping plugs and jigs. A tough and determined fighter, the *'ōmilu* makes long and powerful runs on light tackle. The standard line used is around 10- to 12-pound test. *'Ōmilu* travel in small schools and will attack a school of baitfish in rapid succession. A well-retrieved plug can be effective when this fish is traveling in small schools; it is almost certain that one will take the plug.

The best baits to use when you're after *'ōmilu* are the *hīnālea* and the jumping jack. The best way to use the jumping jack is to whip it live around reef areas. It is especially effective in white water areas

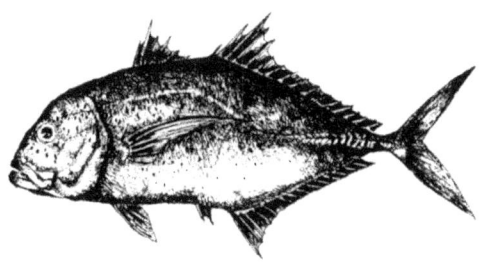

'Ōmilu (2 feet)

and close to the ocean bottom. If the tide is right and *'ōmilu* are around, you'll have more than your share of action.

Two cut baits that the *'ōmilu* likes especially are sections of *'ōpelu* and *akule*. It also will take squid and shrimp without hesitation, as well as strips of *menpachi, 'āweoweo,* and *lai*. Another effective way to catch *'ōmilu* is to chum extensively. Chumming seems to draw them quickly, and once around they will take almost any bait thrown at them. The bait must sink very, very slowly and act much like the sinking chum dispersed in the area.

There is a type of fly called the *palu* fly that resembles any type of chum you might ladle into the water. For this reason, you shouldn't work the fly as you would a conventional fly; merely let it sink down with the rest of the *palu*. One of the best ways to get a fish to take a *palu* fly is to work the fly so that it looks like *palu* hitting the water. If the chum is tossed very high and allowed to hit the water with a splat! and the *ulua* or *'ōmilu* takes it, then repeat this step with another piece. Toss the fly in next and allow it to hit the water the same way. Acting on reflex, the fish will come up and take the fly without hesitation.

Since one of its favorite foods is the jumping jack, the most effective plugs and jigs to use to catch this fish are black in color. The dark black jigs or plastic-bodied Touts make tremendous baits for the *'ōmilu*. Working the surface of the inshore reefs with the black lures, or bouncing the jigs on the bottom are equally effective techniques.

Yellow is another color popular with *'ōmilu*. Yellow-feathered jigs and hair jigs make for some quick action with this reef predator, as do gold spoons, especially when worked in see-saw patterns and with deep strokes. Green has also proven to be a good choice. You won't find too many jigs in this "flavor," but it has been used by some creative individuals with astounding success. One of the possible reasons for its success is that many of the small reef fishes are basically green in color.

One color that I have shied away from in the past is red; lately, however, I've found it to be a very, very good producer. A friend of mine used to use only red jigs and Touts and had great success. I couldn't catch a fish with red to save my soul until I realized that fish of the night are red. Fish like the *'ala'ihi, menpachi,* and *'āweoweo* have all been favorite baits of the slide-bait fisherman for generations and generations, so it stands to reason that red would work in deep waters or close to the bottom. And so I did try just that. I worked the jig down deep and close to the rocks, where red fish are usually found. Strikes occurred more consistently, and as a result, I added another color to the arsenal of colors I have faith in.

'Ōmilu can also be hooked and landed on flies that have black and red as basic colors. Blue-backed beer-belly flies and small white flies also work. The fly has to be retrieved very, very fast so that it is always on the surface and zipping along. Poppers also work to some extent, as do standard black streamer flies.

'ŌPELU (Mackerel Scad)
Decapterus pinnulatus

The *'ōpelu* makes one of the best cut baits for shore fishermen, although its meat is rather soft and flaky, and doesn't sit on the hook too well. Most anglers salt the cut sections to make them hard and firm. It normally takes about twelve hours for the meat to lose all of its moisture and become firm.

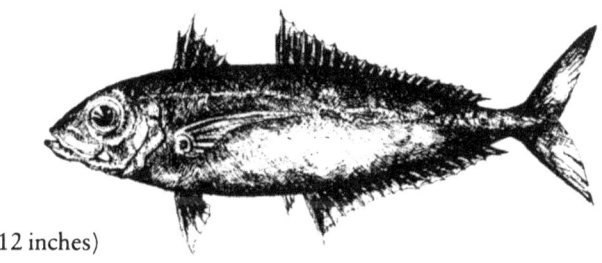

'Ōpelu (12 inches)

If you can get live *'ōpelu* on your hook, then you will have a bait that is second to none. Hooked live and allowed to swim along the shoreline, it will draw *ulua* strikes that are unbelievable. As a dead slide bait, it is not too good because the small reef fish make short work out of it. The *'ōpelu* isn't normally hooked by shore fishermen, but it has been snagged when traveling in big schools in harbors and bays. Once an *'ōpelu* is snagged, it is allowed to swim with the hook still embedded in its side. *Ulua* and *kāhala* follow *'ōpelu* schools and will attack any that is acting abnormally. *Ulua* that have tipped the scales over 100 pounds have been landed this way, and all with heavy spinning tackle and some great determination. The average-size ones normally run from approximately 35 to 65 pounds.

The *'ōpelu* is good eating. It is good both raw and fried. When fried, the meat is firm and moist and very tasty. It is super when dried: the fish is filleted into two sections and allowed to dry whole. It makes great beer *pūpū,* and when served with hot rice and *chazuke* (tea), it is beyond compare. This fish is often served in some Kona restaurants, and it commands a fairly good price on the market. If the market doesn't get the fish, the commercial fishermen will. It is great bait for *'ahi* and other deep-sea fish.

TA'APE (Blue-Lined Snapper)
Lutjanus kasmira

The *ta'ape* is a snapper that was imported and transplanted from the Marquesas. It was first introduced in Kaneohe Bay, Oahu, on 23 June 1958; again on 24 June 1958; and a few years later in December 1961. It has since flourished and can be seen traveling in great schools in bays, harbors, and channels.

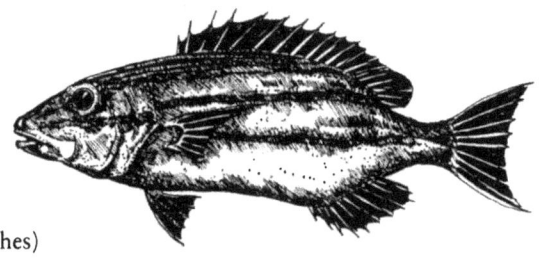

Ta'ape (10 inches)

The *ta'ape* is much like the *to'au*, and tends to be found with schooling *to'au*. Both fish feed mostly on shrimp and other reef animals. *Ta'ape* is easily caught with hook and line, and has been known to grow up to fifteen or sixteen inches in length. It is a great fighting fish on ultralight tackle and will give you a thrill for a short period of time.

The fish is mostly yellow and has three to four blue lines running the length of its body. It makes for good *ulua* bait and will last a long time on the hook. If you decide not to use it for bait, it makes great table fare too. The fish is not as robust as the *to'au*, but good eating nonetheless. It is a good idea to land a lot of them and then fillet and dry them under the sun. Properly dried and salted they make great *pūpū* for the beer drinkers in the house.

TO'AU (Red and Green Snapper)
Lutjanus fulvus

Although commonly called a perch, the *to'au* (the Tahitian name) is really a snapper. The fish was introduced several times by the Hawaii Fish and Game in October 1956, June 1958, August 1961, and again in December 1961. The *to'au* now thrives in large schools in harbors and outer reefs of the Hawaiian chain. Unfortunately the *to'au* and *ta'ape* are not liked very much by bottom fishermen, who feel that these fish are over-grazing their fishing grounds and are contributing to the decline of the *'ehu* and *'ōpakapaka* (snapper) population. This has never been substantiated, however.

To'au (10 inches)

The *to'au* is a robust, bright-yellow fish. Since it travels in such large schools, it can be hooked and landed fairly quickly. On ultralight tackle it is a good fighter and quick biter; the only problem is that it tends to swallow a lot of bait. It doesn't seem to like lures too much, but will take a fly that is small and white.

This fish is good to eat because it has a lot of moist and succulent meat. It is very good steamed or fried, and is even better cooked over an open fire or filleted and dried under the hot sun.

ULUA, BLACK (Black Jack)
Caranx lugubris

The black *ulua* is much like the white *ulua* in its habits and character; they differ only in coloration and fighting style. The angling techniques fishermen use for black *ulua* are the same as those used for the white *ulua*. The baits are also essentially the same. Black *ulua* are strong and intelligent fighters. They like to strike and then run

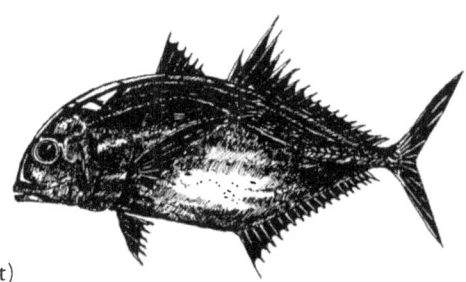

Black *Ulua* (4 feet)

quickly under rocks or into coral caverns. They have been known to travel in big schools, ravaging schools of other reef fish. The angler that spins heavily can get very frustrated when he sees a huge black *ulua* take his plug, since this almost certainly will mean the plug will be lost and the fish will escape.

ULUA, KAGAMI (Threadfin Jack)
Alectis ciliaris

This is one of the most beautiful of all the *ulua*. It looks much like a brilliant mirror (*kagami* in Japanese). The Hawaiian name for this fish is *ulua kihikihi;* it is also called "African Pompano." A jack, the *kagami* battles much like the typical *ulua*—deep and strong. The *kagami* will hit small yellow jigs and other jigs that can be bounced along the bottom. They don't chase lures very often and are rarely hooked on slide-bait rigs.

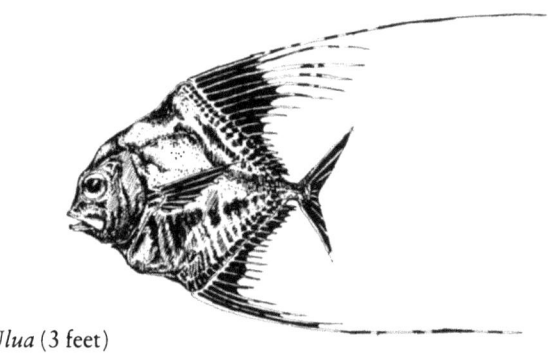

Kagami Ulua (3 feet)

The juvenile *kagami* is diamond-shaped, and has two distinct, long filaments that trail from its dorsal and anal fins. The older the *kagami* gets, the shorter the filaments become. This fish doesn't get very big in Hawaii, averaging around twenty pounds. Being that it is so skinny, the *kagami* doesn't have much meat to eat, although the larger ones do have good sections of beautiful whitish meat. The meat is good fried, and because the *kagami* hardly has any scales, an entire fillet can be eaten whole.

ULUA, WHITE (Forskal's Indo-Pacific Jack Fish)
Caranx ignobilis

The white *ulua* is the most sought after shoreline fish in Hawaii. A true predator of the inshore reefs, the *ulua* is almost purely an ambush fish. It loves to ambush its prey by concealing itself in either shoreline

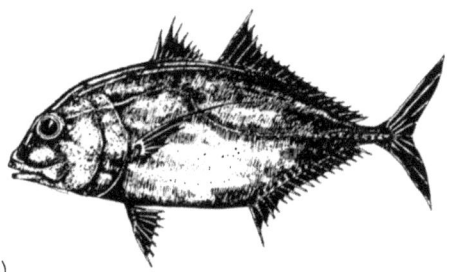

White *Ulua* (4 feet)

white waters or inshore coral reef mazes. It is no wonder the white *ulua* is the most efficient of inshore predators. They tend to roam in small packs; later, when they get larger, they become loners.

The *ulua* feeds mostly at night, favoring the darkest nights. Although the white *ulua* feeds in shallow areas, most of its feeding is done in deep areas with reefs that drop off very abruptly and that therefore provide easy escapes.

One of the nicest things about the white *ulua* is that it will hit a number of baits, as well as a wide assortment of lures and flies. Whether it be a large deerhair jig or expensive hardwood plug, the white *ulua* will hit anything that it thinks is edible. The techniques to use with your lure will change every day. On some days the lure will work best if whipped across the surface like a frightened minnow; on other days, if jigged in extra deep waters in an erratic pattern. So, the practical fisherman after the wily white predator will be able to adapt to any and all techniques as befit the day and fish.

The white *ulua* also has been known to frequent inshore bays and harbors. They roam the calm shorelines looking for small reef fish and bottom-dwelling crustaceans. The octopus is one of its favorite foods, as are crabs, lobsters, eels, and a host of reef fish. Some of the reef fish that are his favorites are the *mamo, halalū, menpachi, ʻāweoweo,* mullet, *enenue, ʻōpelu, palani, paoʻo,* and *weke*. Some of the white *ulua*'s favorite cut baits are filleted moray eel, squid strips, filleted *ʻōpelu,* and sections of *akule* or of the white belly of a shark.

The slide bait technique is the most effective way to catch white *ulua,* mainly because it can be used efficiently at night, in various kinds of weather, and in deep water. It was created to accommodate the large baits the *ulua* loves. Some of these baits are so big they aren't measured in inches but by the pound.

Some big white *ulua* have been known to take huge chunks of *kāhala* bait meant for huge sharks. In one instance, the *ulua* was such a pig that it ate the bait whole and got hooked on the shark hook. It was later eaten by a roaming shark, which left only the *ulua*'s head. The *ulua*'s weight was estimated at approximately 120 pounds. Basic bait casting also works as well as just hanging sections of moray eel from steep cliffs with a long stiff rod. Whichever you choose, the *ulua* will accommodate you if you are persistent.

The white *ulua* can grow to enormous sizes. Some individuals claim they have seen *ulua* that were well over 200 pounds. With the largest on record tilting the scales at 198 pounds, it is not surprising that there is a 200-pounder still out there. The largest known was landed by shore caster Roy Gushiken and weighed in at 137.9 pounds.

WAHANUI (Fork-Tailed Snapper)
Aphareus furcatus

Some people call this fish *hanui* or *gurutsu* (its Japanese name). The fish looks and fights very much like a smallmouth bass. It has a large mouth, thus the name *waha*, "big mouth." Its mouth is jointed like an *ulua*'s or a bass'. It can open its mouth wide enough to gobble up large baitfish with no problem at all.

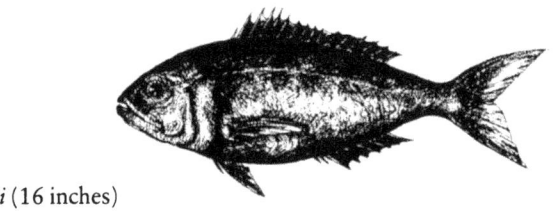

Wahanui (16 inches)

The *wahanui* tends to live on the outer edges of the reef and in midwater. It is frequently hooked by whippers, and is not an especially strong fish. On medium tackle the *wahanui* is not much of a battler, but on ultralight tackle the fish puts up a superb fight.

Basically a predator, the *wahanui* will take any plug or lure that acts like a wounded minnow. Yellow and gold are its favorite colors. Yellow or orange jigs work great when jigged over deep reefs and drop-offs. Yellow flies tied behind a whipping lead has also taken its toll on the *wahanui* population.

As an eating fish, the *wahanui* is rather bland, especially after it has been in the freezer a while. It tends to get very dry and unappetizing and so should be eaten right away. Being a hefty-size fish (growing to approximately five pounds), it has a lot of meat and makes a good-size meal. The best way to prepare the *wahanui* is to either bake or steam it. This keeps the fish a little more moist and flavorful. Some onions and garlic salt can make it more than favorable to the family.

Not many people think of the *wahanui* as baitfish, but it makes good live bait for *ulua*. The fish is a good size and frisky when hooked quickly and slid down your line. It will survive many long hours on the hook, and because of its endurance it is a good target for big, big *ulua*.

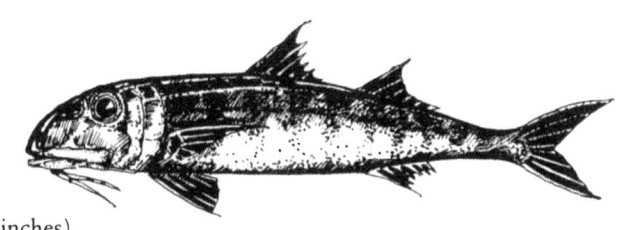

Weke (12 inches)

WEKE (Goatfish Family)
MULLIDAE

The *weke* is a bottom dweller. Young *weke* are called ʻ*oama* and are usually caught during the months of July and August. A school may contain hundreds, even thousands of *weke,* and can be found by looking for a small ring of anglers armed with handpoles and bait. The best baits to use for this fish are salted crab and shrimp. The best place to put the bait is close to the bottom, being that the fish is a bottom feeder. With its two thin bottom feelers it will dig up the bottom to look for small, sand-dwelling shrimp and crabs.

The baby *weke* make supreme baits for *pāpio* and other reef predators. If they are used as live bait and drifted out under a floater or simply dunked off piers or cliffs, the *ulua* or other fish will take the bait without hesitation.

The adult *weke* (also called *weke ʻula* in the case of Pfluger's Goatfish) prefers deep waters and also feeds on the bottom. The best way to catch one is by dunking in sandy ocean bottoms and keeping a close watch on your rod tip. Another way is to make a long cast and drag the bait on the sand in a start–stop motion. This movement will arouse the *weke*'s curiosity. Once he comes to the bait, it is only a matter of time before he takes it. For the very deep water *weke,* the best bait is cut up sections of *'ōpelu*. Live *'ōpae* (river shrimp) will work even better.

Deep fried and eaten whole, the *'oama* makes for a good meal. The larger *weke* are also good fried or steamed whole. Add a few slices of onions and some soy sauce to the dish and you've got a meal that could compete against cooked trout any day.

GLOSSARY

aho	small rope, usually handmade
aku	tuna
hibachi	charcoal brazier
ika	cuttlefish; squid
kala	unicorn surgeonfish
kupipi	grey damselfish
manini	Sandwich Island surgeonfish (reef fish)
nehu	Hawaiian anchovy
'o'opu	goby (several types are found both in fresh water and salt water)
'ōpae	small shrimp; also called *shirosa*
palu	to "chum" or throw bits of ground-up fish into the water to lure fish to the fishing spot
poke	slices of meat cut crosswise
puhi	moray eel
pūpū	h'ors d'oeuvre
sashimi	Japanese dish consisting of thinly sliced raw fish
shirosa	Japanese name for *'ōpae* (shrimp)
tabi	Japanese cloth shoes
tako	octopus
tohei	conger eel; also called white eel

REFERENCES

Keane, Martin J. *Classic Rods and Rodmakers.* New York: Winchester Press, 1976.

McNally, Tom. *Tom McNally's Complete Book of Fisherman's Knots.* Chicago: J. Philip O'Hara, Inc., 1975.

1983 World Record Game Fishes. Fort Lauderdale, Florida: International Game Fish Association, 1983.

Sosin, Mark J., ed. *Angler's Bible.* New Jersey: Stoeger Publishing Co., 1975.

Tinker, Spencer Wilkie. *Fishes of Hawaii.* Hawaii: Hawaiian Service, Inc., 1978.

GAMEFISH INDEX

'ahi, yellowfin tuna, *Thunnus albacares*, 125
āholehole, Hawaiian flag fish, *Kuhlia sandvicensis*, 8, 115, 135, 221–222
aku, skipjack tuna, *Euthynnus* (=*Katsuwonus*) *pelamis*, 129
akule, bigeyed scad, *Trachurops crumenophthalmus*, 130, 210, 222–223, 229, 238, 244
'ala'ihi, squirrelfish, *Holocentrus* genus, 239
'ama'ama, mullet (pond), *Mugil cephalus*, 8, 9, 223–224, 244
awa, milkfish, *Chanos chanos*, 225, 235
awaawa/awa-'aua, ladyfish, ten-pounder, tarpon, *Elops hawaiensis*, 226
'āweoweo, Schneider's bigeye fish, *Priacanthus cruentatus*, 8, 85, 115, 133, 226–227, 238, 239, 244
enenue/nenue, ash-colored rudderfish, pilotfish, *Kyphosus fuscus*, 8, 133, 227–228, 244
halalū/hahalalū, juvenile bigeyed scad (akule), *Trachurops crumenophthalmus*, 8, 222, 223, 244. See also akule
hīnālea, wrasse, *Labridae* family, 131, 135–139, 238
kāhala, amberjack, yellowtail fish, *Seriola dumerilii*, 125, 168, 211, 223, 228–229, 244
kākū, Pacific barracuda, *Sphyraena barracuda*, 93, 113, 229
kamanu, rainbow runner, Hawaiian salmon, *Elaqatis bipinnulatus*, 230
kawele'ā, Heller's barracuda, *Sphyraena helleri*, 230–231
kole, surgeonfish, *Ctenochaetus strigosus*, 189
kūmū, red goatfish, *Parupeneus porphyreus*, 8, 113, 114, 133

lai, leatherback, *Scomberoides sancti-petri*, 149–152, 231–232, 238
mahimahi, dolphin fish, *Coryphaena hippurus*, 125, 237
mamo, damselfish, *Abudefduf abdominalis*, 8, 131, 133, 189, 244
manini, surgeonfish, convict tang, *Acanthurus triostegus*, 131
menpachi/mempachi, squirrelfish, *Myripristis murdjan*, 8, 85, 86, 115, 133, 210, 211, 214, 222, 227, 232–233, 238, 239, 244
moano, red goatfish, *Parupeneus multifasciatus*, 8, 113, 142, 178–179
moi, Pacific threadfin, *Polydactylus sexfilis*, 113, 233–234
mū, grandeyed porgy fish, *Monotaxis grandoculis*, 132, 234–235
nehu, Hawaiian anchovy, *Stolephorus purpureus*, 237
'oama, juvenile goatfish (weke), 3, 8, 91, 131, 226, 246
'ō'io, bonefish, *Albula vulpes*, 125, 131, 160, 235–236
'ōmaka, yellow-tailed scad, *caranx mate*, 236–237
'ōmilu, bluefin trevally, *Caranx melampygus*, 47, 150, 162, 168, 237–238
ono, wahoo, *Acanthocybium solandri*, 93
'o'opu 'akupa, freshwater goby, *Eleotris sandwicensis*, 15–16, 49, 91, 116
'o'opu nākea, brackish water to saltwater goby, *Awaous stamineus*, 15–16, 116
'ōpelu, mackerel scad, *Decapterus pinnulatus*, 8, 114, 116, 123, 130, 131, 223, 229, 231, 233, 234, 237, 238, 239–240, 244
palani, surgeonfish, *Acanthurus dussumieri*, 8, 133, 244
pao'o, jumping jack, *Istiblennius zebra*, 16, 140–142, 151, 179, 244

pāpio, juvenile jack *(ulua)*, 3, 8, 47–48, 49, 113, 135, 141–142, 161, 210
ta'ape, blue-lined snapper, *Lutjanus kasmira*, 8, 131, 133, 240–241
to'au, red and green snapper, *Lutjanus fulvus*, 8, 133, 241
uhu, parrotfish, *Scarus perspicillatus*, 132
ulua, jack crevally, *Carangidae* family, 8, 30, 57–63, 66, 95–107, 116–120, 122, 124–128, 132, 133, 136–139, 160, 168, 169, 173, 174, 183–195, 210–211, 223, 236, 240; black, *Caranx lugubris*, 241–242; kihikihi, kagami ulua, threadfin jack, *Alectis ciliaris*, 242–243; white, Forskal's Indo-Pacific jack fish, *Caranx ignobilis*, 243–244. *See also* pāpio
wahanui, fork-tailed snapper, *Aphareus furcatus*, 245
weke, goatfish, *Mullidae* family, 113, 114, 133, 169, 244, 246. *See also* 'oama
weke 'ula, goatfish, *Mulloidichthys vanicolensis* or *M. pflugeri*, 246

GENERAL INDEX

'A'ama (crab), 235
Abu-Garcia reels, 26, 27
Aerators, 16, 140
Albright Knot, 84–85, 95, 103, 164, 183
Ambassadeur reels, 27
Apte, Stu, 18, 19
Atlapac reels, 26, 27–28, 189

Bait-casting reels, 24
Bait-casting rods, 51–53
Baits: dead, 116–133; for handpole fishing, 15–16; live, 132–142; size of, 14, 133–135
Balloon Stopper Rig, 112, 113
Bamboo handpole, 1–5, 40, 49, 58–59; selection of, 2; tempering, 5
Bank Sinker, 202–203
Berner, Juliana, 39
Big Island Leader, 95
Bimini Twist Knot, 77, 78–79, 95, 98, 99, 103, 111, 164, 173, 183
Blood Knot, 77, 81, 82
Book of Saint Albans, The, 39
Boron rods, 45, 65
Boschen, William, 17, 18

Calcutta bamboo, 40
Casting accuracy, 162
Centrifugal tension knob, in bait-casting reels, 25
Chum *(palu),* 105–106, 117, 125–126, 129–130, 131; in handpole fishing, 8
Coleman lantern, 210, 213, 214
Compleat Angler, The, 39
Conversion kits, 21
Cork, for rod grips, 44
Cotton cord loop, 4
Coxe, Joe A., 17
Crab, as bait, 131

Daiwa reels, 26, 27, 30, 49, 171
Deadend Rig, 95, 96, 102
Diamond Jigs. *See* Tin Squids
Double Nail Knot Splice, 77, 84
Double Surgeon's Loop Knot, 83, 103
Drag systems: improving, 33–36; multiple-disk star, 30; single-disk, 30; for surf casting reels, 30; testing of, 34
Dropper Knot, 86, 87

Eel. See *Puhi; Tohei*
Egg Sinker, 113, 114, 203
Egg Sinker Leader, 135, 141
Extension kit, for surf casting reels, 27, 28

Fenglass rods, 49
Fenwick rods, 50, 54, 136, 171
Fiberglass extension poles, for handpole fishing, 5–6
Fiberglass rods, 40–41, 45, 53, 61–63, 65
Figure 8 Knot, 91–92
Fin Nor reels, 30
Fish bags, insulated, 218–219
Fishing depths, 14
Floaters, for handpole fishing, 9
Fly fishing: leaders, 78–79; rods, 40
Fortin, Frère François, 39
Fuji reel seat, 63

Gaffing techniques, 192–193, 195–197
Gaffs: bamboo pole, 194–197; slide, 186, 191–193; swivel, 193–194
Galvanized trolling hook, 121
Glitter shrimp, as lures, 113
Goby Handpole Rig, 15
Graphite rods, 25, 45, 64–66; medium-action, 54
Guides: ceramic, 43, 56, 63; silicon carbide, 43; single-foot, 46, 55, 56; stainless steel, 43; tip top, 44–45

Half-and-half rods, 60, 62, 66–67
Handpole fishing techniques, 13–14
Hanging Spreader Rig, 114–115
Hardy Brothers Company, 18
Harness lugs, 30
Haywire Twist, 97, 98, 113, 115
Headlamps, 16, 141, 215–216
Heavy-weight spinning rods, 55–57
Hemostats, 208
Homer Rhodes Loop Knot, 90, 163, 164
Hooks, 155, 201–202; for handpole fishing, 6–8. See also *Tankichi* hook; Treble hook
Hypolon, for rod grips, 44, 53

Ice chests, 218–219
IGFA (International Game Fish Association), 185
Ika (squid), as bait, 114, 131, 149, 222, 230
Illingworth, Holden, 18
Improved Clinch Knot, 87, 140, 164, 178; for gaff rigs, 194; for handpole fishing, 9

Jansik Special, 89
Japan Fishing Knot, 91
Jigging, 174–177
Jigs, 174–175; *lai* skin, 149–152; lead head, 154–156; plastic body, 156–158
J. Lee Cuddy Associates, 35

Knots, 76–92; for handpole fishing, 9. See also *individual knots*
Konn, Jeff, 173

Lai Skin Jig, 149–152
Lamiglass rods, 63
Lanterns: fluorescent, 214; kerosene, 213–214; white gas, 212–213
Leader material, 204–207
Leaders, 76–77, 92–115; for ultralight whipping, 112–114. See also *individual leaders*
Leadhead Jig, 154–156
Lead sinkers, 202–203; for handpole fishing, 8
Les Ruse Innocentes, 39
Lifesaver-Balloon Rig, 109–111
Lubricants for reels, 22, 32, 35, 37; LPS, 22, 37, 210; Never-Seez, 35; 3-in-1 Oil, 37; WD-40, 22, 37, 210; Wonder Mist, 37
Lures: homemade, 158–159; plastic body, 113–114, 156–158; for ultralight tackle, 47. See also Plugs; *individual lures*

Magnetic brakes, in bait-casting reels, 25
Maintenance manuals, 33, 37
Mallock, Peter, 18

Matsui, Earl, 48
Maxima, 28, 93
Meat hooks, 219–220
Medium-action spinning rods, 53–55
Mighty Midget rods, 49–51; cost of, 50
Miner's light. *See* Headlamps
Minibuckle Rig, 111–112
Mirro-Lure plug, 146–148, 163, 164, 168
Mister Twister body, 113, 114
Monofilament, 72–75; for handpole fishing, 6–8; for ultralight tackle, 47
Mullet Floater Rig, 10
Mustad hooks, 7, 49, 121, 140

Nail clippers, 209–210
Newell, Carl, 29
Newell reels, 30

Octopus *(tako),* 123–127, 230
'Ōpae (river shrimp; *shirosa*), as bait, 139–140, 246

Palomar Knot, 88
Palu (chum), 105–106, 117, 125–126, 129–130, 131; in handpole fishing, 8
Palu bag, 107
Pat Crozier Slip Pin Leader, 108–109
Penn International reels, 28, 30, 189
Penn Senator reels, 26, 27, 28, 30, 63
Perfection Loop Knot, 85–86
Pflueger-Templar reels, 26, 27, 28, 189
Phillippe, Samuel, 40
Pigtail bend, 96, 100, 182–183
Pliers, 207–208
Plugs, 144–146, 172; Boone's Chugger, 172; Cordell's Near Nuthing, 171; Cordell's Striper Pencil Popper, 171; Heddon's Chugger Spook; Hawaiian Pili, 171; modification of, 146–147; sinking, 146, 166; surface chugger, 145–146, 159, 169–173; techniques, 52; *ulua,* 172
Puhi (eel), 94, 97, 98, 99, 104–105, 124; as bait, 113, 116–122; as *palu* (chum), 105–107
PVC case, 67–71
Pyramid Sinker, 203

Ranne, Gary, 150
Reef fish, as bait, 131
Reels: bait-casting, 24–26; evolution of, 17–19; fixed spool, 18; maintaining, 31–36; repair kit, 36–38; selecting, 19–21; spinning, 21–24; star-drag, 18; surf casting, 25–31
Reel seats, 30, 44; for bait-casting rods, 53; graphite, 44, 63; for medium-action spinning rods, 55; stainless steel, 44
Repairs, 36–38
Rod cases, 67–71

GENERAL INDEX

Rod components, 43–45
Rods: bait-casting, 51; bamboo, 40, 58; boron, 45, 64–66; fiberglass, 40, 45, 53, 60, 61–63; graphite, 45, 54, 64–66; half-and-half, 60, 62, 66–67; heavyweight spinning, 55–57; history of, 39–41; medium-action spinning, 53–55; Mighty Midget, 49–51; selecting, 41–45; ultralight, 45–48; *ulua* pole, 57–63
Rod sacks, 71
Rod taper, 41–43
Rope, polypropylene, 191–192
Roy Dean Products Co., 35
Rubber Ball Floater, 11

Sabre rods, 53, 62
Safety line, 30
Sandy Beach Slide-Bait Rig, 99, 100
Sevalon (braided wire), 92, 182, 205–206; for catching *puhi*, 117
Shark, as bait, 116, 127–129
Shimano reels, 26
Shrimp, as bait, 15, 134–135, 139–140, 222, 223, 233, 234, 246. See also '*Ōpae*
Skirted spool, 20–23
Slide-Bait Leader, 94; Big Island, 95; Pat Crozier, 108, 109; Sandy Beach, 99, 100; Ted Tokunaga MD-TP, 101–107
Slide-Bait Rig, 97, 134, 181–182
Snails, 15
Spider Hitch Knot, 80, 103, 183
Spinning, 163–174; baits for, 135–137
Spinning reels, 18, 21–24
Split-cane rod, 40
Spoons, 152–154; techniques using, 177–179
Squid *(ika)*, 114, 131, 149, 230
Straight Splice Knot, 77
Sugimoto, Barry and Pauline, 63

Surgeon's Knot, 80–81, 163
Swivels, 183, 200–201; for handpole fishing, 8

Tabis, 16
Tackle boxes, 216–218
Tail carriers, 219–220
Tako (octopus), 123–127
Tankichi hooks, 97, 100, 105, 125, 127, 137, 138, 202
Taper, 41–43; of Lamiglass rod, 63; of *ulua* rod, 60
Theodore, Ernie, 47
Three-and-a-Half-Turn Clinch Knot, 88
Tiger Tail Rig, 98, 99
Tin Squids (Diamond Jigs), 148, 149
Tohei (white eel), as bait, 122–123
Toilet Paper Rig, 101–105
Tokunaga Fishing Supply, 49
Tonkin cane, for bamboo poles, 3
Torpedo leads, 203
Treble hooks, 137, 138, 172
Trilene Knot, 92
Twist weld wire leader, 206–207

Ultralight spinning reels, 23
Ulua fishing, 26; baits, 116–129, 224, 236, 240, 244; hooks, 201, 202; lures, 148; rigs, 97; rods, 45–48, 57–67; tackle, 181–183; techniques, 183–188, 244; and tides, 188–191
Underwrapping, 45, 56
Uni-Knot Splice, 77, 82, 83

Vom Hofe, Julius, 17

Walton, Iziak, 39
Washers, 23, 33–36
Wire Bank Sinker, 203
Wright, Stan, 46, 93, 150, 173

ABOUT THE AUTHOR

Michael R. Sakamoto is an associate editor of *Hawaii Fishing News*. He has been published in such magazines as *Saltwater Sportsman, Fishing World* (published in Australia), and *Rod and Rifle;* and he is the author of *Oscar's Fishing Guidebook,* a book for fishermen between the ages of 7 and 10.

Sakamoto was born and raised in Hawaii, and he is an IGFA representative for the city of Hilo. Also an IGFA record holder, his fishing experience includes everything from handpole fishing to deep-sea trolling. He has fished not only the waters of all the Hawaiian islands but also of Truk Lagoon and Christmas Island. His favorite form of fishing is fly fishing for *ulua* and whipping for any reef fish that will hit his lure.

www.ingramcontent.com/pod-product-compliance
Lightning Source LLC
Chambersburg PA
CBHW071426150426
43191CB00008B/1057